The CCNA 2.0™ Cram Sheet

This Cram Sheet contains key facts about CCNA 2.0. Review this information right before you enter the test room, paying special attention to those areas where you need the most support. You can transfer any of these facts onto a blank sheet of paper before beginning the exam, although knowledge is better than memorization.

INTERNETWORKING BASICS

1. The primary advantage of bridging is increased bandwidth available on a segment because of the decreased number of devices in the collision domain.

2. Switches have the same basic functionality as bridges but usually have more ports. Each switch port is a separate collision domain, and each port provides dedicated bandwidth.

3. Virtual local area networks (VLANs) can be used to make a group of switch ports into a separate, isolated LAN. Routing is required for communication between VLANs.

4. VLANs can function across multiple switches when they are connected by a trunk connection. Inter-switch linking (ISL) is used to create a trunk connection between Fast Ethernet ports on Cisco switches.

5. Switches make it possible to run Ethernet devices in full-duplex mode. In full-duplex mode, two devices share the Ethernet wire simultaneously and exclusively, enabling faster throughput because no collisions are possible.

6. Store-and-forward switching reads the entire frame before making a forwarding decision; cut-through switching reads only the first six bytes—the destination media access control (MAC) address—to make a forwarding decision. Store-and-forward switching performs error checking; cut-through switching does not.

7. The primary advantages of routers are:
   - Allow you to connect dissimilar LANs
   - Provide multiple paths to a destination network
   - Allow the interconnection of large and complex networks

8. Connection-oriented communication uses a nonpermanent path for data transfer. It involves three steps: establish the connection, transfer the data, and terminate the connection. Connectionless communication uses a permanently established link. Example of connection oriented is TCP and connectionless is UDP.

OPEN SYSTEMS INTERCONNECT (OSI) MODEL

9. The layers of the OSI model are 7-application, 6-presentation, 5-session, 4-transport, 3-network, 2-data link, and 1-physical.

10. Encapsulation, or tunneling, takes frames from one network system and places them inside frames from another network system.

11. The presentation layer concerns itself with data representation, data encryption, and data compression. It supports different protocols for text, data, sound, video, graphics, and images such as ASCII, MIDI, MPEG, GIF, and JPEG.

12. The session layer establishes, manages, and terminates sessions between applications. Network file system (NFS), structured query language (SQL), and remote procedure calls (RPCs) are examples of session layer protocols.

43. The interface between the customer network and the WAN provider network occurs between the data terminal equipment (DTE) and the data communication equipment (DCE). DTE devices are usually routers. DCE devices are usually modems, channel service units/data service units (CSUs/DSUs), and terminal adapter/network terminations 1 (TA/NT1s).

44. Frame Relay is a high-speed, packet-switching, WAN protocol that operates at the data link layer. It runs on nearly any type of serial interface, uses frame check sequence (FCS) as its error-checking mechanism, and relies on a discard eligibility bit for congestion management. A virtual circuit must connect two DTE devices within a Frame Relay network. Permanent virtual circuits (PVCs) are more widely used than switched virtual circuits (SVCs) in Frame Relay networks.

45. Data link connection identifier (DLCI) serves as the addressing scheme within a Frame Relay network. Local Management Information (LMI) is a set of enhancements to Frame Relay that was developed by Cisco, StrataCom, Northern Telecom, and DEC. Cisco routers support LMI variations for American National Standards Institute (ANSI), Q933a, and Cisco.

46. DLCIs are mapped to network layer addresses through inverse ARP or by using the **frame-relay map** command. (Important command to know)

47. Committed Information Rate (CIR) is the rate, in bits per second, at which data is transferred across the Frame Relay network.

48. A single physical interface can be configured with several virtual subinterfaces. Each subinterface can be configured with different addressing information. Subinterfaces can be created and accessed using the serial interface number followed by a period and a number (such as serial 0.78).

49. The commands to configure Frame Relay on a router are:

    - **Router (config)# encapsulation frame-relay cisco**
    - **Router (config)# frame-relay lmi-type cisco**
    - **Router (config)# interface serial 0**
    - **Router (config-if)# frame-relay interface-dlci <dlci number>**

50. The basic commands to monitor Frame Relay activity on a router are **show frame-relay pvc**, **show frame-relay lmi**, **show frame-relay map**, and **debug frame-relay lmi**.

51. Password Authentication Protocol (PAP) uses a two-way handshake to authenticate Point-to-Point Protocol (PPP) connections and transmits username/password information in clear text. Challenge Handshake Authentication Protocol (CHAP) uses a three-way handshake and relies on secret, encrypted passwords and unique IDs to authenticate PPP.

52. The commands to configure PPP on a router are:

    - **Router (config)# username <name> password <password>**
    - **Router (config)# interface serial 0**
    - **Router (config-if)# encapsulation ppp**
    - **Router (config-if)# ppp authentication chap**

53. The basic commands to monitor PPP activity on a router are **show interface** and **debug ppp chap**.

54. Integrated services digital network (ISDN) can be ordered as either basic rate interface (BRI) or primary rate interface (PRI). ISDN functions represent devices or hardware functions within ISDN. Reference points describe the logical interfaces between functions.

55. ISDN can be used to:

    - Add bandwidth for telecommuting
    - Improve Internet response time
    - Carry multiple network layer protocols
    - Encapsulate other WAN services

56. Dial-on-demand routing (DDR) works with ISDN to establish and terminate connections. It uses access lists to look for interesting traffic.

57. The commands to configure ISDN on a router are:

    - **Router (config)# isdn switch-type <switch-type>**
    - **Router (config)# dialer-list <dialer-group> protocol <protocol-name> permit**
    - **Router (config-if)# interface bri 0**
    - **Router (config-if)# encapsulation PPP**
    - **Router (config-if)# dialer-group <number>**
    - **Router (config-if)# dialer map <protocol> <next-hop address> name <hostname> speed <number> <dial-string>**
    - **Router (config-if) dialer idle-timeout <seconds>**

58. The basic commands to monitor ISDN and DDR activity on a router are **show controller bri**, **show interface bri**, and **show dialer**.

59. ISDN is faster than a basic modem.

60. ISDN can carry voice, data, video.

61. ISDN is replacing regular phone lines.

62. ISDN has a faster call setup than regular phone lines.

27. Interior Gateway Routing Protocol (IGRP) can be configured on a router with the following commands:

- **Router (config)# router igrp <autonomous system number>**

- **Router (config-router)# network <network>**

TRANSMISSION CONTROL PROTOCOL/ INTERNET PROTOCOL (TCP/IP)

- File Transfer Protocol (FTP)   21
- Telnet   23
- Simple Mail Transfer Protocol (SMTP)   25
- Domain Name System (DNS)   53
- TFTP   69
- Simple Network Management   161, 162
  Protocol (SNMP)

28. TCP provides a connection-oriented and reliable service to the applications that use its services with the use of acknowledgments, sequence number checking, error and duplication checking, and the TCP three-way handshake. User Datagram Protocol (UDP) provides a connectionless and best-effort service to the applications that use its services.

29. Address Resolution Protocol (ARP) maps a known IP address to a physical address. Reverse Address Resolution Protocol (RARP) maps a known physical address to a logical address.

30. Understand the basic concepts of IP addressing. Dotted-decimal notation is the decimal representation of a 32-bit IP address. The dotted-decimal notation represents the four octets of bits by performing binary-to-decimal conversion for each octet and providing a decimal value for each octet.

31. Know the decimal representation of classes A, B, and C addresses as well as the number of networks and nodes each supports.

- Class A   1 through 126
- Class B   128 through 191
- Class C   192 through 223

32. Recognize the default mask for each class of IP address.

- Class A   255.0.0.0
- Class B   255.255.0.0
- Class C   255.255.255.0

33. The most important basic commands used to monitor IP with Cisco routers are **show ip interface**, **show ip protocol**, and **show ip route**.

34. The network number and broadcast address for a given subnet are the first and last IP addresses, respectively. The range of usable IP addresses is all addresses between the network number and broadcast address. In binary format, the network

number has all of the host bits of the address set to 0. The broadcast address has all of the host bits set to 1.

35. Know how to do subnetting tasks very quickly. It will save you valuable time in the end.

INTERNETWORK PACKET EXCHANGE (IPX)

36. IPX addresses consist of a network number and a node number. The node number is the node's MAC address.

37. IPX can be configured on a router with the following commands:

- **Router (config)# ipx routing**
- **Router (config)# interface ethernet 0**
- **Router (config-if)# ipx network <network> encapsulation sap**

38. Recognize the common commands used to monitor IPX activity on a router: **show ipx interface**, **show ipx route**, **show ipx servers**, **show ipx traffic**, **debug ipx routing activity**, and **debug ipx sap activity**.

ACCESS LISTS

39. A list of the import access list numeric identifiers is as follows:

- 1 through 99   IP standard access list
- 100 through 199   IP extended access list
- 800 through 899   IPX standard access list
- 900 through 999   IPX extended access list
- 1000 through 1099   Service Advertisement Protocols (SAP) access list

40. Two rules for applying a wildcard mask to an IP address are:

- A 1 bit in the wildcard mask indicates that the corresponding bit in the IP address can be ignored. Thus, the IP address bit can be either 1 or 0.

- A 0 in the wildcard mask indicates that the corresponding bit in the IP address must be strictly followed. Thus, the value must be exactly the same as specified in the IP address.

41. The difference in the capabilities of IP extended access lists in comparison with IP standard access lists is that standard access lists filter IP traffic based on source IP address or address range. IP extended access lists filter traffic based on source and destination addresses, ports, and many other fields.

42. Know that the last line of any access list is deny any any (implicit).

CORIOLIS™
Certification Insider Press

13. The transport layer sits between the upper and lower layers of the OSI model. The transport layer performs flow control by buffering, multiplexing, and parallelization. It provides end-to-end data transport services by:

- Segmenting upper-layer applications
- Establishing an end-to-end-connection
- Sending segments from one end host to another
- Ensuring reliable data transport

14. The primary functions of the network layer of the OSI model are path determination and packet switching. In addition, remember that the network layer is the domain of routing.

15. The primary functions of the data link layer of the OSI model are:

- Allows the upper layers of the OSI model to work independently of the physical media
- Performs physical hardware addressing
- Provides optional flow control
- Generates error notification

ROUTER BASICS

16. EXEC includes the following:

- Context-sensitive help for syntax checking, command prompting, and keyword completion. Use the question mark (?) to activate context-sensitive help.
- Command history that provides a record of recent commands. Use the Up and Down Arrow keys to scroll through the history list. Tab completes a partially entered command.
- Enhanced editing that enables commands retrieved from command history to be changed quickly then re-executed. The **terminal editing** and **terminal no editing** commands enable and disable enhanced editing.
- Use the TAB key to allow the router to complete commands after you get a %incomplete command% message

17. Examine the status of a router with the following commands: **show version**, **show memory**, **show protocols**, **show running-config** (or **write terminal**), **show startup-config** (or **show configuration**), **show interfaces**, and **show flash**.

18. The Cisco Discovery Protocol (CDP) displays summary information about directly connected devices and operates at the data link layer. The **show cdp neighbors** command displays ID, local and remote port, holdtime, platform, and capability information. The **show cdp entry <device id>** command displays information about a specific device including all layer 3 addresses and Internetwork Operating System (IOS) versions.

ROUTER CONFIGURATION

19. The command to back up a router configuration file (copy a configuration file from a router to a Trivial File Transfer Protocol [TFTP] server) is **copy running-config tftp**. The command to restore a configuration file (copy a configuration file from a TFTP server to a router) is **copy tftp running-config**.

20. The commands to set the enable, enable secret, console, and auxiliary passwords on a router are as follows:

- **Router(config)#enable** *password*
- **Router(config)#enable secret** *password*
- **Router(config)#line aux** *0* and **Router (config-line)#login** and **Router(config-line)#password** *password*
- **Router(config)#line con** *0* and **Router (config-line)#login** and **Router(config-line)#password** *password*
- **Router(config)#line vty** *0 4* and **Router (config-line)#login** and **Router(config-line)#password** *password*

21. To create a banner for a router and a description for an interface, use the **banner motd** (message of the day) and **description** commands.

ROUTING PROTOCOLS

22. Convergence occurs when all routers in an internetwork agree on optimal routes. A routing loop occurs when a packet bounces back and forth between two or more routers. A routing loop is sometimes called counting to infinity.

23. Distance vector routing protocols send all of their route tables to their neighbors. Link state protocols send the state of their own interfaces to every router in the internetwork.

24. Counting to infinity is a problem for distance vector routing protocols. It can be eliminated or mitigated by using the following techniques: maximum hop count, split horizon, route poisoning, and hold-down timers.

25. Router resource usage, bandwidth consumption, and update synchronization are problems for link state routing protocols. They can be eliminated or reduced by using the following techniques:

- Lengthening update frequency
- Exchanging route summaries
- Using time stamps or sequence numbers

26. Routing Information Protocol (RIP) can be configured on a router with the following commands:

- **Router (config)# router rip**
- **Router (config-router)# network <network>**

CCNA™

Sheldon Barry

CCNA™ Exam Cram

Limits of Liability and Disclaimer of Warranty

Trademarks

The Coriolis Group, LLC
14455 N. Hayden Road
Suite 220
Scottsdale, Arizona 85260

(480) 483-0192
FAX (480) 483-0193
www.coriolis.com

Library of Congress Cataloging-in-Publication Data
Barry, Sheldon
    CCNA / by Sheldon Barry.
        p.   cm. -- (Exam cram)
    Includes index.
    ISBN 1-58880-232-9
    1. Electronic data processing personnel--Certification.   2. Computer networks--Examinations--Study guides.   I. Title.   II. Series.

QA76.3 .B366   2001
005.74--dc21

                                        2001053695
                                        CIP

President and CEO
Roland Elgey

Publisher
Al Valvano

Associate Publisher
Katherine R. Hartlove

Acquisitions Editor
Sharon Linsenbach

Product Marketing Manager
Jeff Johnson

Project Editor
Dan Young

Technical Reviewer
Dennis Suhanovs

Production Coordinator
Todd Halvorsen

Cover Designer
Carla Schuder

Printed in the United States of America
10 9 8 7 6 5 4 3 2 1

CORIOLIS™

The Coriolis Group, LLC • 14455 North Hayden Road, Suite 220 • Scottsdale, Arizona 85260

A Note from Coriolis

Our goal has always been to provide you with the best study tools on the planet to help you achieve your certification in record time. Time is so valuable these days that none of us can afford to waste a second of it, especially when it comes to exam preparation.

Over the past few years, we've created an extensive line of *Exam Cram* and *Exam Prep* study guides, practice exams, and interactive training. To help you study even better, we have now created an e-learning and certification destination called **ExamCram.com**. (You can access the site at **www.examcram.com**.) Now, with every study product you purchase from us, you'll be connected to a large community of people like yourself who are actively studying for their certifications, developing their careers, seeking advice, and sharing their insights and stories.

We believe that the future is all about collaborative learning. Our **ExamCram.com** destination is our approach to creating a highly interactive, easily accessible collaborative environment, where you can take practice exams and discuss your experiences with others, sign up for features like "Questions of the Day," plan your certifications using our interactive planners, create your own personal study pages, and keep up with all of the latest study tips and techniques.

We hope that whatever study products you purchase from us—*Exam Cram* or *Exam Prep* study guides, *Personal Trainers*, *Personal Test Centers*, or one of our interactive Web courses—will make your studying fun and productive. Our commitment is to build the kind of learning tools that will allow you to study the way you want to, whenever you want to.

Help us continue to provide the very best certification study materials possible. Write us or email us at **learn@examcram.com** and let us know

Visit ExamCram.com now to enhance your study program.

how our study products have helped you study. Tell us about new features that you'd like us to add. Send us a story about how we've helped you. We're listening!

Good luck with your certification exam and your career. Thank you for allowing us to help you achieve your goals.

ExamCram.com Connects You to the Ultimate Study Center!

Look for these other products from The Coriolis Group:

CCNP Routing Exam Cram
by Eric McMasters, Brian Morgan, and Mike Shroyer

CCNP Remote Access Exam Cram
by Craig Dennis and Eric Quinn

CCNP Support Exam Cram
by Matthew E. Luallen

CCNP Switching Exam Cram
by Richard A. Deal

Also recently published by Coriolis Certification Insider Press:

Linux+ Exam Cram
by Michael Jang

CCSA Exam Cram
by Tony Piltzecker

MCSE ISA Server 2000 Exam Cram
by Diana Bartley and Gregory Smith

"To strive, to seek, to find, and not to yield."
—*Tennyson's* Ulysses 1842

About the Author

Sheldon Barry (B.A, B.ED, CCNA, CCAI, MCSE, MCT) is a technology trainer, writer, and consultant in Newfoundland, Canada. He is currently employed as Coordinating Instructor at Memorial University of Newfoundland in the postgraduate Information Technology Program (**www.ce.mun.ca/ppd/it_diploma.html**). Some of his previous employment positions have included technical writing, educational content consulting, high-school department head, and high-school teacher.

Sheldon completed a Bachelor of Arts from Memorial University of Newfoundland in 1994 and then went on to complete a Bachelor of Education from Memorial in 1995. Since then Sheldon has been working on a Masters of Education (Information Technology) Degree, which he is expected to complete by Spring 2002.

He currently enjoys life with his wife, Kelly, and his two little girls, Sarah and Anna, and he loves to play soccer and golf.

Sheldon can be reached at **sheldonb@mun.ca**.

Acknowledgments

. . . .

The acknowledgement section of this book is the most difficult to do because so many people have helped and supported me through its creation that I have room to mention only a few of them. So to all the people that helped I say thank you.

I want to first thank my wife, Kelly, and two children, Sarah and Anna, who have managed to keep smiles on their faces even though I sat with a laptop in the evenings for many weeks to get this book completed. Thank you.

I want to thank Sharon Linsenbach of The Coriolis Group. She is the Acquisitions Editor who approached me and made this possible. Also I want to thank my Project Editors: Cheryl Gilbert and Dan Young. These two people are the ones that kept me on task when I needed the extra push to keep stringent time lines.

I also want to thank my Technical Reviewer and Copyeditor, Dennis Suhanovs and Bart Reed, respectively, for carefully going through each line of the book to ensure that accuracy and quality were upheld.

Contents at a Glance

Chapter 1   Cisco Certification Exams   1

Chapter 2   Internetworking Concepts: An Overview   11

Chapter 3   The TCP/IP Model   35

Chapter 4   Network Hardware   51

Chapter 5   Maintaining the Network   63

Chapter 6   Router Configuration and
             Software Management   75

Chapter 7   IP Addressing and Routing   107

Chapter 8   Internet Package Exchange (IPX)   147

Chapter 9   Router Access Lists   165

Chapter 10   LAN Switching   189

Chapter 11   Extending Switch Functionality   207

Chapter 12   Wide Area Networking   225

Chapter 13   Sample Test   263

Chapter 14   Answer Key   287

Table of Contents

Introduction xix

Self-Assessment xxix

Chapter 1
Cisco Certification Exams 1
    The Exam Situation   2
    Exam Layout and Design   3
    Using Cisco's Exam Software Effectively   5
    Exam-Taking Basics   5
    Question-Handling Strategies   6
    Mastering the Inner Game   6
    Additional Resources   7

Chapter 2
Internetworking Concepts: An Overview 11
    Networking Fundamentals   12
        Transmission Media   12
        Media Access Methods   13
        Data Transmission Methods   14
    Network Standards   15
    The OSI Model   15
    Application Layer   17
    Presentation Layer   18
    Session Layer   18
    Transport Layer   19
        Segment Upper-Layer Applications   19
        Establish End-to-End Connections   19
        Send Segments from One Host to Another   20
        Ensure Reliable Data Transport   21

Network Layer   21
    Path Determination   22
    Packet Switching   22
Data Link Layer   22
    LLC Sublayer 802.2   23
    Media Access Control Sublayer 802.3   24
    Framing   24
Physical Layer   25
    Encapsulation and De-Encapsulation   26
Practice Questions   29
Need to Know More?   34

Chapter 3
The TCP/IP Model 35

Background and History of TCP/IP   36
The TCP/IP Layers   36
    Application Layer   37
    Transport Layer   38
    Internet Layer   42
    Network Access Layer   44
Practice Questions   45
Need to Know More?   50

Chapter 4
Network Hardware 51

Network Hardware Roles   52
    Hubs   52
    Bridges   52
    Switches   54
    Routers   54
Problems Associated with the Expanding Network   56
    Latency   56
    Collisions   57
    Broadcasts   57
Practice Questions   58
Need to Know More?   62

Chapter 5
Maintaining the Network 63

Testing Other Devices   64

    Telnet   64

    Ping   64

    Traceroute   65

    The **show interface** Command   66

    Trivial File Transfer Protocol   67

Practice Questions   70

Need to Know More?   74

Chapter 6
Router Configuration and Software Management 75

Router Elements   76

    Router Modes   76

    Router Components   78

    Router Status   78

Managing Configuration Files   84

    Types of Configuration Files   84

    Displaying the Running and Startup Configuration Files   85

    Configuring the Running and Startup Configuration Files   86

    Backing Up and Restoring Configuration Files   87

Router Passwords   89

    The **enable password** and **enable secret** Password Commands   89

    The **console** and **auxiliary** Password Commands   89

    The **virtual terminal** Password Command   90

Router Identification and Banner   90

Initial Configuration of a Cisco Router   91

Upgrading Cisco IOS Software   94

    Backing Up the Current IOS   94

    Upgrading the IOS   96

    Reloading the Router   97

Practice Questions   98

Need to Know More?   105

Chapter 7
IP Addressing and Routing 107
    IP Addressing   108
        Dotted Decimal Notation   108
        IP Classes   110
        Subnetting   112
    Configuring and Verifying IP Addresses   119
        IP Host Names   119
        Verifying IP Addresses   119
    Monitoring IP   121
        The **show ip interface** Command   121
        The **show ip protocol** Command   122
        The **show ip route** Command   123
    Routing Activities   124
    Routing Algorithms and Protocols   124
        Goals of Routing Protocols   124
        Types of Routing Protocols   127
        Routing Metrics   130
    Distance Vector vs. Link State   131
        Distance Vector Overview   131
        Link State Overview   132
        Network Discovery   133
        Topology Changes   134
        Distance Vector Problems   135
        Distance Vector Remedies   135
        Link State Problems   136
        Link State Remedies   136
    Routing Protocol Configuration and Review   137
        RIP   137
        IGRP   139
    Practice Questions   140
    Need to Know More?   146

Chapter 8
Internet Package Exchange (IPX) 147
    NetWare Protocol Suite   148
        Upper Layers   148
        Network Layer   149
        Data Link and Physical Layers   149

IPX Addressing   149

IPX Encapsulation   150

IPX Routing   150

IPX Service Advertisement   151

Configuring IPX   152

Monitoring IPX   153

Troubleshooting IPX   156

Practice Questions   158

Need to Know More?   163

Chapter 9
Router Access Lists 165

IP Access Lists   166

    IP Standard Access Lists   167

    IP Extended Access Lists   172

IPX Access Lists   176

    IPX Standard Access Lists   177

    IPX Extended Access Lists   178

Monitoring and Verifying Access Lists   180

Practice Questions   182

Need to Know More?   187

Chapter 10
LAN Switching 189

Layer 2 Switching Technology   190

    Discovering MAC Addresses   190

    Filtering and Forwarding   190

    Preventing Loops   191

    Spanning Tree Protocol   192

Cisco LAN Switching Methods   194

    Store-and-Forward Switching   194

    Cut-Through Switching   194

    Fragment-Free Switching   195

Cisco Switches   195

    Switch Startup   196

    Configuring the Switch   197

    Configuring TCP/IP Options   200

    Using the Web Interface   201

Practice Questions   202

Need to Know More?   206

Chapter 11
Extending Switch Functionality **207**

Virtual Local Area Networks (VLANs)   208

Frame Tagging   210

Trunk Connections   211

    Interswitch Link (ISL)   211

    VLAN Trunking Protocol (VTP)   211

Configuring VLANs   213

    Enabling VTP   214

    Enabling Trunking   214

    Creating the VLAN   216

    Assigning the VLAN to Ports   216

Practice Questions   218

Need to Know More?   223

Chapter 12
Wide Area Networking **225**

WAN Services   226

HDLC Overview   229

PPP Overview   229

    PPP Physical Layer   230

    PPP Connections   230

    PPP Authentication   231

    LCP Configuration Options   232

Configuring PPP   233

Monitoring PPP   234

ISDN Overview   235

    Basic Rate Interface and Primary Rate Interface   236

    ISDN Protocols   236

    Functions and Reference Points   236

    DDR   238

Configuring ISDN   238

Monitoring ISDN   240

Frame Relay   243

    Virtual Circuits   244

    DLCI   245

    LMI   245

Configuring Frame Relay   246
Nonbroadcast Multiaccess   247
Subinterfaces   247
Monitoring Frame Relay   248
Practice Questions   252
Need to Know More?   262

Chapter 13
Sample Test 263

Chapter 14
Answer Key 287

Glossary 303

Index 321

Introduction

Welcome to *CCNA Routing and Switching Exam Cram, 3rd Edition*. The main goal of this book is to provide enough information to prepare you to successfully pass the Cisco Certification Exam 640-507, "Cisco Certified Network Associate 2.0." This introduction explains Cisco's certification programs in general and talks about how the *Exam Cram* series can help you to prepare for Cisco's certification exams.

Although the book will be a super tool to prepare you for the examination, it should be noted that a significant portion of the examination will be based on Cisco routers and switches as well as the commands relevant to those devices. Therefore, it is imperative that you get practical hands-on experience with these devices before attempting the examination.

The Cisco Certification Program

When you start the Cisco Career Certification process, you first must determine the career path you wish to master. Cisco offers a wide variety of certifications; however, they are designed to follow two distinct career paths, with multiple tracks along each path. In an effort to summarize the material, this book presents each career path and the tests required for proceeding along each path. Cisco Systems Inc. offers a wide variety of training courses designed to facilitate the certification process. You can find the recommended training courses and a more in-depth analysis of each test at **www.cisco.com/warp/public/10/wwtraining/ certprog/index.html**. One thing to remember when selecting the best path for you is that Cisco certifications are valid for three years, and you either have to have your path finished or recertify.

Network Installation and Support Certifications

The Routing and Switching Network Installation and Support certification career path is for professionals who support networks with Cisco local area network (LAN) and wide area network (WAN) routers and switches. This path has three core certifications: CCNA, CCNP, and CCIE. Each core certification contains two different exams that will fulfill the requirement. The exams are:

Cisco Certified Network Associate (CCNA) 2.0
CCNA Exam 640-507

The skills expected of a CCNA include installing, configuring, and operating simple-routed LAN networks, routed WAN networks, and switched LAN networks.

CCNA WAN Switching Certification (CCNA)
CCNA Exam 640-410

The skills expected of a CCNA include the foundation knowledge to install and configure WAN switched networks.

Cisco Certified Network Professional (CCNP) 2.0

The skills expected of a CCNP include the ability to install, configure, operate, and troubleshoot complex routed LAN networks, routed WAN networks, switched LAN networks, and dial access services. Two different test options are available for achieving the CCNP.

Test option 1:

➤ 640-507 CCNA Certification

➤ 640-509 Foundation 2.0

➤ 640-506 Support 2.0

Test option 2:

➤ 640-507 CCNA Certification

➤ 640-503 Routing 2.0

➤ 640-504 Switching 2.0

➤ 640-505 Remote Access 2.0

➤ 640-506 Support 2.0

The only difference between test option 1 and 2 is the second set of tests required for test option 2. These tests are designed to cover the same material as the Foundation 2.0 Exam in test option 1, but they are broken up to reduce the test time and make the certification process more manageable.

CCNP WAN Switching (CCNP)

The skills expected of a CCNP include the advanced skills required to configure, install, operate, and troubleshoot WAN switched networks.

The exams required to obtain this certification are:

➤ 640-410 (CCNA exam)

➤ 640-419 (MSSC exam)

➤ 640-425 (BSSC exam)

➤ 640-411 (MACC exam)

➤ 640-469 (CWMIO exam)

CCIE—Routing and Switching

The CiscoCertifiedInternetworkingExpert is the pinnacle of career certifications in the Cisco certification process. The skills expected of a CCIE include the ability to install, configure, operate, and troubleshoot complex routed LAN networks, routed WAN networks, switched LAN networks, ATM LANE networks, and dial access services. Also, a CCIE is expected to diagnose and resolve network faults, use packet/frame analysis and Cisco debugging tools, and document and report the problem-solving processes applied. The CCIE exam is split into a written test and a grueling laboratory test:

➤ Routing and Switching CCIE Written Exam

➤ Routing and Switching CCIE Lab Test

For more information about the CCIE Routing and Switching certification, visit Cisco's CCIE Routing and Switching Web page at **www.cisco.com/warp/public/625/ccie/certifications/routing.html**.

Network Engineering and Design Certifications

The Routing and Switching Network Engineering and Design certification career path is for professionals who want to design Cisco-based networks that predominantly include routed LAN networks, routed WAN networks, and switched LAN networks. This career path has two core certifications.

Cisco Certified Design Associate (CCDA)
Design Cisco Networks DCN Exam 640-441

The skills expected of a CCDA include the ability to design simple routed LAN networks, routed WAN networks, and switched LAN networks.

Cisco Certified Design Professional (CCDP) 2.0

The skills expected of a CCDP include designing complex routed LAN networks, routed WAN networks, and switched LAN networks. The test assumes prerequisite knowledge and skills to install, configure, and operate these networks. Two different test options are available for achieving the CCDP.

Test option 1:

➤ 640-507 CCNA Certification

➤ 640-441 CCDA Certification

➤ 640-509 Foundation 2.0

➤ 640-025 Cisco Internetworking Design 3.0

Test option 2:

➤ 640-507 CCNA Certification

➤ 640-441 CCDA Certification

➤ 640-503 Routing 2.0

➤ 640-504 Switching 2.0

➤ 640-505 Remote Access 2.0

➤ 640-025 Cisco Internetworking Design 3.0

The only difference between test option 1 and 2 is the third set of tests required for test option 2. These tests are designed to cover the same material as the Foundation 2.0 Exam in test option 1, but they are broken up to reduce the test time and make the certification process more manageable.

Taking a Certification Exam

You can register for the CCNA 2.0 exam online through Sylvan Prometric's Web site at **www.2test.com**.

You can also call 1-800-755-3926 to register for the exam. We strongly recommend that you take the time to review Cisco's Exam Web sites mentioned previously. The cost of the exam at the time of book publication is $100(U.S. currency). This fee can be paid by credit card, personal check, or money order. When you call, reference exam number 640-507; this is the Sylvan Prometric examination number for the CCNA 2.0 examination.

You will be taking the test at a Sylvan Prometric Testing Center at the location you choose. When you arrive at the testing location, sign in with the test coordinator and have two forms of identification ready—one of which must be a photo ID. The test coordinator will give you a set of rules for you to read and abide by during the test. You will also receive some scratch paper and a pencil, or a dry-erase board and marker. The amount of scratch paper required to take the test will vary for each individual, but we recommend that you get as much as possible to be safe. If you are given a dry-erase board, ask for two of them so you don't have to erase previously written material to make extra room for notes or calculations during the test. The test coordinator will take you to a room with a number of computer stations divided by walls. You will have the option of taking a tutorial on the exam before the time starts for the test. If this is your first Cisco test, we recommend that you review this material.

A Cram Sheet has been provided at the beginning of this book with material that most often appears on the test. If it helps you, write down as much as you can remember on your scratch paper before taking the test. You can use the time provided to take the tutorial to make these notes. The test will consist of approximately 65–70 questions. If you have spent the time studying the material and are confident you understand it as presented in this book, you will be well equipped to tackle the test head on.

After you have completed the test, the results will be available online immediately. After you have received your passing score, you will be prompted to print your results. Make sure you do not leave the testing center without a printed and officially stamped printout of the exam results, because this is your only true verification that you have passed the exam. After you have seen this printout, conclude the exam and see the test coordinator.

CCNA Exam Test Format

At the time of book publication, the CCNA 2.0 exam has approximately 65–70 questions. For up-to-date information on the exam details, refer to the Cisco Web site at **www.cisco.com**. The CCNA exam uses the typical certification test format of asking multiple-choice questions, with one or more answers per question. What makes some questions more difficult is that more than five answer choices are listed, thus reducing the power of eliminating answers and choosing from the remaining answers. The nice part is that the number of required answers is given for each question.

How to Prepare for an Exam

The CCNA exam requires test-taking skills that many of us learned in high school or college. This section will be a refresher for many and important for all.

The first thing to focus on during the test is time management. The exam time limits are generally always set with the assumption that each question will take you no more than one- to one-and-a-half minutes per question. Don't worry about how long it takes you to finish an individual question, but divide the test into checkpoints to monitor your progress during the test.

You must answer each question. In fact, the test engine will not let you proceed if you have not selected an answer or if you have not chosen the correct number of answers. You will not be allowed to go back to a question after you've answered it. If you get stuck on a question, check to see how much time you have left and whether you are on schedule to finish in adequate time. If you don't have time to spare, make an educated guess and move on.

Another very important item to remember is to read every question and answer it carefully. Many of the questions refer to exact commands required to implement a function on a router. It is important to know the different syntax and to recognize small differences in commands. This book will highlight areas of the exam that might be tricky.

Make sure to read every answer before choosing one. Often, one answer might sound great; however, another answer will be more correct than the first. Remember to read all the answers before choosing the best one. In addition, reading questions out loud often makes them easier to understand and, therefore, easier to answer.

About the Book

If you're preparing for a first-time test, we've structured the topics in this book to build on one another. Therefore, some topics in later chapters make more sense after you've read earlier chapters. That's why we suggest you read this book from front to back for your initial test preparation. If you need to brush up on a topic or get ready for a second try, use the index or table of contents to go straight to the topics and questions you need to study. After this book has helped you become a CCNA, you now have a very good reference book at your disposal.

Given all of the book's elements and its specialized focus, we've tried to create a tool that will help you to prepare for—and pass—Cisco Exam 640-507, "Cisco Certified Network Associate 2.0." Please share your feedback about the book with us, especially if you have ideas about how we can improve it for future test takers. We'll consider everything you say carefully, and we'll respond to all suggestions.

Send your questions or comments to us at **learn@examcram.com**. Please remember to include the title of the book in your message; otherwise, we'll be forced to guess which book you're writing about. And we don't like to guess—we want to *know*! Also, be sure to check out the Web pages at **www.examcram.com**, where you'll find practice tests, information updates, commentary, clarifications, and more on documents for each book that you can either read online or download for later use.

Thanks, and enjoy the book!

Skills Acquired from Certification Preparation

The CCNA (Cisco Certified Network Associate) certification indicates a foundation in and apprentice knowledge of networking for the small office/home office (SOHO) market. CCNA certified professionals can install, configure, and operate LAN, WAN, and dial access services for small networks (100 nodes or fewer), including but not limited to the use of these protocols: IP, IGRP, IPX, serial, AppleTalk, Frame Relay, IP RIP, VLANs, RIP, Ethernet, and access lists.

Exam Specifics

As of book publication time, according to the Cisco Web site (**www.cisco.com/ warp/public/10/wwtraining/certprog/testing/current_exams/640-507.html**), the following topics provide general guidelines for the content likely to be included on the CCNA exam. However, other related topics may also appear on any specific delivery of the exam.

Bridging/Switching:

➤ Name and describe two switching methods.

➤ Distinguish between cut-through and store-and-forward LAN switching.

➤ Describe the operation of the Spanning Tree Protocol and its benefits.

➤ Describe the benefits of virtual LANs.

OSI Reference Model and Layered Communications:

➤ Describe data-link and network addresses and identify key differences between them.

➤ Define and describe the function of the MAC address.

➤ List the key internetworking functions for the OSI Network layer.

➤ Identify at least three reasons why the industry uses a layered model.

➤ Describe the two parts of network addressing; then identify the parts in specific protocol address examples.

➤ Define and explain the five conversion steps of data encapsulation.

➤ Describe connection-oriented network service and connectionless network service and then identify their key differences.

➤ Identify the parts in specific protocol address examples.

➤ Describe the advantages of LAN segmentation.

➤ Describe LAN segmentation using bridges.

➤ Describe LAN segmentation using routers.

➤ Describe LAN segmentation using switches.

➤ Describe the benefits of network segmentation with bridges.

➤ Describe the benefits of network segmentation with routers.

➤ Describe the benefits of network segmentation with switches.

Network Protocols:

➤ Describe the different classes of IP addresses (and subnetting).

➤ Identify the functions of the TCP/IP network-layer protocol.

➤ Identify the functions performed by ICMP.

➤ Configure IP addresses.

➤ Verify IP addresses.

➤ List the required IPX address and encapsulation type.

Routing:

➤ Define flow control and describe the three basic methods used in networking.

➤ Add the RIP routing protocol to your configuration.

➤ Add the IGRP routing protocol to your configuration.

WAN Protocols:

➤ Recognize key Frame Relay terms and features.

➤ List commands to configure Frame Relay LMIs, maps, and subinterfaces.

➤ List commands to monitor Frame Relay operation in the router.

➤ State a relevant use and context for ISDN networking.

➤ Identify ISDN protocols, function groups, reference points, and channels.

➤ Identify PPP operations to encapsulate WAN data on Cisco routers.

Network Management:

➤ Configure standard access lists to figure IP traffic.

➤ Configure extended access lists to filter IP traffic.

➤ Monitor and verify selected access list operations on the router.

LAN Design:

➤ Describe full- and half-duplex Ethernet operations.

➤ Describe network congestion problems in Ethernet networks.

➤ Describe the features and benefits of Fast Ethernet.

➤ Describe the guidelines and distance limitations of Fast Ethernet.

Cisco Basics, IOS, and Network Basics:

➤ Examine router elements.

➤ Manage configuration files from the privilege EXEC mode.

➤ Control router passwords, identification, and banners.

➤ Identify the main Cisco IOS software commands for router startup.

➤ Log in to a router in both user and privilege modes.

➤ Check an initial configuration using the **setup** command.

➤ Use the context-sensitive help facility.

➤ Use the command history and editing features.

➤ List the commands to load Cisco IOS software from Flash memory, a TFTP server, or ROM.

➤ Prepare to back up, upgrade, and load a backup Cisco IOS software image.

➤ List problems that each routing type encounters when dealing with topology changes and describe techniques to reduce the number of these problems.

➤ Prepare the initial configuration of your router and enable IP.

Additional Resources

As you prepare for the examination, you may feel that you want more information on topics, and that is perfectly normal. It is essential that you check the Cisco Web site at www.cisco.com and verify that the exam details have not changed since the time of this book's publication. Here are a few sites that Cisco has provided for you to complement your certification needs:

➤ http://www.cisco.com/go/certifications

➤ http://www.cisco.com/go/training

➤ http://www.cisco.com/edu/academies

➤ http://www.cisco.com/go/e-learning

Self-Assessment

The Self-Assessment in this *Exam Cram* book will help you to evaluate your readiness to tackle the Cisco Certified Network Associate (CCNA) certification. It should also help you to understand what you need to know to master the topic of this book, namely, CCNA Exam 640-507. But before you tackle this assessment, let's talk about the information technology (IT) networking profession and understand the opportunity Cisco certifications can create for you.

IT Networking Opportunities

The demand for experienced and skilled IT networking professionals is forecast to grow tremendously over the next decade. In addition, the supply of skilled IT networking professionals does not meet the current demand, thus requiring IT organizations to pay a premium for these skills. The demand for IT networking professionals at all levels is increasing, and it's creating an opportunity for both the novice and the expert to increase their personal net worth to corporate America.

The beauty of IT networking is that the industry builds from a core set of technical skills into a wide variety of diverse and highly challenging technical focuses. Mastery of the IT networking foundation skills enables an individual to learn more complex subjects at a more rapid pace. Many professionals attempt or are forced to learn the more complex subjects of IT networking before they truly understand the basic networking skills. These people often become frustrated, and their ability to learn new skills is drastically reduced, because they never took the time to master the foundation skills.

The CCNA exam is an excellent starting point or checkpoint for determining if you have mastered the basic skills of IT networking. We cannot emphasize enough the advantages you will realize by mastering these skills before attempting to understand the more complex subjects of IT networking.

Mastering the basic skills before attempting to understand the more difficult technologies is critical to your success. Now for the good news: The CCNA exam is designed for IT networking professionals of all levels. It tests the basic foundations skills required to be successful in the profession.

If you are a novice IT networking professional, this book is focused on assisting you to obtain possibly your first IT certification. If you are an experienced IT professional, this book gives you the opportunity to go back and master the basic skills and substantially increase your ability to learn more complex technologies quickly.

Choosing Cisco Systems Career Certifications as a starting point for your career certification process is the right step. Cisco Systems currently owns 80 percent of the internetworking arena. Cisco is the dominant player in corporate network infrastructures and the Internet. Individuals who have Cisco Certifications find jobs, period.

CCNAs in the Real World

In the next section, we describe an ideal CCNA candidate, knowing full well that only a few real candidates will meet this ideal. In fact, our description of that ideal candidate might seem downright scary. But take heart: Although the requirements to obtain CCNA certification may seem pretty formidable, they are by no means impossible to meet. You should be keenly aware, however, that it does take time, require some expense, and consume substantial effort to get through the process.

You can get all the real-world motivation you need from knowing that many others have gone before, so you will be able to follow in their footsteps. If you're willing to tackle the process seriously and do what it takes to obtain the necessary experience and knowledge, you can take—and pass—all the certification tests involved in obtaining a CCNA. In fact, we've designed this *Exam Cram* to make it as easy on you as possible to prepare for these exams. But prepare you must!

The Ideal CCNA Candidate

Just to give you some idea of what an ideal CCNA candidate is, here are some relevant statistics about the background and experience such an individual might have. Don't worry if you don't meet these qualifications or even come very close—this is a far from an ideal world, and where you fall short is simply where you'll have more work to do.

➤ Academic or professional training in network theory, concepts, and operations.

➤ Two years or more of professional networking experience in a LAN environment, including experience with Ethernet, token ring, modems, switches, and other networking media. This must include installation, configuration, upgrade, and troubleshooting experience.

➤ Two years or more in a WAN environment that includes hands-on experience with Frame Relay, High-level Data Link Control (HDLC), or Integrated Services Digital Network (ISDN) architecture, installation, configuration, maintenance, and troubleshooting.

➤ A thorough understanding of key networking protocols, routing protocols, and addressing, including Transmission Control Protocol/Internet Protocol (TCP/IP), Internet Packet Exchange/Sequence Packet Exchange (IPX/SPX), Routing Information Protocol (RIP), and Interior Gateway Routing Protocol (IGRP).

Fundamentally, this boils down to a bachelor's degree in computer science, plus three years of work experience in a technical position involving network design, installation, configuration, and maintenance. We believe that well under half of all certification candidates meet these requirements and that, in fact, most meet less than half of these requirements—at least, when they begin the certification process. Many have survived this ordeal and have been certified, and you can survive it too—especially if you heed what our Self-Assessment can tell you about what you already know and what you need to learn.

How Prepared Are You?

The following series of questions and observations is designed to help you figure out how much work you must do to pursue CCNA certification and what resources to consult on your quest. Be absolutely honest in your answers, or you'll end up wasting money on exams that you're not yet ready to take. You'll not find right or wrong answers, only steps along the path to certification. Only you can decide where you really belong in the broad spectrum of aspiring candidates.

Two things should be clear from the outset:

➤ Even a modest background in computer science will be helpful.

➤ Hands-on experience with Cisco products and technologies is an essential ingredient to certification success.

Educational Background

1. Have you ever taken any computer-related classes? [Yes or No]

   If Yes, proceed to Question 2.

   If No, proceed to Question 3.

2. Have you taken any networking concepts or technologies classes? [Yes or No]

If Yes, you will probably be able to handle networking terminology, concepts, and technologies. If you're rusty, brush up on basic networking concepts and terminology, especially the Open Systems Interconnect (OSI) model, TCP/IP, IPX/SPX, and networking technologies such as Ethernet, token ring, fiber distributed data interface (FDDI), and WAN links.

If No, you might want to read one or two books in this topic area. The two best books that we know of are *Computer Networks, 3rd Edition*, by Andrew S. Tanenbaum (Prentice Hall, 1996, ISBN 0133499456) and *Computer Networks and Internets*, by Douglas E. Comer (Prentice Hall, 1997, ISBN 0132390701).

Skip to the next section, "Hands-on Experience."

3. Have you done any reading about networks? [Yes or No]

If Yes, review the requirements stated in the first paragraphs after Question 2. If you meet those requirements, move on to the next section, "Hands-on Experience."

If No, consult the recommended reading list. A strong background will help you to prepare for the CCNA exam better than just about anything else.

Hands-on Experience

The single most important key to success on all of the Cisco tests is hands-on experience, especially with Cisco routers. If we leave you with only one realization after taking this Self-Assessment, it should be that you can't find any substitute for time spent installing, configuring, and using the various Cisco equipment on which you'll be tested repeatedly and in depth.

4. Have you installed, configured, and worked with Cisco routers? [Yes or No]

If Yes, make sure that you understand addressing, TCP/IP, IPX/SPX, and routing protocols. Be sure to study WAN services like Frame Relay and ISDN.

If you haven't worked with Cisco routers, we recommend that you obtain access to at least two routers, so that you can exercise the concepts that you will be learning.

5. Have you installed, configured, and worked with Cisco switches? [Yes or No]

If Yes, make sure that you understand the concepts and benefits of network segmentation and the types of LAN switching.

If No, you will need to obtain access to a switch.

Before you even think about taking any Cisco exam, make sure that you've spent enough time with the related equipment and software to understand how to install, configure, monitor, and troubleshoot it. This will help you during the exam and in real life.

Testing Your Exam-Readiness

Whether you attend a formal class on a specific topic to get ready for an exam or use written materials to study on your own, some preparation for the CCNA certification exam is essential. At $100 a try, pass or fail, you want to do everything you can to pass on your first try. That's where studying comes in.

For any given subject, consider taking a class if you've tackled self-study materials, taken the test, and failed anyway. The opportunity to interact with an instructor and fellow students can make all the difference in the world, if you can afford that privilege. For information about Cisco classes, visit the Training and Certification Web page at **www.cisco.com/training**. If you can't afford to take a class, visit the Training and Certification Web page anyway, because it also includes pointers to free practice exams and other self-study tools. Even if you can't afford to spend much at all, you should still invest in some low-cost practice exams from commercial vendors, because they can help you to assess your readiness to pass a test better than any other tool. All of the following Web sites offer practice exams online:

➤ The Coriolis Group's Study Resource Center at **www.examcram.com/ studyresource/practiceexam**.

➤ CCPrep.com at **www.ccprep.com** (requires membership)

➤ Network Study Guides at **www.networkstudyguides.com** (pay as you go)

6. Have you taken a practice exam on your chosen test subject? [Yes or No]

If Yes and you scored 70 percent or better, you're probably ready to tackle the real thing. If your score isn't above that crucial threshold, keep at it until you break that barrier.

If No, obtain all of the free and low-budget practice tests you can find (see the previous list) and get to work. Keep at it until you can break the passing threshold comfortably.

When it comes to assessing your test readiness, no better way exists than to take a good-quality practice exam and pass with a score of 70 percent or better. When we're preparing ourselves, we shoot for 80-plus percent, just to leave room for the "weirdness factor" that sometimes shows up on exams.

Assessing Readiness for Exam 640-507

In addition to the general exam-readiness information in the previous section, you can do several things to prepare for the CCNA exam. As you're getting ready for Exam 640-507, visit the Cisco Web site at **www.cisco.com**. Its open forum or technical tips sections are great places to ask questions and get good answers or to watch the questions that others ask (along with the answers, of course).

For OSI model, TCP/IP, and basic router configuration preparation in particular, we'd also like to recommend that you check out one or more of the following resources as you prepare to take Exam 640-507:

➤ Shawn McNutt, Mark Poplar, Jason Waters, David Stabenaw. *CCNA Routing and Switching Exam Prep.* The Coriolis Group, Scottsdale, AZ, 2000. ISBN 1-57610-440-0.

➤ Chappell, Laura. *Introduction to Cisco Router Configuration.* Cisco Systems Inc., MacMillan Publishing Company, Indianapolis, IN, 1998. ISBN 0-7645-3186-7.

➤ Comer, Douglas. *Internetworking with TCP/IP: Principles, Protocols, and Architecture, Vol. 1.* Prentice Hall, Englewood Cliffs, NJ, 1995. ISBN 0-1321-6987-8.

➤ Stallings, William. *Handbook of Computer Communications Standards: The Open Systems Interconnection (OSI Model and OSI-Related Standards), Vol. 1.* Prentice-Hall, Englewood Cliffs, NJ, 1990. ISBN 0-02415-521-7.

Stop by your favorite bookstore or online bookseller to check out one or more of these resources.

One last note: It makes sense to stress the importance of hands-on experience in the context of the CCNA exam. As you review the material for that exam, you'll realize that hands-on experience with the various router configurations and monitoring commands is invaluable. There are also sites available on the Internet that will allow you access to routers via a telnet connection. It may cost you a few dollars up front but it is cheaper than buying equipment and will pay dividends when you pass the exam.

Onward, through the Fog

When you've assessed your readiness, undertaken the right background studies, obtained the hands-on experience that will help you to understand the products and technologies at work, and reviewed the many sources of information to help you to prepare for a test, you'll be ready to take a round of practice tests. When your scores come back positive enough to get you through the exam, you're ready to go after the real thing. If you follow our assessment regime, you'll not only know what you need to study, but when you're ready to make a test date. Good luck!

Cisco Certification Exams

Terms you'll need to understand:

✓ Radio button

✓ Checkbox

✓ Exhibit

✓ Multiple-choice question formats

✓ Careful reading

✓ Process of elimination

Techniques you'll need to master:

✓ Preparing to take a certification exam

✓ Practicing (to make perfect)

✓ Making the best use of the testing software

✓ Budgeting your time

✓ Saving the hardest questions until last

✓ Guessing (as a last resort)

✓ Breathing deeply to calm frustration

Exam taking is not something that most people anticipate eagerly, no matter how well prepared they are. In most cases, familiarity helps ameliorate test anxiety. In plain English, this means that you will probably not be as nervous when you take your fourth or fifth Cisco certification exam as when you take your first.

Whether it is your first exam or your tenth, understanding the details of exam taking (how much time to spend on questions, the environment you will be in, and so on) and the exam software will help you to concentrate on the material, rather than on the setting. Likewise, mastering a few basic exam-taking skills should help you to recognize—and perhaps even outfox—some of the tricks and gotchas you are bound to find in some of the exam questions.

This chapter, besides explaining the exam environment and software, describes some proven exam-taking strategies that you can use to your advantage.

The Exam Situation

When you arrive at the exam-testing center, you must sign in with an exam coordinator and show two forms of identification, one of which must be a photo ID. After you have signed in and your time slot arrives, you will be asked to deposit any books, bags, or other items you brought with you. Then, you will be escorted into a closed room. Typically, the room will be furnished with one to half a dozen computers, and each workstation will be separated from the others by dividers designed to keep you from seeing what is happening on someone else's computer.

You will be furnished with a pen or pencil and a blank sheet of paper, or, in some cases, an erasable plastic sheet and an erasable felt-tip pen. You are allowed to write any information you want on both sides of this sheet. Before the exam, memorize as much of the material that appears on the Cram Sheet (inside the front cover of this book) as you can and write that information on the blank sheet as soon as you are seated in front of the computer. You can refer to your rendition of the Cram Sheet anytime you like during the test, but you will have to surrender the sheet when you leave the room.

Most test rooms feature a wall with a large picture window. This permits the exam coordinator standing behind it to monitor the room, to prevent exam takers from talking to one another, and to observe anything out of the ordinary that might happen. The exam coordinator will have preloaded the appropriate Cisco certification exam—for this book, that's Exam 640-507—and you will be permitted to start as soon as you are seated in front of the computer.

It is very important to make sure to check Cisco's official Web site for up-to-date and accurate information regarding exams. The information presented in this book is accurate at the time of publication.

All Cisco certification exams allow a certain maximum amount of time in which to complete the work (this time is indicated on the exam by an on-screen counter/ clock, so you can check the time remaining whenever you like). Exam 640-507 consists of approximately 65 randomly selected questions. You may take up to 75 minutes to complete the exam.

All Cisco certification exams are computer-generated and use a multiple-choice format. From time to time, you may be prompted to enter actual configuration commands as if you were at the command-line interface. It is important not to abbreviate the commands in any way when this type of question is posed. Although this may sound quite simple, the questions are constructed not only to check your mastery of basic facts and figures about Cisco router configuration, but also to require you to evaluate one or more sets of circumstances or requirements. Often, you will be asked to give more than one answer to a question. Likewise, you might be asked to select the best or most effective solution to a problem from a range of choices, all of which are technically correct. Taking the exam is quite an adventure, and it involves real thinking. This book shows you what to expect and how to deal with the potential problems, puzzles, and predicaments.

Exam Layout and Design

Some exam questions require you to select a single answer, whereas others ask you to select multiple correct answers. The following multiple-choice question requires you to select a single correct answer. Following the question is a brief summary of each potential answer and why it is either right or wrong.

Question 1

What is the key piece of information on which routing decisions are based?

○ a. Source Network layer address

○ b. Destination Network layer address

○ c. Source MAC address

○ d. Destination MAC address

Answer b is correct. The destination Network layer, or layer 3, address is the protocol-specific address to which this piece of data is to be delivered. The source Network layer address is the originating host and plays no role in getting the information to the destination; therefore, answer a is incorrect. The source and destination MAC addresses are necessary for getting the data to the router or to the next hop address, but they are not used in pathing decisions; therefore, answers c and d are incorrect.

This sample question format corresponds closely to the Cisco certification exam format—the only difference on the exam is that answer keys do not follow questions. To select an answer, position the cursor over the radio button next to the answer, and then click the mouse button to select the answer.

Let's examine a question that requires choosing multiple answers. This type of question provides checkboxes rather than radio buttons for marking all appropriate selections.

Question 2

> Which of the following services exist at the Application layer of the TCP/IP model? [Choose the three best answers]
>
> ❑ a. SMTP
>
> ❑ b. FTP
>
> ❑ c. ICMP
>
> ❑ d. ARP
>
> ❑ e. TFTP

Answers a, b, and e are correct. SMTP, FTP, and TFTP all exist at the Application layer of the TCP/IP model. Answer c is incorrect because ICMP exists at the Internet layer of the TCP/IP model. Answer d is incorrect because ARP exists at the Network Interface layer of the TCP/IP model.

For this type of question, more than one answer is required. As far as I can tell, such questions are scored as wrong unless all of the required selections are chosen. In other words, a partially correct answer does not result in partial credit when the test is scored. For Question 2, you have to check the boxes next to items a, b, and e to obtain credit for a correct answer. Notice that picking the right answers also means knowing why the other answers are wrong!

These two basic types of questions can appear in many forms; they constitute the foundation on which all of the Cisco certification exam questions rest. More complex questions include so-called *exhibits*, which are usually network scenarios, screen shots of output from the router, or pictures from the course materials. For some of these questions, you will be asked to make a selection by clicking on a checkbox or radio button on the screenshot itself. For others, you will be expected to use the information displayed therein to guide your answer to the question. Familiarity with the underlying utility is your key to choosing the correct answers.

Other questions involving exhibits use charts or network diagrams to help document a workplace scenario that you will be asked to troubleshoot or configure. Careful attention to such exhibits is the key to success. Be prepared to toggle frequently between the exhibit and the question as you work.

Using Cisco's Exam Software Effectively

Unlike some exams by Cisco and other companies, the CCNA 2.0 exam software does not allow you to mark questions or review them later. You may not skip questions or go back to them later. In fact, the test engine will not let you proceed if you have not selected an answer or if you have not chosen the correct number of answers.

With this in mind, time management is very important during the test. You cannot save difficult or lengthy questions to do at the end of the exam. For this reason, it will be helpful to monitor your progress by checking the clock periodically during the test. Make sure that you are one-third of the way through the test when one-third of your time is up. The test has approximately 65 questions and allows 75 minutes, so that gives you just over 1 minute per question, so think fast and move on.

Exam-Taking Basics

The most important advice about taking any exam is this: Read each question carefully. Some questions are deliberately ambiguous, some use double negatives, and others use terminology in incredibly precise ways.

Here are some suggestions for how to deal with the tendency to jump to an answer too quickly:

➤ Make sure you read every word in the question. If you find yourself jumping ahead impatiently, go back and start over.

➤ As you read, try to restate the question in your own terms. If you can do this, you should be able to pick the correct answers much more easily.

➤ Breathe. Deep rhythmic breathing is a stress reliever. Breathe in for a count of four, hold it for two, and then exhale for a count of four. You will be surprised how this can clear your mind of the frustration that clouds it and allow you to regain focus.

Above all, try to deal with each question by thinking through what you know about Cisco routers and their configuration—the characteristics, behaviors, facts, and figures involved. By reviewing what you know (and what you have written down on your information sheet), you will often recall or understand things sufficiently to determine the answer to the question.

Question-Handling Strategies

Based on exams I have taken, some interesting trends have become apparent. For questions that require a single answer, two or three of the answers will usually be obviously incorrect, and two of the answers will be plausible—of course, only one can be correct. Unless the answer leaps out at you (if it does, reread the question to look for a trick; sometimes those are the ones you are most likely to get wrong), begin the process of answering by eliminating those answers that are most obviously wrong.

Things to look for in obviously wrong answers include spurious menu choices or utility names, nonexistent software options, and terminology you have never seen. If you have done your homework for an exam, no valid information should be completely new to you. In that case, unfamiliar or bizarre terminology probably indicates a bogus answer.

Numerous questions assume that the default behavior of a particular utility is in effect. If you know the defaults and understand what they mean, this knowledge will help you cut through many Gordian knots.

As you work your way through the exam, another counter that Cisco thankfully provides will come in handy—the number of questions completed and questions outstanding. Budget your time by making sure that you have completed one-quarter of the questions one-quarter of the way through the exam period and three-quarters of them three-quarters of the way through.

If you are not finished when 70 minutes have elapsed, use the last 5 minutes to guess your way through the remaining questions. Remember, guessing is potentially more valuable than not answering; blank answers are always wrong, but a guess may turn out to be right. If you do not have a clue about any of the remaining questions, pick answers at random. The important thing is to submit an exam for scoring that has an answer for every question.

Mastering the Inner Game

In the final analysis, knowledge breeds confidence, and confidence breeds success. If you study the materials in this book carefully and review all of the exam questions at the end of each chapter, you should become aware of those areas where additional learning and study are required.

Next, follow up by reading some or all of the materials recommended in the "Need to Know More?" section at the end of each chapter. The idea is to become familiar enough with the concepts and situations you find in the sample questions that you can reason your way through similar situations on a real exam. If you know the material, you have every right to be confident that you can pass the exam.

After you have worked your way through the book, take the practice exam at the end of the book. This will provide a reality check and help you to identify areas that you need to study further. Make sure that you follow up and review materials related to the questions you miss on the practice exam before scheduling a real exam. Take the real exam only when you have covered all of the ground and feel comfortable with the whole scope of the practice exam.

 If you take the practice exam and do not score at least 70 percent correct, you need additional practice.

Armed with the information in this book and with the determination to augment your knowledge, you should be able to pass the certification exam. You need to work at it, however, or you will spend the exam fee more than once before you finally pass. If you prepare seriously, you should do well. Good luck!

Additional Resources

A good source of information about Cisco certification exams comes from Cisco itself. Because its products and technologies (and the exams that go with them) change frequently, the best place to go for exam-related information is online.

If you haven't already visited the Cisco Certified Professional site, do so right now. The Career Certifications home page resides at **www.cisco.com/warp/public/10/wwtraining/certprog/index.html**, as shown in Figure 1.1.

Note: Because things change regularly on the Cisco site, the home page might not be available at this address or it might have been replaced by something new and different. If this is the case, read the sidebar titled "Coping with Change on the Web."

The menu options in the left column of the home page point to the most important sources of information in the Career Certifications pages. Here's what to check out:

➤ *Career Certifications*—This Web link is a detailed breakdown of all Cisco certifications, exams and paths that one can take to become a Cisco Certified Professional.

Figure 1.1   The Cisco Connection Online home page.

➤ *Exam Information*—This Web link will detail what to expect on the exam and will enable the candidate to show show networking knowledge and expertise.

➤ *Tracking System*—This section is a secure Web site that provides a record of exam history, certification information, and personal information for the many Cisco professionals.

These are just the high points of what's available on the Cisco Certified Professional pages. As you browse through them—and we strongly recommend that you do—you will probably find other informational tidbits that are interesting and compelling.

Coping with Change on the Web

Sooner or later, all the information we have shared with you about the Cisco Certified Professional pages and the other Web-based resources mentioned throughout the rest of this book will go stale or be replaced by newer information. In some cases, the URLs you find here might lead you to their replacements; in other cases, the URLs will go nowhere, leaving you with the dreaded "404 File not found" error message. When that happens, do not give up.

There's always a way to find what you want on the Web if you are willing to invest some time and energy. Most large or complex Web sites—and Cisco's qualifies on both counts—offer a search engine. Looking back at Figure 1.1, you can see that a Search button appears on the page. As long as you can get to Cisco's site (it should stay at **www.cisco.com** for a long while yet), you can use this tool to help you find what you need.

The more focused you can make a search request, the more likely the results will include information you can use. For example, you can search for the string "training and certification" to produce a lot of data about the subject in general, but if you are looking for the preparation guide for Exam 640-507, "CCNA Routing and Switching," you will be more likely to get there quickly if you use a search string similar to the following:

```
"Exam 640-507" AND "preparation guide"
```

Finally, feel free to use general search tools—such as **www.search.com**, **www.altavista.com**, and **www.excite.com**—to search for related information. The bottom line is this: If you can't find something where the book says it lives, intensify your search.

Internetworking Concepts: An Overview

Terms you'll need to understand:

✓ Open Systems Interconnection (OSI) Model

✓ Ethernet

✓ Twisted Pair Cabling

✓ Coaxial Cabling

✓ Fiber-Optic Cabling

✓ Carrier Sense Multiple Access with Collision Detection (CSMA/CD)

✓ Token Ring

✓ Encapsulation

Techniques you'll need to master:

✓ Describing data-link and network addresses and identifying key differences between them

✓ Defining and describing the function of the MAC address

✓ Listing the key internetworking functions for the OSI Network layer

✓ Identifying at least three reasons why the industry uses a layered model

✓ Defining and explaining the five conversion steps of data encapsulation

The first step in preparing for the CCNA certification is making sure you have a solid understanding of basic networking concepts. You will rely on these fundamentals as you learn to design and configure Cisco routed and switched internetworks. You will need to understand different network topologies, transmission media, and protocols. In addition, you must know the components that make up a network—hubs, bridges, routers, switches, and so on. This chapter will provide an overview of these basic internetworking concepts and a detailed look at the Open Systems Interconnection (OSI) model.

Networking Fundamentals

This section briefly reviews several basic networking concepts that are the building blocks to CCNA study. Ideally, you should recognize and understand most of the material in this section, using it only as a review. If these concepts are not familiar, make sure you study this section and master this material before proceeding.

The network consists of several components—the physical connections between devices, the intermediate devices that facilitate transmission (such as hubs, routers, and switches), and the protocols used to make everything work. You will examine the following components that make network communication possible:

➤ *Transmission media*—The physical connection between devices

➤ *Media access method*—The rules that define how a device can access the transmission media

➤ *Data transmission methods*—What types of data messages can be sent

➤ *Network transport methods*—The standards, such as Ethernet, that define the media, access, and transmission methods and form a complete system for moving data

Transmission Media

At the bottom of the Open Systems Interconnection (OSI) model are the layers that define how a network is physically connected—that is to say, the wires that carry data from one device to another. This network component is called the *transmission media*. It is important to note that wire is not the only type of transmission media. Several newer technologies, such as microwave, radio, and infrared are used in wireless networks.

The most common types of wire-based transmission media are:

➤ *Twisted pair copper cable*—Commonly referred to as 10/100 BaseT, this is a popular wiring type for local area networks (LANs). Individual copper wires are twisted together to prevent electromagnetic interference (EMI). Twisted pair is very inexpensive and flexible. Twisted pair network cables can reliably transmit data to a length of 100 meters. The American National Standards Institute classifies twisted pair cable into different "categories" based on the data rate it can sustain. The most common types of cables you will see are Category 3 and Category 5 (also called CAT 3 and CAT 5, respectively). CAT 3 is the minimum cable type required for voice systems and 10Mb Ethernet. CAT 5 is required to support Fast Ethernet. Most new buildings are being prewired with CAT 5 cable. However, many existing cable plants are wired with CAT 3 cable. Shielded and unshielded twisted pair are the two most common types of twisted pair cabling. Unshielded is more susceptible to electromagnetic interference and is the cheaper of the two to purchase.

➤ *Coaxial cable*—Commonly referred to as *10Base2* or *10Base5*, coaxial cable comes in two forms: thick and thin. Thick cable (also called thicknet or 10Base5) was one of the first types of wire used to connect computers. This type of wire is rigid and therefore difficult to work with. The other type of coaxial cable, thin cable (also called thinnet or 10Base2), is easier to work with because of its flexibility. Coaxial cable can support longer distances than twisted pair. The maximum distance for data to travel on 10Base2 is 185 meters, whereas 10Base5 can travel up to 500 meters without suffering attenuation.

➤ *Fiber-optic cable*—Commonly called *100BaseFL*, fiber optic is the newest type of cable available for wiring networks. It consists of a glass core that is encased by a plastic outer covering. Instead of electrical current, fiber-optic cable carries laser light. It can transport data much farther than other wiring types—kilometers instead of feet. It is also immune to EMI. The disadvantages are its cost and difficulty to install and work with. The maximum distance for data to travel on 100BaseFL is 3 kilometers without suffering attenuation.

Media Access Methods

Most networks today are built using some type of shared media. That is, all the devices on the network are connected to the same media channel, whether it's twisted pair, coaxial, or fiber optic. Only one device can access the media at a given time, so there must be some way for devices to share the available media (also called a *channel*).

A *media access method* is a rule or set of rules that defines how devices can share a single media channel. The most common media access methods currently in use are:

➤ *Contention*—Contention is an access method in which devices access the media on a first-come, first-served basis. All devices are contending for the single media channel. The most common type of contention method is Carrier Sense Multiple Access with Collision Detection (CSMA/CD). Ethernet uses this type of access method. Whenever the device needs to send data, it listens to the channel to find out if it is available. If so, the data is sent. If not, it will wait until the channel is free. The problem with this method is that two devices may check the channel at the same time, both detecting that it is free, and both may send data at the same time. When this happens, a collision (or *jam*) occurs, and both devices must retransmit the data.

➤ *Token passing*—Token passing is an access method that is used in ring-connected networks. A signal called the *token* is passed from device to device around the ring so that data can only be transmitted over the media when a device has the token. The token-passing method eliminates collisions and retransmissions. However, the disadvantage is that more processing power is required, and problems can occur if the ring is broken by a malfunctioning device. Token passing is the only true access method that is free of collisions.

➤ *Polling*—Polling is an access method that relies on a central device to control access to the network. Before a device can transmit data onto the network, it must check with this central device, known as a *media access administrator* or *channel access administrator*.

Data Transmission Methods

Once a network device has access to the shared media, how does it format the data in order to get the data to its intended recipient? The answer to this depends on whether the data needs to be sent to a single device or multiple devices on the network. Remember, because all devices are connected to the same physical media, all the devices may "see" all the packets, regardless of their intended recipient. (This is not always the case and will be talked about in Chapter 10.) Each device will examine a packet to determine its recipient. If the packet is addressed to a different device, it will get dropped. There are three methods by which data packets are addressed and transmitted onto the network:

➤ *Unicast*—A unicast packet is one that is sent directly from one device to another. Each network device is identified by a unique hardware address (MAC address), and only the machine whose address matches will process the packet.

➤ *Multicast*—A multicast packet needs to be sent to more than one recipient. This is accomplished by addressing each packet to a multicast group address. Hosts wishing to receive the packet must join this multicast group. Multicasts are typically used with multimedia applications, such as delivering video and audio to end users on a network. IP multicasting applications use Class D addresses to address packets. Class D IP addresses range from 224.0.0.0 to 239.255.255.255. (IP addressing will be discussed in detail in Chapter 10.)

➤ *Broadcast*—A broadcast packet is sent to all receiving devices on the network. A special address is used in place of the recipient's hardware address, indicating that the packet is intended for all network devices.

Network Standards

Several network standards have been developed that define specific topologies, media, access methods, and transmission methods. These standards incorporate all these aspects into a single solution for moving data across a network. Three of the most common standards are:

➤ *Ethernet*—Ethernet has become, by far, the most common standard for LANs. Ethernet uses coaxial, twisted pair, or fiber-optic cable to transmit data using CSMA/CD contention. It operates at the speed of 10Mbps (10 million bits per second). There are faster versions of Ethernet, such as Fast Ethernet, which operates at 100Mbps, and Gigabit Ethernet, which operates at 1,000Mbps. Devices are connected either on a linear bus or star topology.

Note: Ethernet uses a three-part naming convention. Common Ethernet specifications include 10BaseT, 100BaseT, and 10BaseFL. First is a number indicating the speed (in Mbps), such as 10, 100, or 1000. Second is the signaling type, which in almost all cases is baseband, or Base. Finally, there is a value indicating the physical media type. For example, T indicates twisted pair, and F indicates fiber media.

➤ *Token ring*—Token ring was developed by IBM in the 1970s and is still a common network type in use today. Devices on a token ring network are connected in a ring topology. Typically, they are connected to a multistation access unit (MSAU) that simulates the ring topology. Token ring uses either coaxial cable or twisted pair to transmit data using the token-passing method of media access. It operates at speeds up to 16Mbps.

➤ *Asynchronous Transfer Mode (ATM)*— ATM is a newer network standard that can be used for extremely high-speed data transport over long distances. It uses a star topology and relies on polling as the media access method. An ATM switch is the central hub of the star and acts as the channel access administrator. ATM can use coaxial or fiber-optic cable at speeds from 200Mbps to over 1Gbps (1 billion bits per second).

The OSI Model

Computers and programs that share and move data must use common protocols to communicate. A *protocol* is simply a formal description of a set of rules and conventions that defines how devices on a network must exchange information.

If a wide variety of protocols for data communication exists, linking computers into networks becomes extremely difficult. As a result, computer vendors began developing their own protocols. Because protocols were being developed rapidly and for different computer platforms, some vendors developed more than one.

This situation led to the creation of standards for the various computer platforms and systems. In 1984, the International Organization for Standardization (ISO) released the OSI reference model to help computer vendors create interoperable network equipment. Since then, the OSI reference model has become the primary architectural model for intercomputer communication. Most network vendors now relate their products to the OSI reference model in order to educate customers about the product's features and capabilities. Each technology addressed in this book can be mapped to one of the layers in the OSI model. As a result, the OSI model is a valuable tool available for people who need to learn about network technologies.

Note: ISO does not stand for International Standards Organization. ISO is not an acronym for anything. The International Organization for Standardization borrowed its name from the Greek word isos, *which means equal. Creating an acronym for the organization's three official languages (English, French, and Russian) would be incredibly difficult.*

This model divides the functions of networking—moving data from one device to another—into seven distinct and separate tasks or layers. In a nutshell, this basically means that different types of computer systems can communicate with each other because of these standards.

Each of the seven layers within the OSI model represents a specific and separate network function. Standards and protocols have been defined for each layer. When two systems are communicating over the network, data is being sent down the layers at the sending device and back up the protocol stack at the receiving device. This division of separate network functions in a stack provides the following benefits:

➤ The interrelated aspects of network operations are divided into simpler components.

➤ Complex internetworking components can be divided into discrete subsets.

➤ Hardware and software engineers can focus their designs and development efforts in a modular fashion.

➤ Enhancements to one area are isolated from another area.

➤ Standard interfaces for plug-and-play compatibility between vendors can be defined.

For example, the OSI model details how data should be communicated from a word processing application residing on one computer through a network medium (such as a copper wire) to a word processing application residing on another computer.

 In order to pass the exam, you must study and understand the OSI model inside and out. Whenever I prepare for an exam, I use a mnemonic to help me remember the specific order of things. For the OSI model, I remember the order by repeating the phrase, "All (Application) People (Presentation) Seem (Session) To (Transport) Need (Network) Data (Data Link) Processing (Physical)."

The problem of moving data among different computer systems over a network is significant. Using a divide-and-conquer approach, the OSI reference model addresses this problem by dividing the transmitting and receiving of data process into seven smaller layers. This layered approach does not constrain or define how a vendor's implementation should be; it simply provides a framework in which vendors can build their specific products. In other words, a network implementation or product does not conform to the OSI model, but it conforms to the standards and protocols developed from the OSI model.

As we discuss the OSI model in more detail, keep in mind that the upper layers are Application, Presentation, Session, and Transport, and the lower layers are Network, Data Link, and Physical. The upper layers deal with how communication occurs between the differing systems, whereas the lower layers deal with network-related issues and how the data is to be transferred.

Application Layer

The Application layer (layer 7) is the layer closest to the user. This layer communicates with user applications and selects the appropriate network applications for those user applications. In addition, layer 7 identifies and establishes the availability of application resources in order to synchronize applications, negotiate error recovery, and provide data integrity. A few examples of the most common uses of layer 7 applications are email, word processing, and browsing the Web.

Any of the user applications can require services from one or more of the network applications. For example, a database application on one server may require remote access to a database on another server and, also, the ability to transfer database information back and forth.

Presentation Layer

The Presentation layer (layer 6) ensures that information received from the Application layer is readable by the Application layer of the destination peer. Simply put, the Presentation layer concerns itself primarily with how the data is presented to the application by way of translation. Because there are standards for the way data is to be formatted, operations such as encryption, decryption, compression, and decompression are part of this layer's usage. The Presentation layer accomplishes this task by performing several functions:

➤ It performs code formatting and conversion to ensure that applications have readable information.

➤ It negotiates data-transfer syntax between applications that use different data formats.

➤ It performs data encryption and decryption to ensure that the data cannot be viewed or altered by unauthorized parties.

➤ It performs data compression to make optimal use of its channel (a single communication path on a system).

The Presentation layer must support a wide variety of data types, some of which are listed in Table 2.1.

Session Layer

The Session layer (layer 5) establishes, manages, and terminates sessions between applications. A *session* consists of a dialogue between Presentation layers on two or more systems. The Session layer also synchronizes and coordinates service requests and responses between the systems. Common layer 5 protocols include:

➤ *Network Filing System (NFS)*—Developed by Sun Microsystems, NFS provides transparent remote access to network resources via TCP/IP on Unix workstations.

➤ *Structured Query Language (SQL)*—Developed by IBM, SQL provides a simple method of accessing information on local or remote systems.

Table 2.1 Presentation layer data types and standards.	
Data Type	**Standards**
Text and data	ASCII, EBCDIC, and encrypted
Sound and video	MIDI, MPEG, and QuickTime
Graphics and images	PICT, TIFF, GIF, and JPEG

➤ *Remote procedure call (RPC)*—RPCs are procedures that are built on a client and executed on a local or remote server.

 The Application, Presentation, and Session layers provide standardization so that applications can share data and communicate with one another more easily. Layers 7, 6, and 5 do not concern themselves with how the data will arrive at its destination.

Transport Layer

The Transport layer (layer 4) is situated between the upper and lower layers. As its name implies, the Transport layer provides end-to-end data transport services to the upper layers. To further clarify, layer 4 provides the following services to the upper layers:

➤ It segments upper-layer applications.

➤ It establishes an end-to-end connection.

➤ It sends segments from one end host to another.

➤ It ensures reliable data transport.

Segment Upper-Layer Applications

One service provided by the Transport layer is the capability to segment upper-layer applications. Layer 4 accomplishes this task by transporting the data segment by segment. Each segment created is autonomous. Different applications send successive segments on a first-come, first-served basis to the Transport layer. The applications can destine the segments for a single system or several different systems. For example, a file transfer can occur between two different systems. Conversely, a single email message may be sent to one or more recipients. The Transport layer tracks and manages the various segments sent to and from both applications using port numbers. These port numbers are standard for each application and must be set by the application before the Transport layer receives the segment. Because the source and destination applications use predefined port numbers, the Transport layers at the source and destination systems can pass the segments easily to and from the appropriate upper-layer applications.

Establish End-to-End Connections

The second service that the Transport layer provides is establishing an end-to-end connection between the source and destination systems. Layer 4 establishes this connection through a series of *handshakes*, which involve one system making a request to another system prior to a connection being established. Handshakes occur during the establishment of a connection between two systems and address matters such as synchronization and connection parameters.

Send Segments from One Host to Another

Another service that is provided by the Transport layer occurs after the connection has been established and data transfer between the two systems has begun. The Transport layer is responsible for sending the segments from one system to another and verifying that all the segments arrive at the destination, which is known as an *acknowledgment*. As data is transferred between the two systems, data can be discarded for many reasons, but the most common reason is *congestion*, which may occur during data transfer if one computer generates traffic faster than the network can transfer it. Also, if several computers send traffic simultaneously to a single destination or through a single gateway, that destination or gateway may not be able to process the data quickly enough. The Transport layer handles congestion by *flow control*, a mechanism that ensures a sending system does not overwhelm the receiving system with data.

As the Transport layer sends segments from one system to another, it can use any of these three methods of flow control:

➤ Buffering

➤ Multiplexing

➤ Parallelization

Buffering

The first method of flow control involves *buffering*. Each system has a certain amount of memory available for buffering information. The Transport layer of the receiving system ensures that sufficient buffers are available and that data is not transmitted at a rate that exceeds the rate at which the receiving system can process it. When the buffers on the receiving system are full, a "not ready" message is sent to the sending system to suspend data transmission until the data in the buffers has been processed. A "ready" message is sent from the receiving system to the sending system when the data in the buffers has been processed.

Multiplexing

The second method of flow control involves *multiplexing*. Occasionally, the upper layers require slower service than a channel can provide. As a result, the channel's bandwidth becomes underutilized. In this case, the Transport layer multiplexes conversations by interweaving packets from different segments and transmitting them. The Transport layer at the receiving end sorts the packets (using the header information that was encapsulated) and re-creates the original segments.

Parallelization

The third method of flow control involves *parallelization*. If the upper layers require faster service than a channel can provide, the Transport layer may be able to combine multiple channels (paralleling the flow of the data) to increase the effective bandwidth for the upper layers.

Note: Operating systems such as Unix and MVS support parallelization, whereas some personal computers do not.

Ensure Reliable Data Transport

The final service that is provided by the Transport layer involves the reliable transport of the segments. Reliable transport depends on a connection-oriented relationship between the sending and receiving systems to ensure that the following tasks are completed successfully:

➤ Send an acknowledgment to the sending system for each segment that was received successfully.

➤ Retransmit any segments that were not acknowledged by the receiving system.

➤ Discard any duplicate segments.

➤ Return segments to their original sequence at the receiving system.

➤ Provide congestion avoidance and control.

Therefore, reliable transport ensures that segments are not lost, damaged, duplicated, or received out of sequence. Upon successful receipt of segments, the receiving system sends acknowledgments to the sending system.

Network Layer

The primary purpose of the Network layer is to determine the best path from one network to another and to route messages in that direction. It is at this layer that a router utilizes its capabilities. Essentially, a router will receive a packet and then determine whether it is to be sent to a locally connected network. If it is determined that this is not the case, the router will search its internal routing table to determine the best path the packet should take for delivery to its destination. In the event that the router does not know the destination address, the packet may be discarded, depending on the configuration. The process of routing includes path determination and packet switching. Path determination requires the use of routing protocols to optimize the routing process. In addition, the Network layer employs routed protocols that provide a logical two-part addressing scheme to identify paths and assign costs to different destinations. The steps in path determination and packet switching are discussed in the next sections.

Remember that the primary purposes of the Network layer are:

➤ Packet switching

➤ Path determination

Path Determination

The Network layer performs path determination via routers, routing protocols, and routed protocols. A router utilizes a routing protocol to determine the best path between itself and a destination. Typically, routing protocols utilize layer 3 or logical addressing—an inherent part of most routed protocols—to identify and differentiate between two destinations.

Packet Switching

The final purpose of the Network layer is to perform packet switching from one network to another. The process of packet switching refers to a router receiving a packet on one network interface and switching it to another interface en route to its destination. This process relies on the determination of an optimal path by the routing protocol so that the best interface can be identified for reaching the packet's destination. When the best path has been identified, the router takes the packet from one interface and forwards it to another interface on the most optimal path to the packet's destination.

Data Link Layer

The data link layer is responsible for translating messages from the network layer into bits for the physical layer and also formatting messages into frames. The Data Link layer encapsulates data in the format of a frame. In this layer, the MAC address of a node is most relevant because it is the MAC address that uniquely identifies every individual node on a network. *Do not confuse this with the function of a router.* A router does not concern itself with individual nodes; the router only cares about the network location which nodes are connected to. This layer is divided into two sublayers: the LLC sublayer and the MAC sublayer. The LLC and MAC sublayers work together to perform all the functions required of the Data Link layer. The Data Link layer performs the following functions:

➤ Allows the upper layers of the OSI model to work independently of the type of media used at the Physical layer.

➤ Provides optional flow control and frame sequencing.

➤ Provides error notification.

➤ Performs physical hardware addressing to ensure that all devices in an internetwork have a unique identification.

LLC Sublayer 802.2

The LLC sublayer performs more of the software functions of the Data Link layer. Its primary function is to allow the upper layers to communicate with other devices in connectionless or connection-oriented environments. Because confusion often occurs regarding the difference between connection-oriented and connectionless communication, an explanation of the difference between the two follows.

Connection-Oriented vs. Connectionless Communication

Connection-oriented communication involves using a nonpermanent path for data transfer. In order for two systems to communicate, they must establish a path that will be used for the duration of their connection. Connection-oriented communication involves three steps:

1. Establish the connection.

2. Transfer the data.

3. Terminate the connection.

Connection-oriented services generally are able to reserve a guaranteed throughput rate. Data is sent sequentially over the established path for the duration of the connection. This is useful for transmitting data for services that don't tolerate delays and packet resequencing, such as many voice and video applications.

Connectionless communication involves using a permanently established link. Path selection and bandwidth allocation are done dynamically. Applications that can tolerate some delay or resequencing are typically based on connectionless service. An example of connectionless would be UDP.

Functions of the LLC Sublayer

The LLC sublayer performs the following functions:

➤ *Allows upper layers to perform independently of the LAN/WAN protocol or physical media*—The LLC sublayer allows upper-layer protocols such as IP and IPX to act independently of the LAN topology or protocol. This is a major benefit because you can change the LAN protocols or media without affecting the upper layers. This autonomy is available because the LLC sublayer is not tied to a specific MAC protocol.

➤ *Provides SAPs for the lower MAC sublayer to communicate with the upper-layer functions*—The LLC sublayer provides a common set of Service Access Points (SAPs) so that the MAC sublayer can send information to the upper-layer services. The SAPs help the LLC sublayer determine where to send the data received from the MAC sublayer.

➤ *Performs flow control for upper-layer protocols*—The Data Link layer is capable of using ready/not ready codes to indicate when it or its upper layers are capable of receiving more information. This allows communicating devices to throttle back on the communication data rate and minimizes the amount of data that has to be sent twice due to dropped packets.

➤ *Performs sequencing of frames*—The Data Link layer is capable of resequencing any frames that are received in the wrong order. This enables frames to use different paths to reach its destination and makes it more efficient and faster.

Media Access Control Sublayer 802.3

The MAC sublayer interfaces with the Physical layer and media. In comparison with the LLC sublayer, the MAC sublayer is responsible for performing more of the hardware functions of the Data Link layer.

The MAC sublayer maintains the physical address of a device. The physical address is also referred to as the *MAC address*. The MAC address is a 48-bit address expressed as 12 hexadecimal digits. The first six digits contain the unique identification of the manufacturer, and the last six digits comprise the serial number assigned by the manufacturer. Typically, a workstation has a piece of hardware called a *network interface card* (NIC) that has a MAC address burned into the read-only memory (ROM). The MAC address uniquely identifies this interface from any other interface in the world. The Institute of Electrical and Electronics Engineers (IEEE) developed a set of unique identification codes and distributes these codes to manufacturers. Each manufacturer is assigned a different identification code. Examples of MAC addresses are shown in Table 2.2.

The first column shows the entire physical address; it is typically shown in this format. The second column displays the first six digits; these identify the manufacturer code assigned by the IEEE. The last column displays the last six digits that are assigned by the manufacturer as a product serial number.

Framing

The MAC sublayer is also responsible for framing data as it is received or transmitted onto the physical media. All WAN/LAN protocols implement specific frame formats; however, they all perform a subset of the following functions:

Table 2.2 MAC address examples.		
MAC Address	**Manufacturer Code**	**Serial Number**
FF34.2345.12AB	FF34.23	45.12AB
45AB.2348.ABDD	45AB.23	48.ABDD

➤ Add a header and/or trailer to the transmitted packet, indicating the protocol, frame length, and error-checking mechanism.

➤ Perform error checking on received frames.

➤ Strip the header off the received frame and pass the data to the LLC sublayer.

➤ Determine whether any frames on the Physical layer are destined for this device.

Physical Layer

The Physical layer performs the mechanical and electrical engineering functions of the OSI model. Because the Physical layer specifies the conversion of 1s and 0s into an electrical current or pulse of light, it must communicate with its peer layers regarding the signals for activating, maintaining, and deactivating a physical circuit. Numerous standards are specified for the Physical layer, as defined by the OSI. For exam purposes, you need only to concern yourself with the standards for Ethernet technologies.

Table 2.3 provides a quick reference guide to help you do some last-minute studying. This table will be very beneficial to you come exam time because it is condensed.

Table 2.3	OSI quick reference.		
Layer	**Function**	**Example**	**Device**
Application	Specialized network functions such as file transfer, virtual terminal, electronic mail, and file servers	Email, WWW, FTP, Gopher, and MS Word	Gateway
Presentation	Data formatting and character code conversion and data encryption	ASCII, EBCDIC, JPEG, GIF, TIFF, and MPEG	Gateway
Session	Negotiation and establishment of a connection with another node	Remote Procedure Call (RPC), Zone Information Protocol (ZIP), and Session Control Protocol (SCP)	Gateway
Transport	Provision for reliable end-to-end delivery of data	Transmission Control Protocol (TCP), Name Binding Protocol (NBP), and OSI transport protocols (SPX)	Gateway
Network	Routing of packets of information across multiple networks	Border Gateway Protocol (BGP), Open Shortest Path First (OSPF), and Routing Information Protocol (RIP)	Router

(continued)

Table 2.3	OSI quick reference. *(continued)*		
Layer	Function	Example	Device
Data Link	Transfer of addressable units of information, frames, and error checking	Frame Relay; Link Access Procedure, Balanced (LAPB); Synchronous Data Link Control (SDLC); Point-to-Point Protocol (PPP); and SMDS Interface Protocol (SIP)	Bridge
Physical	Transmission of binary data over a communications network	Ethernet/IEEE 802.3, Fast Ethernet, FDDI, Token Ring/IEEE 802.5, High-Speed Serial Interface (HSSI), SMDS Interface Protocol (SIP)	Repeater

Encapsulation and De-Encapsulation

For peer-to-peer communication to occur, data must move through the layers within a single system before going across the network to another system. For example, the Application layer must send its Protocol Data Units (PDUs) to the Presentation layer. The Presentation layer then sends its PDUs to the Session layer, and so on down the protocol stack, until the Physical layer sends bits across the network. The concept of encapsulation is essential to understanding how the OSI model operates. What you need to remember is that each layer of the OSI has to add protocol information to the data as it is being sent through the various layers. This is done through the PDU.

Each layer (source layer), however, includes control information with its PDUs that informs its peer layer (destination layer) what should be done with the PDUs. This control information is included in a PDU by the source layer through a process known as *encapsulation*. The control information is read and processed by the destination layer through a process known as *de-encapsulation*. During the encapsulation process, a layer adds header information to the data it received from the layer directly above it. In some cases, a layer will add information to the end of the data block; this is known as a *trailer*. In either case, the layer then passes the newly created package of data to the layer directly beneath it.

During the encapsulation process, the information changes from layer to layer as each layer adds header information to the PDU it receives from the layer directly above it. Although header information is added as the information moves down the protocol stack, the contents or original data does not change. In other words, the original data continues to be wrapped and header information added as it is sent from layer to layer.

1. A user creates an email message. The upper layers convert and format the message for use on the internetwork. The message is sent from the session layer to the transport layer as data.

2. The Transport layer receives the data, converts the data into segments, and includes header information with each segment to ensure that the email systems at both ends of the internetwork can communicate reliably. The Transport layer sends the segments (segment header and data) to the Network layer.

3. The Network layer receives the segments from the Transport layer, converts the segments into packets, and adds its header information—that is, logical source and destination addresses—to each packet. The Network layer then sends the packets (packet header and segments) to the Data Link layer.

4. The Data Link layer receives the packets from the Network layer, converts the packets into frames, and adds its header and trailer information, that is, physical source and destination addresses, to each frame. The Data Link layer then sends the frames (frame header and packets) to the Physical Layer.

5. The Physical layer receives the frames from the Data Link layer and converts the frames into a pattern of electrical voltages that represent 0s and 1s, called *bits*. The 0s and 1s (bits) can then be transmitted on the network medium.

The de-encapsulation process takes place whenever a system receives bits on the network. De-encapsulation is simply the reverse of encapsulation: A layer reads its corresponding header information, processes the header, removes the header information, and, if necessary, sends the PDU to the layer directly above it for further processing. The encapsulation and de-encapsulation processes can occur several times on a single data stream during its transmission across an internetwork to its final destination.

When the entire process of encapsulation and de-encapsulation involves taking data from one network system and placing it inside frames from another network system, it is called *tunneling*.

Quick Reference Steps of Data Encapsulation

Here is a quick reference on the encapsulation process before taking your examination:

1. User information is converted to data (upper layers).

2. Data is converted to segments (Transport layer).

3. Segments are converted to packets or datagrams (Network layer).

4. Packets and datagrams are converted to frames (Data Link layer).

5. Frames are converted to bits (Physical layer).

Practice Questions

Question 1

What layer of the OSI model would a router operate at?

○ a. Physical

○ b. Data Link

○ c. Transport

○ d. Network

The correct answer is d. A router uses network addresses to decide the path determination, which is of course the Network layer. Hubs operate at the Physical layer, switches operate at the Data Link layer, while a gateway would be an example of a Transport layer device. Therefore, answers a, b, and c are incorrect.

Question 2

What layer of the OSI model does a bridge operate at?

○ a. Physical

○ b. Data Link

○ c. Transport

○ d. Network

The correct answer is b. A bridge relies on the MAC address of individual nodes to determine whether the data is to be forwarded on or not. Repeaters operate at the Physical layer, so answer a is wrong. Answer c is wrong because gateways work at the Transport layer. Routers operate at the Network layer, so answer d is also incorrect.

Question 3

A MAC address is divided into a 48-bit address scheme. For the MAC address FF34.2345.12AB, which part represents the vendor code?

○ a. FF34

○ b. 2345

○ c. FF34.23

○ d. 45.12AB

The correct answer is c. The first six digits identify the manufacturer code assigned by the IEEE. The manufacturer assigns the last six digits as a product serial number.

Question 4

What is the correct order of the encapsulation process with relation to the OSI model?

○ a. Physical, Data Link, Network, Transport, upper layers

○ b. Session, Network, Transport, Data Link, Physical

○ c. Session, Transport, Network, Data Link, Physical

○ d. Presentation, Session, Network, Data Link, Physical

The correct answer is c. User information is converted to data at the upper layers; data is converted to segments at the Transport layer; segments are converted to packets or datagrams at the Network layer; packets and datagrams are converted to frames at the Data Link layer; frames are converted to bits at the Physical layer. Therefore, answers a, b, and d are incorrect.

Question 5

10BaseT has a maximum distance for data travel of _____.

○ a. 100 meters

○ b. 185 meters

○ c. 500 meters

○ d. 3 kilometers

The correct answer is a. 10BaseT (or *twisted pair cabling*) cannot exceed 100 meters without the use of additional devices.

Question 6

Which of the following refer to twisted pair cabling? [Choose the best answers]

  ○ a.   Commonly called STP

  ○ b.   Commonly called UTP

  ○ c.   Can transmit data up to 100 meters without signal loss

  ○ d.   Is not susceptible to EMI

The correct answers are a, b, and c. Twisted pair cabling has two types, STP and UTP, and can carry data up to 100 meters without suffering signal loss. Answer d is incorrect because one of the limitations of twisted pair is that it is susceptible to electromagnetic interference.

Question 7

Which is an advantage of a layered network model?

  ○ a.   Accelerates evolution

  ○ b.   Reduces complexity

  ○ c.   Simplifies learning

  ○ d.   All of the above

  ○ e.   Both a and b

The correct answer is d. The layered approach addresses many issues, including the ability to accelerate evolution, because individual layers can be upgraded. It certainly reduces complexity, because each layer is broken down and has specific functions; in other words, it is easier to deal with pieces rather than the whole. Lastly, it simplifies learning. The ability to break down each layer and look at protocols, devices, and so on that operate at each layer makes the layered approach an easy learning tool.

Question 8

> When data is encapsulated, which OSI layer is responsible for converting a segment into a packet?
>
> ○ a. Physical
>
> ○ b. Data Link
>
> ○ c. Network
>
> ○ d. Transport

The correct answer is c. Answer a is incorrect because at the Physical layer, frames are converted to bits. At the Data Link layer, packets are converted into frames, so answer b is incorrect. At the Transport layer, data is converted to segments, which makes answer d incorrect also.

Question 9

> A repeater functions at which OSI layer?
>
> ○ a. Layer 1
>
> ○ b. Layer 2
>
> ○ c. Layer 3
>
> ○ d. Layer 4

The correct answer is a. A repeater serves no function other than to pass information and broadcasts. Because of this, it has no purpose for path determination or selection. An example of layer 2 devices would be a switch, layer 3 would be a router, and layer 4 would be a gateway. Therefore, answers b, c, and d are incorrect.

Question 10

> What does a router route?
>
> ○ a. Layer 1 bits
>
> ○ b. Layer 2 frames
>
> ○ c. Layer 3 packets
>
> ○ d. Layer 4 segments

The correct answer is c. Remember from our chapter reading that we said a router operates at the Network layer. The Network layer is actually layer 3, and the segments are broken down into packets during the encapsulation process. A switch would forward data based on layer 2 frames. A layer 4 device, such as a gateway, would forward segments. Data and bits are sent across the physical media in the layer 1 phase.

Need to Know More?

Lammle, Todd, Donald Porter, and James Chellis. *CCNA Cisco Certified Network Associate*. Sybex Network Press. Alameda, CA, 1999. ISBN 0-7821-2381-3.

This book is a great supplement for learning the technologies tested on the CCNA exam.

McNutt, Shawn, Mark Poplar, Jason Waters, and David Stabenaw. *CNNA Routing and Switching Exam Prep*. The Coriolis Group. Scottsdale, AZ, 2000. ISBN 1-57610-440-0.

This book is a great complement to the *CNNA Exam Cram* book. It has expanded coverage and detailed information about CNNA exam topics.

Syngress Media, with Richard D. Hornbaker, CCIE. *Cisco Certified Network Associate Study Guide*. Osborne/McGraw-Hill. Berkeley, CA, 1998. ISBN 0-07882-487-7.

Another great book for review before taking the CCNA exam.

The TCP/IP Model

Terms you'll need to understand:

✓ Transmission Control Protocol (TCP)

✓ Internet Protocol (IP)

✓ Defense Advanced Research Projects Agency (DARPA)

✓ Advanced Research Project Agency network (ARPAnet)

✓ File Transfer Protocol (FTP)

✓ User Datagram Protocol (UDP)

✓ Telnet

✓ Simple Mail Transfer Protocol (SMTP)

✓ Simple Network Management Protocol (SNMP)

✓ Domain Name System (DNS)

✓ TCP three-way handshake

✓ Internet Control Message Protocol (ICMP)

✓ Address Resolution Protocol (ARP)

✓ Reverse Address Resolution Protocol (RARP)

Techniques you'll need to master:

✓ Describing the connection-oriented network service and the connectionless network service and identifying their key differences

✓ Identifying the functions of the TCP/IP Network layer protocol

✓ Identifying the functions performed by the Internet Control Message Protocol (ICMP)

This chapter discusses the Transmission Control Protocol/Internet Protocol (TCP/IP) suite of protocols. The birth and evolution of the Internet was made possible by the creation of the TCP/IP protocol suite. This chapter begins by providing a brief background of TCP/IP. Understanding its humble beginnings allows you to truly appreciate the enormity of its use in our world today.

To continue to build on the foundation of internetworking, the TCP/IP protocol suite is mapped to the Open Systems Interconnection (OSI) model. Each of the TCP/IP protocols maps roughly to one of the seven layers of the OSI model. Each of the TCP/IP layers is discussed and broken down to a level of detail to prepare you for the CCNA exam. The purpose and function of many of the TCP/IP protocols are discussed in this chapter. IP addressing and subnetting are covered in Chapter 7.

Background and History of TCP/IP

The importance of TCP/IP in today's society was not expected during its early development. In the early 1970s, Stanford University received funding from the Defense Advanced Research Projects Agency (DARPA) to create a protocol that could exploit the advantages of a packet-switched network and allow for communication between dissimilar networks.

DARPA wanted a protocol that could connect different networks and be robust enough to choose among multiple paths to a final destination. DARPA believed that the flexibility inherent to a packet-switched network might be the solution. Stanford University, consequently, produced the IP suite to fulfill these wishes. Meanwhile, DARPA built a hardware infrastructure designed to use IP as the software and called it *ARPAnet*, which later evolved into the Internet. The IP suite is commonly referred to as *TCP/IP* in reference to the two best-known protocols.

The IP suite was developed to operate across the networks of a wide variety of institutions. The IP suite allowed networks with different information formats, data rates, error characteristics, and data unit sizes to share a common suite of protocols. It is the adaptability of the IP suite that has made it the most widely used protocol today. Nearly every computer vendor supports at least part of this suite. The TCP/IP suite of protocols has literally evolved from a government-funded research program, into packet-switched networks, into a ubiquitous media.

The TCP/IP Layers

Each layer of the TCP/IP model plays an important function and role in the delivery of data. In each layer, I will look at protocols that operate at each layer.

Application Layer

The Application layer consists of a set of services that provides ubiquitous access to all types of networks. Applications utilize the services to communicate with other devices and remote applications. A large number of TCP/IP services are provided at the Application layer. Table 3.1 lists several Application layer protocols and their associated port numbers.

 You should be familiar with the most commonly used port numbers, as they may very well test you on these on the examination.

FTP

File Transfer Protocol (FTP) is used to copy a file from one host to another host, regardless of the physical hardware or operating system (OS) of each device. FTP identifies a client and server during the file transfer process. In addition, it provides a guaranteed transfer by using the services of TCP. The services that TCP provides are explained in more detail in the next section of this chapter.

TFTP

Trivial File Transport Protocol (TFTP) was designed to be a lean FTP service. The goal was to develop a protocol that could fit into the limited read-only memory (ROM) space of diskless machines. TFTP is a connectionless protocol that uses the services of UDP for transport. TFTP is used to copy files from one host (server) to another host (client). In many cases, TFTP is used to copy software to a device as it boots up. A common use of a TFTP server is to upgrade the IOS of a Cisco router.

Telnet

The Telnet service allows users to act as though their terminals are attached to another device. This process is referred to as *terminal emulation*. Telnet is a very

Table 3.1	TCP/IP Application layer services.	
Service	**Function**	**Port Number**
FTP	File transfer	21
TFTP	File transfer	69
Telnet	Terminal emulation	23
SMTP	Mail transfer	25
SNMP	Network management	161, 162
DNS	Domain name resolution	53

useful protocol in internetworking, because it allows network administrators to view and configure remote devices in the network from one location. Telnet uses the services of TCP to provide a connection-oriented session. An example of using the Telnet service between two devices follows:

```
Router#telnet 204.99.4.36
Trying 204.99.4.36 ... Open
Phoenix>
```

SMTP

Simple Mail Transport Protocol (SMTP) is used to pass mail messages between devices. It uses TCP connections to pass the email we've all grown to love between two mail hosts.

SNMP

Simple Network Management Protocol (SNMP) is used to obtain data on remote devices. Typically, a network-management station uses SNMP to poll the devices in a network and to retrieve data regarding the devices' current and past conditions. In SNMP, the network-management machine is referred to as the *manager*, and all the remote devices are considered *agents* of the manager. Each of the agents maintains a management information database (MIB) locally that constantly stores information about that device. The manager systematically polls each of its agents, requesting information from their databases. It then manipulates and organizes the data into a useful format for reporting or displaying on the network-management monitor.

DNS

Domain Name Service (DNS) is used to translate hostnames or computer names into IP addresses, such as **www.examcram.com,** or vice versa. DNS is a hierarchical database of names and their associated IP addresses. DNS is what allows people to enter a word-based address for any device on the Internet. When this occurs, that person's device requests a DNS lookup from a DNS server. The DNS server replies with the IP address associated with that hostname.

Transport Layer

The Transport layer provides an end-to-end connection between two devices during communication by performing sequencing, acknowledgments, checksums, and flow control. The Transport layer allows the Application layer to ignore the complexities of the network and focus on its primary job. This layer is also responsible for sending data that it receives from the Network layer to the appropriate application. An application using the services of the Transport layer can use two different protocols: UDP and TCP. Both protocols fulfill the Transport layer responsibilities; however, they provide two very different levels of service.

TCP

TCP provides a connection-oriented, reliable service to the applications that use its services. TCP was designed to add some reliability into the world of IP networking. A description of the main functions of TCP follows:

➤ *Segments Application layer data stream*—TCP accepts data from applications and segments it into a desirable size for transmission between itself and the remote device. The segment size is determined while TCP is negotiating the connection between the two devices. Either device can dictate the segment size; however, the receiving station is given priority.

➤ *Provides acknowledgment timers*—TCP maintains timers to identify when packets have taken too long to get to their destination. When an acknowledgment is not received for an IP packet before the expiration of the timer, TCP resends the packet to the destination.

➤ *Enables sequence number checking*—TCP/IP uses sequence numbers to ensure that all packets sent by an application on one device are read in the correct order by an application on another device. The packets might not be received at the Transport layer in the correct order, but TCP sequences them in their original order before passing them to the Application layer.

➤ *Provides buffer management*—Any time two devices are communicating, the possibility exists that one device can send data faster than the other can accept it. Initially, the receiving device puts the extra packets into a buffer and reads them when it gets a chance. When this data overflow persists, however, the buffer is eventually filled and packets begin to drop. TCP performs some preventive maintenance called *flow control* to avoid this scenario.

➤ *Initiates connection with three-way handshake*—TCP uses the concept of the three-way handshake to initiate a connection between two devices. A TCP connection begins with device A sending a request to synchronize sequence numbers and initiate a connection (a SYN message). Device B receives the message and responds with a SYN message with the sequence number increased by one. Device A responds by sending an acknowledgement message (an ACK) to device B, indicating that the device received the sequence number it expected.

➤ *Performs error and duplication checking*—TCP uses a checksum to identify packets that have changed during transport. If a device receives a packet with a bad checksum, it drops the packet and does not send an acknowledgment for it.

Therefore, the sending device resends the packet (hopefully, it will not change during transport this time). In addition, any time TCP receives a duplicate packet, it drops the duplicate.

➤ *Performs acknowledgment windowing to increase efficiency of bandwidth use*—Any time a TCP device sends data to another device, it must wait for the acknowledgment that this data was received. To increase the efficiency of bandwidth utilization, TCP can change the window size. If the window size is increased to 2, the sending device requires only one acknowledgment for every two packets sent. TCP sets the window size dynamically during a connection, allowing either device involved in the communication to slow down the sending data rate based on the other device's capacity. This process is often referred to as *sliding windows* because of TCP's ability to change the window size dynamically. The default window size as suggested by the RFCs is six packets.

TCP Header Format

The TCP header is designed to support all the functions mentioned previously and many more. The TCP header is 20 bytes and encapsulated in an IP packet during transport.

The purpose of each of the fields in the TCP header is as follows:

➤ *Source port*—Identifies the port at which upper-layer source processes receive TCP services.

➤ *Destination port*—Identifies the port at which upper-layer destination processes receive TCP services.

➤ *Sequence number*—Allows the receiving device to order data correctly before passing it to an application or to detect missing frames.

➤ *Acknowledgment number*—Identifies which TCP octet is expected next.

➤ *Header length*—Gives the length of the header in 32-bit words. This is necessary because the TCP header can have optional fields in it that can extend the header.

➤ *Reserved*—Reserved for later use. Always set to zero.

➤ *Code bits*—Identifies what type of segment is being sent. For example, the code bit can designate a SYN or ACK segment type.

➤ *Window*—Identifies the number of bits a device is willing to accept.

➤ *Checksum*—Provides a field that is verified by the receiving device to ensure that data was not manipulated during transport.

➤ *Urgent pointer*—Indicates the end of urgent data.

➤ *Options*—Identifies the maximum TCP segment size. This is the only option that is currently defined.

➤ *Data*—Identifies the payload.

UDP

UDP is a Transport layer protocol that provides a subset of the functionality of TCP. UDP, however, requires considerably fewer network resources to perform its job than TCP does. UDP is a connectionless protocol because it does not require acknowledgments or sequence numbers to communicate. UDP simply receives data from the Application layer, applies the proper header, and sends the datagram on its merry way. This is why UDP is referred to as a *best-effort protocol*.

UDP Header Format

The UDP header requires only 8 bytes for all its information. In comparison with TCP's 20-byte header, the UDP header is very small and requires minimal bandwidth.

The purpose of each of the fields in the UDP header are as follows:

➤ *Source port*—Identifies the port at which upper-layer source processes receive UDP services

➤ *Destination port*—Identifies the port at which upper-layer destination processes receive UDP services

➤ *Header length*—Identifies the length of the UDP in bytes

➤ *Checksum*—Provides a checksum that covers the UDP header and data

Ports

We have mentioned the purpose of ports in our explanation of TCP and UDP. This section provides a more detailed look at ports and sockets. A port number identifies a sending or destination application. Every application running on a host uses certain ports or ranges of ports to communicate with applications running on other hosts. It is by these port numbers that TCP or UDP determines which application to pass the data to in the Application layer. A total of 65,535 ports exist; however, only a subset of these ports is most commonly used. These ports are referred to as the *well-known ports*.

The well-known ports have a value between 0 and 1,023. When an application on one device wants to communicate with an application on another device, it must specify the address of the device (IP address) and identify the application (port number). The combination of the sending and destination port numbers and the sending and destination IP addresses defines a socket. A *socket* can be used to uniquely define any UDP or TCP connection. Here are some of the most commonly used ports and their associated applications:

➤ FTP—23

➤ Telnet—23

➤ DNS—53

➤ HTTP—80

➤ POP3—110

Notice that each port number is assigned either to UDP or TCP. All the well-known port numbers are defined in Request for Comment (RFC) 1700.

Internet Layer

The Internet layer is responsible for path determination and packet switching. The Internet layer utilizes a logical addressing scheme to make intelligent decisions regarding path determination and packet switching. The Internet layer performs the actual relay of packets from an originating network to a destination network in an efficient manner. Every packet is viewed by IP, which determines its destination by using a routing table. The routing table helps establish the best path for the packet to be sent.

IP

Internet Protocol (IP) is the transport for TCP, UDP, and Internet Control Message Protocol (ICMP) data. IP provides an unreliable service. It lets the upper-layer protocols, such as TCP, or application-specific devices worry about reliability. In addition, IP performs as a connectionless service because it handles each datagram as an independent entity. IP performs packet switching and path determination by maintaining tables that indicate where to send a packet based on its IP address. The format of the IP packet header is provided below.

The purpose of each of the fields in the IP header is as follows:

➤ *Bit version*—Identifies the current version of IP. The current IP version is 4 (or IPv4).

➤ *Header length*—Identifies the number of 32-bit words in the header.

➤ *Type-of-service (TOS)*—Used to provide quality of service for IP data transport. The TOS field is broken into a 3-bit precedence bit and 4 TOS bits.

➤ *Total length*—Provides the total length of the IP datagram in bytes.

➤ *Identification*—Uniquely identifies every packet from the sending device. This field, along with the flags and fragment offset fields, is used for packet fragmentation and reassembly.

➤ *Time-to-live (TTL)*—Sets an upper limit on the number of routers that can switch the packet. It is used to drop packets that are in routing loops.

➤ *Protocol field*—Identifies the protocol to pass the packet to upstream. For example, this protocol could be TCP, UDP, ICMP, or Internet Group Management Protocol (IGMP).

➤ *Checksum*—Provides a cyclical redundancy check of the IP header only.

➤ *Source IP address*—Identifies the IP address of the sending device.

➤ *Destination IP address*—Identifies the IP address of the destination device.

➤ *Options*—Identifies a variable-length list of optional information for the packet.

ARP

Address Resolution Protocol (ARP) bridges the gap between physical and logical addressing by mapping a known IP address to a physical address. Therefore, if two devices want to communicate, the first device can send a broadcast ARP requesting the physical address for a specified IP address. The receiving device responds with its IP address, and the first device maintains this entry in its ARP cache. If a device does not exist on the same subnet, the sending device addresses the default gateway's physical address and sends the packet to the default gateway.

RARP

Reverse Address Resolution Protocol (RARP) provides the exact opposite type of mapping from ARP—that is, RARP maps a known physical address to a logical address. Diskless machines that do not have a configured IP address when started typically use RARP. These devices send a broadcast requesting an IP address. In such a scenario, a device on the same local area network (LAN) is designed to respond to this broadcast request and supply the IP address for that physical address.

It is vital that you understand the difference between when ARP versus RARP is applicable. One instance in which RARP is used involves diskless machines, because diskless machines do not have an IP address during the boot sequence.

ICMP

Internet Control Message Protocol (ICMP) communicates error messages and control messages between devices. Thirteen different types of ICMP messages are defined. The ICMP protocol allows devices to check the status of other devices, query the current time, and perform other functions. The most used function of ICMP is the ping utility. The most common ICMP messages are as follows:

➤ *Destination unreachable*—Indicates that a certain device cannot be contacted

➤ *Time exceeded*—Indicates that a certain device could not be reached within a specified time limit

➤ *Echo*—Requests an echo reply to determine device reachability

➤ *Echo reply*—Replies to an echo request indicating that a host is reachable

The **ping** command is extremely useful in troubleshooting network problems. An extended **ping** command is also available in the Cisco Internetwork Operating System (IOS). An extended ping is performed by using the IP **ping** command. After executing this command, you will be given the option to alter many of the variables in the **ping** command, including the number of attempts and the size of the packet.

Network Access Layer

This layer provides access to the LAN. The physical addressing and network-specific protocols exist at this layer. Token Ring, Ethernet, and Fiber Distributed Data Interface (FDDI) are some examples of Network Interface layer protocols.

For quick reference, Table 3.2 details the TCP/IP model's layers and their associated protocols.

Table 3.2 The TCP/IP model.	
Layer	**Protocols**
Application layer	Telnet, TFTP, FTP, and SNMP
Transport layer	TCP and UDP
Internet layer	ICMP, ARP, RARP, IP, and BOOTP
Network Access layer	Ethernet, Fast Ethernet, Token Ring, and FDDI

Practice Questions

Question 1

Which of the following terms does not identify a layer of the TCP/IP model?

○ a. Application

○ b. Transport

○ c. Presentation

○ d. Internet

○ e. Network Access

The correct answer is c. Only the OSI model uses the Presentation layer; therefore, this term does not identify a layer of the TCP/IP model. Answers a, b, d, and e all identify separate layers of the TCP/IP model.

Question 2

Which of the following services exist at the Application layer of the TCP/IP model? [Choose the best answers]

❑ a. SMTP

❑ b. FTP

❑ c. ICMP

❑ d. ARP

❑ e. TFTP

The correct answers are a, b, and e. SMTP, FTP, and TFTP all exist at the Application layer of the TCP/IP model. Answer c is incorrect because ICMP exists at the Internet layer of the TCP/IP model. Answer d is incorrect because ARP exists at the Network Interface layer of the TCP/IP model.

Question 3

> If you wanted to locate the hardware address of a local device, which protocol would you use?
>
> ○ a. ARP
>
> ○ b. RARP
>
> ○ c. ICMP
>
> ○ d. PING

The correct answer is a. If you know the IP address and you are trying to find the hardware (MAC) address, ARP is the choice. Answers c and d are incorrect because a ping command is used to verify network connectivity and sends ICMP packets to determine this. RARP, answer b, is incorrect because it will find the identity of an IP address.

Question 4

> Which of the following services is used to translate hostnames into IP addresses?
>
> ○ a. SNMP
>
> ○ b. SMTP
>
> ○ c. IP
>
> ○ d. UDP
>
> ○ e. DNS

The correct answer is e. DNS is used to translate word-based addresses into IP addresses, or vice versa. SNMP and SMTP are TCP/IP Application layer services, but they do not perform address translation. SNMP is used to monitor remote devices, and SMTP is used to send email between devices. IP is not a service but rather a protocol used for addressing. Therefore, answers a, b, and c are incorrect. Finally, UDP is a Transport layer protocol used for packet sequencing, which makes answer d incorrect.

Question 5

Which of the following functions is not performed by TCP?

○ a. Flow control

○ b. Sequencing

○ c. Error checking

○ d. Subnetting

The correct answer is d. Subnetting is not a function performed by TCP; it is a process used to create more networks out of classful IP addresses. Answer a is incorrect because TCP does indeed provide flow control in the form of sliding windows and buffer management. Answer b is incorrect because TCP provides sequencing to ensure that datagrams are read in the correct order on the receiving side. Finally, answer c is incorrect because TCP provides error checking by applying a checksum to the TCP header and encapsulated data.

Question 6

Which of the following functions do UDP and TCP both perform? [Choose the best answers]

☐ a. Destination and source port numbers

☐ b. Flow control

☐ c. Dynamic datagram size allocation

☐ d. Checksum

☐ e. Acknowledgments of datagram receipt

The correct answers are a and d. Answer a is correct because the destination and source port numbers are provided in both the UDP and TCP headers. In addition, answer d is correct because both TCP and UDP provide for a checksum in the header to verify accurate delivery. Answer b is incorrect because only TCP performs flow control–type activities in the form of buffer management and sliding windows. Answer c is incorrect because UDP does not set datagram sizes dynamically, but rather assigns each datagram the same size. Finally, only TCP provides reliability in its data transport. Therefore, answer e is incorrect, because UDP does not generate acknowledgments for the receipt of datagrams.

Question 7

> Which of the following are functions of the Internet layer? [Choose the two best answers]
>
> ❑ a. Path determination
>
> ❑ b. Packet switching
>
> ❑ c. Code formatting
>
> ❑ d. Reliability
>
> ❑ e. Physical addressing

The correct answers are a and b. Answer a is correct because the Internet layer uses the logical address of a packet to determine the best path to take to a destination. In addition, the Internet layer uses the logical address to make packet-switching decisions. Therefore, answer b is correct. Answer c is incorrect because code formatting is performed by the TCP/IP Application layer, not the Internet layer. Answer d is incorrect because the Internet layer does not provide reliability but rather relies on the TCP/IP Transport and Application layers to provide the reliability. Answer e is incorrect because physical addressing is a function of the TCP/IP Interface layer.

Question 8

> Which of the following are characteristics of the protocol ARP? [Choose the two best answers]
>
> ❑ a. It resides at the Network layer.
>
> ❑ b. It resides at the Network Interface layer.
>
> ❑ c. It maps a known IP address to a MAC address.
>
> ❑ d. It maps a known MAC address to an IP address.

The correct answers are a and c. Answer a is correct because the protocols ARP, RARP, ICMP, and IP exist at the Network layer. Answer c is correct because devices use ARP to determine the physical address (MAC address) for a known IP address. Answer b is incorrect because LAN protocols such as Token Ring, Ethernet, and FDDI exist at the Network Interface layer. Answer d is incorrect because the process of mapping a known MAC address to an unknown IP address is accomplished by RARP.

Question 9

Which Transport layer protocol provides connectionless services?

- ○ a. UDP
- ○ b. TCP
- ○ c. ICMP
- ○ d. IP
- ○ e. FTP

The correct answer is a. UDP is a Transport layer protocol that provides a best-effort connectionless service. Answer b is incorrect because TCP provides a connection-oriented Transport layer service through the use of acknowledgments and sequence numbers. Answer c is incorrect because ICMP is an Internet layer protocol used for control messaging. Answer d is incorrect because IP is an Internet layer protocol used for addressing and path determination. Answer e is incorrect because FTP is an Application layer protocol used for transferring files between two devices.

Question 10

Which of the following would be examples of when to use RARP? [Choose the two best answers]

- ❑ a. When you don't know the MAC address
- ❑ b. When you don't know the IP address
- ❑ c. When you are using a diskless machine
- ❑ d. When you are logging into a domain

The correct answers are b and c. RARP will send out a packet that includes a machine's MAC address if the IP is unknown, thus making a incorrect and b correct. Answer c is correct because RARP is most often used in diskless machines during the boot-up sequence to obtain a valid IP address. Answer d is incorrect because in order to log into a domain, you would have to have an IP address, which you do not have until RARP performs its functions.

Need to Know More?

 Chappell, Laura. *Introduction to Cisco Router Configuration*. Cisco Systems Inc., Macmillan Computer Publishing. Indianapolis, IN, 1998. ISBN 0-7645-3186-7.

The first three chapters cover some great OSI material.

 Lammle, Todd, Donald Porter, and James Chellis. *CCNA Cisco Certified Network Associate*. Sybex Network Press. Alameda, CA, 1999. ISBN 0-7821-2381-3.

Chapter 4 covers IP addressing.

 McNutt, Shawn, Mark Poplar, Jason Waters, and David Stabenaw. *CCNA Routing and Switching Exam Prep*. The Coriolis Group. Scottsdale, AZ, 2000. ISBN 1-57610-440-0.

This book has a very detailed chapter on TCP/IP.

 Stevens, W. Richard. *TCP/IP Illustrated, Volume 1*. Addison-Wesley Professional Computing Series. Reading, MA, 1994. ISBN 0-201-63346-9.

 Syngress Media, with Richard D. Hornbaker, CCIE. *Cisco Certified Network Associate Study Guide*. Osborne/McGraw-Hill. Berkeley, CA, 1998. ISBN 0-07-882487-7.

Chapter 2 covers IP addressing.

 Tittel, Ed, Kurt Hudson, and J. Michael Stewart. *TCP/IP Exam Cram*. The Coriolis Group. Scottsdale, AZ, 1998. ISBN 1-57610-195-9.

 www.cisco.com/univercd/cc/td/doc/cisintwk/ito_doc/ip.htm on Cisco's Web site provides some excellent information regarding IP.

Network Hardware

Terms you'll need to understand:

✓ Hub

✓ Bridge

✓ Switch

✓ Router

✓ Latency

✓ Collision

✓ Broadcast

Techniques you'll need to master:

✓ Understanding LAN segmentation using bridges

✓ Learning the benefits of network segmentation
with bridges

✓ Understanding LAN segmentation using switches

✓ Learning the benefits of network segmentation
with switches

The first step in preparing for CCNA certification is making sure you have a solid understanding of basic hardware. You will rely on these fundamentals as you learn to design and configure Cisco routed and switched internetworks. You will need to understand the role that each piece of hardware plays in the overall network design and functionality. In addition, you must know the components that make up a network—hubs, bridges, routers, switches, and so on. This chapter will provide an overview of these basic network concepts and roles.

Network Hardware Roles

The problems of network congestion can be addressed by segmenting the network into smaller sections. Four tools are commonly used in today's networks to perform this segmentation: hubs, bridges, switches, and routers. In the following sections, you will take a look at the role each device plays within a network infrastructure.

Hubs

Hubs are nonintelligent devices operating at layer 1 (Physical layer) of the OSI model. Hubs are used at the lowest level of desktop connectivity. Actually, many companies are phasing out hubs for desktop connectivity in favor of a switch port for every device.

A hub can be thought of as a physical extension to the Ethernet wire. A hub does not view or process any data that crosses it. It simply receives data on any wire plugged into it and electronically repeats this data to all other wires.

The characteristics of hubs can be summarized as follows:

➤ All devices share bandwidth.

➤ All devices are in the same collision domain.

➤ All devices are in the same broadcast domain.

Bridges

A bridge is used to physically separate a LAN into multiple segments. A bridge operates at layer 2 (Data Link layer) of the OSI model, making installation simple because a bridge is transparent to higher-layer protocols such as Transmission Control Protocol/Internet Protocol (TCP/IP) and Internetwork Packet Exchange (IPX). All you need to do to make a bridge work is plug a segment into each of its ports and turn it on.

Each port on a bridge constitutes a separate segment. A single device can be plugged into a port, thus getting its own segment. Alternatively, a hub can be plugged into a bridge port, thus connecting any devices on the hub to its own segment. Each segment becomes a separate collision domain. For this reason, a bridge can provide a simple and effective way to improve the performance of a network experiencing excessive line utilization or collisions. Broadcasts, however, are still forwarded to all segments. These characteristics are summarized as follows:

➤ Each segment is a separate collision domain.

➤ All segments are in the same broadcast domain.

Because a bridge is a layer 2 device, all bridging decisions are based on layer 2 hardware Media Access Control (MAC) addresses. By listening to all frames on each segment, the bridge learns which devices are present on each segment and builds a forwarding table based on this information. Figure 4.1 shows an example of a network that is separated into two segments with a bridge.

When a device on segment 1 sends out a frame for a host on segment 2, the bridge will forward the frame. However, if the same host sends a frame to a computer on its own segment, the bridge will simply drop the frame because it will be picked up by the destination computer without the aid of the bridge. The bridge only sends a frame to a segment if it is destined for a host on that segment.

By using this method of segmentation, the network functions as if everything were on one big segment—but with line-utilization and collision rates reduced in each segment.

So far, I have been describing the behavior of bridging when dealing with unicast frames. How does a bridge handle multicast or broadcast frames?

The answer to this question lies in the fact that a bridge is a transparent device. That is, the bridge must make many smaller segments function exactly like one large segment would. For this reason, any broadcast or multicast frames are still sent to all segments connected to the bridge.

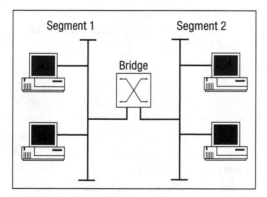

Figure 4.1   Network segmentation.

The most important concept to understand about bridges is the way they deal with different types of traffic. Bridges simply forward nonlocal and broadcast traffic. They drop local traffic because an Ethernet bridge assumes the frame has already reached its destination.

Switches

Switching is a major enhancement to bridging. A switch provides much of the same functionality as a bridge, because both are layer 2 devices. In addition, both solve collision problems, and both forward all broadcasts and multicasts. Like a bridge, a switch can be implemented into most existing network infrastructures with little or no upgrading or reconfiguration. Also like a bridge, a switch offers the following characteristics:

➤ Each segment is a separate collision domain.

➤ All segments are in the same broadcast domain.

Compared to bridges, switches offer increased throughput performance and port density, and greater flexibility. Switches provide higher port densities than bridges, so network administrators typically place fewer users on each switch port. The term *port density* refers to the number of ports on one physical device—in this case, a switch. Minimizing the number of users per port increases the total bandwidth available per user. In most cases, each computer or server is given its own port, thereby granting it dedicated access to the physical media. In the case of Ethernet technology, servers or users realize 10Mbps, 100Mbps, or even 1,000Mbps of bandwidth. Furthermore, most switches are capable of providing full-duplex media access. It is the architecture of the switch that allows the tremendous rates and high port densities.

Switching technology will be examined in detail in Chapter 10.

Each port on a switch provides dedicated bandwidth. For example, if five devices are plugged in to a Fast Ethernet switch, all five devices can utilize the full 100Mbps of bandwidth.

Routers

A router is yet another tool that can be used to segment a network. Routers operate at layer 3 (Network layer) of the OSI model. Unlike bridges, which are virtually transparent and easy to implement, routers are much more intrusive in a network. They forward and filter packets based on layer 3 addresses, such as IP addresses. This means that a network-addressing scheme must be carefully planned and laid out before you can successfully implement routers into a network.

One important feature that distinguishes a router from a bridge or switch is the fact that it does not forward broadcasts by default. Like a bridge, a router creates separate collision domains, but it also creates separate broadcast domains. In comparison to a hub, bridge, or switch, a router has the following characteristics:

➤ Each segment is a separate collision domain.

➤ Each segment is a separate broadcast domain.

Whereas bridging and switching physically segment LANs, routing provides a method to isolate traffic into logically and physically distinct LANs. Why do we want to do this? Logically separating LANs allows for different types of LAN technologies (token ring, FDDI, Ethernet, and so on) to communicate with one another without concern for the LAN technology being used. You have seen that bridges can provide some options for connecting dissimilar LANs; however, the functionality bridges provide is dwarfed in comparison to that provided by routers. Routers provide the intelligence necessary for the interconnection of complex networks.

Routers provide the logic for implementing security, fragmenting packets, converting between technologies, and a variety of other functions. Routers don't concern themselves with individual hosts on a network but rather focus on taking the best path to the network of a host. Routers only have to determine the best way to forward a packet to a destination network. Furthermore, routers effectively terminate LAN broadcast domains.

The additional functionality included in routers does not come without costs. The amount of latency for sending packets across routers is estimated at 30 to 40 percent more than that of LAN media. These numbers have been drastically reduced with the introduction of new technologies into routers. However, the amount of time required to make layer 3 decisions continues to be higher than layer 2 decisions.

In summary, here are the advantages of routers:

➤ They connect dissimilar LANs.

➤ They provide multiple paths to a destination network.

➤ They allow for a richer set of functionality than bridges and switches.

➤ They allow for the interconnection of large and complex networks.

Here are the disadvantages of routers in comparison to bridges and switches:

➤ They increase latency to forward packets.

➤ They increase maintenance complexity.

As you prepare for the CCNA examination, you will most certainly have to know at which layers of the OSI model the aforementioned devices operate. A router uses the IP address of a device to base its forwarding decisions on and operates at the Network layer (layer 3) of the OSI model. A hub is a device that has no brains. It forwards on broadcasts, line noise, and so on. Because of this, you can tell that a hub operates at the Physical layer (layer 1) of the OSI model. A bridge, as you'll recall, bases its forwarding decisions on the MAC address of a device, which makes it a layer 2 device (Data Link layer).

Although this information may seem simplistic at this point, the ability to quickly recognize this information is a super way of saving time for more complicated scenario-based questions, which you will undoubtedly face.

Problems Associated with the Expanding Network

Most of the technologies you're studying in preparation for the CCNA exam were developed as a means to solve some of the problems that existed in traditional LANs. I will use Ethernet as the basis for discussion in the following section due to its dominance in the marketplace.

Ethernet is an efficient and reliable means of sharing data between computers when used in the environment for which it was designed. At the time this standard was developed, typical networks rarely exceeded a few hundred devices, and 4Mbps or 10Mbps was adequate bandwidth to support the network applications being used.

Now, compare that with the needs of today's typical medium to large corporate networks. The number of network devices requiring support is often in the thousands. In addition, newer applications are demanding ever-increasing amounts of bandwidth to support applications such as real-time voice and video conferencing.

Latency

One of the first issues that must be addressed when dealing with an expanding local area network is the fact that all devices are sharing the same physical media. As more devices are placed on the wire, chances become greater and greater that the wire will be busy as each device requires access. The time during which the device must wait for access to the wire is called *latency*.

As you can imagine, there's a certain threshold where adding new devices begins to noticeably impact performance. The actual number of devices that can be supported varies greatly, depending on the types of network applications being used.

Collisions

Collisions are another problem for an overcrowded Ethernet network. By design, a network device must check to make sure the wire is free before transmitting data. However, there is a small chance that every time a device transmits data, another device will transmit data at exactly the same time and a collision will occur. In this event, both devices stop, wait a random amount of time, and then try to retransmit the data. Collisions are not necessarily bad. By design, they will happen in an Ethernet network. However, a high collision rate can seriously impact network performance, and the likelihood of a collision happening increases with each new device added into the network.

In order to combat the problem created by collisions in an Ethernet network, you must segment the network into smaller collision domains. This can be accomplished by using bridges, switches, or routers.

Broadcasts

Another issue related to overcrowding an Ethernet segment is the *broadcast storm*. A *broadcast* is a frame sent to every device on the segment. As such, every network interface card (NIC) is required to process the frame, regardless of whether it is actually intended for that device. A *broadcast storm* is an event that occurs when multiple simultaneous broadcasts are sent across a network.

Broadcasts are a very important component in today's network-enabled operating systems because they are typically used to help users find resources. However, more hosts on a segment mean more broadcasts that must be processed by every machine on the segment. Excessive broadcasts can have a very negative impact on network performance.

Segmenting the network into separate broadcast domains can alleviate broadcast problems. A router is often used to accomplish this.

Note: Switches can also be used to segment a network into separate broadcast domains by using VLANs. However, for devices to communicate between VLANs, a router is required.

Practice Questions

Question 1

> Which of the following are advantages of using a bridge to segment a LAN? [Choose the two best answers]
>
> ❏ a. A bridge isolates local traffic to only one physical segment of the LAN.
>
> ❏ b. A bridge logically segments a LAN, thus isolating nonlocal and broadcast traffic from local traffic.
>
> ❏ c. A bridge can extend the physical distance of a LAN by amplifying the electrical signal of the physical media.
>
> ❏ d. A bridge provides security and a high level of protocol-conversion capabilities.

The correct answers are a and c. A bridge isolates local traffic to its originating physical segment. It also can extend the physical media by amplifying the electrical signal between two physically segmented LANs. Answer b is incorrect because a bridge does not logically separate LANs. Therefore, broadcast traffic is forwarded to all nodes on the logical LAN. In addition, nonlocal LAN traffic must be forwarded at a minimum between the physical LAN of the originating and destination nodes. Answer d is incorrect because bridges do not provide security or a high level of protocol-conversion capabilities. Bridges do provide limited protocol conversion capabilities between token ring and Ethernet LANs, however.

Question 2

> Which of the following are advantages of routing compared to bridging and switching? [Choose the two best answers]
>
> ❏ a. Routing provides the functionality to allow complex networks with dissimilar technologies to be connected.
>
> ❏ b. Routing provides reduced latency.
>
> ❏ c. Routing provides a higher level of security.
>
> ❏ d. Routing allows faster throughput than bridges and switches because it does not have to consider layer 3 addressing.

Answers a and c are correct. Routing provides a rich set of functionality when compared to bridges and switches. The ability of routers to identify the best path between two networks (using different technologies and layer 3 addressing schemes) allows routers to interconnect complex and dissimilar networks. Routers also increase the level of security on networks. Answer b is incorrect because routers typically have higher latency when compared to bridges and switches. Answer d is incorrect because switches and bridges usually have a higher throughput than routers.

Question 3

Which technology has the slowest forwarding rates?

○ a. Routing

○ b. Bridging

○ c. Switching

The correct answer is a. Routing has slower forwarding rates when compared to bridging and switching due to the fact that routers must process more data per frame (they must examine up to layer 3) than bridges and switches (they process up to layer 2).

Question 4

At which layer of the OSI model would a bridge operate?

○ a. Physical

○ b. Data Link

○ c. Network

○ d. Transport

The correct answer is b. A bridge uses MAC addresses to base its forwarding decisions on, which is a layer 2 technology. Answer a is incorrect because the Physical layer is responsible for data transmission. Answer c is incorrect because the Network layer is responsible for routing of data and uses IP addresses to base its decisions on. Answer d is incorrect because the Transport layer is responsible for flow control.

Question 5

Which of the following are characteristics of hubs? [Choose the two best answers]

❑ a. All segments are in the same collision domain.

❑ b. Each segment is a separate collision domain.

❑ c. All segments are in the same broadcast domain.

❑ d. Each segment is a separate broadcast domain.

The correct answers are a and c. With hubs (as opposed to bridges, switches, and routers), all devices share bandwidth and are part of a single collision domain and broadcast domain. For this reason, answers b and d are incorrect.

Question 6

Which of the following are characteristics of bridges? [Choose the two best answers]

❑ a. All segments are in the same collision domain.

❑ b. Each segment is a separate collision domain.

❑ c. All segments are in the same broadcast domain.

❑ d. Each segment is a separate broadcast domain.

The correct answers are b and c. In a bridge, each port (segment) is a separate collision domain. However, broadcasts are forwarded across all bridged ports, so all segments are in the same broadcast domain. Therefore, answers a and d are incorrect.

Question 7

Which of the following are characteristics of switches? [Choose the two best answers]

❑ a. All segments are in the same collision domain.

❑ b. Each segment is a separate collision domain.

❑ c. All segments are in the same broadcast domain.

❑ d. Each segment is a separate broadcast domain.

Answers b and c are correct. Like bridges, each port on a switch is a single collision domain, but all ports are in the same broadcast domain. For these reasons, answers a and d are incorrect.

Question 8

Which of the following are characteristics of routers? [Choose the two best answers]

❑ a. All segments are in the same collision domain.

❑ b. Each segment is a separate collision domain.

❑ c. All segments are in the same broadcast domain.

❑ d. Each segment is a separate broadcast domain.

The correct answers are b and d. Each port on a router is both a separate collision and broadcast domain. This is one advantage of using routers as opposed to bridges or switches. Therefore, answers a and c are incorrect.

Question 9

Routers perform all the following functions except which one?

○ a. Logically segment a network

○ b. Break up broadcast domains

○ c. Connect dissimilar LANs

○ d. Reduce latency

The correct answer is d. A router increases latency because it has to make best-path selections as well as segment the LAN. Answers a, b, and c are incorrect because they are all, in fact, functions that a router can perform.

Need to Know More?

 Chappell, Laura. *Introduction to Cisco Router Configuration*. Cisco Systems Inc., Macmillan Computer Publishing. Indianapolis, IN, 1998. ISBN 0-7645-3186-7. This book provides a great overview of the concepts tested on the CCNA exam.

 Ford, Merilee, H. Kim Lew, Steve Spanier, and Kevin Downes. *Internetworking Technologies Handbook 2nd Edition*. Macmillan Computer Publishing. Indianapolis, IN, 1998. ISBN 1-56205-102-3. This book is full of resourceful information on internetworking technologies.

 Lammle, Todd, Donald Porter, and James Chellis. *CCNA Cisco Certified Network Associate*. Sybex Network Press. Alameda, CA, 1999. ISBN 0-7821-2381-3. This book is a great supplement for learning the technologies tested on the CCNA exam.

 McNutt, Shawn, Mark Poplar, Jason Waters, and David Stabenaw. *CCNA Routing and Switching Exam Prep*. The Coriolis Group. Scottsdale, AZ, 2000. ISBN 1-57610-440-0. This book is a great complement to the *CCNA Exam Cram* book. It has expanded coverage and detailed information about CCNA exam topics.

 Syngress Media, with Richard D. Hornbaker, CCIE. *Cisco Certified Network Associate Study Guide*. Osborne/McGraw-Hill. Berkeley, CA, 1998. ISBN 0-07882-487-7. Another great book for review before taking the CCNA exam.

 Visit **www.cisco.com/univercd/cc/td/doc/product/software/ios113ed/ 113ed_cr/switch_c/xcisl.htm** for a great article titled *Configuring Routing between VLANs with ISL Encapsulation*.

Maintaining the Network

Terms you'll need to understand:

✓ Cisco Discovery Protocol (CDP)

✓ Telnet

✓ Ping

✓ Traceroute

✓ TFTP

Techniques you'll need to master:

✓ Explaining the command modes available on a router

✓ Understanding the CDP

✓ Accessing a router remotely

✓ Testing the network connectivity of a router

✓ Copying an internetwork operating system (IOS) to and from a TFTP site

This chapter introduces the basics of maintaining a network using specific devices and resources.

Testing Other Devices

Several methods exist for accessing and testing connectivity to other devices. The approach to testing and troubleshooting should follow the principles of the Open Systems Interconnection (OSI) model. As discussed in earlier chapters, each layer depends on its lower layers for successful communication with its peer layers at the remote host. In other words, if layer 3 on one system can communicate with layer 3 on another system, then layers 1 and 2 of both systems are operating properly.

Several useful tools are available within the IOS to assist in testing and troubleshooting problems, including Telnet, Ping, Traceroute, the **show interface** command, and the Trivial File Transfer Protocol (TFTP).

Telnet

Telnet operates at the Application layer and is an application that provides a virtual terminal. You can connect to a remote router that supports Transmission Control Protocol/Internet Protocol (TCP/IP). Telnet helps to answer the question, Can I access the router remotely across the internetwork? If a Telnet session can be established, all the lower layers are operating properly. If not, one of the lower layers on the local or remote router is experiencing a problem. The following example depicts the **telnet** command:

```
r2#telnet 172.16.41.4
Trying 172.16.41.4... Open
User Access Verification

Password:
r4>
```

Ping

Ping operates at the Network layer. It is a basic echo protocol that determines whether IP packets are being received by the remote hosts as well as the response time across the internetwork. Simply put, Ping checks end-to-end connectivity. Ping sends a specific number of echo requests and waits a specified amount of time for an equal number of echo replies. Ping helps to answer the question, Are my packets being routed successfully? If 100 percent of the echo replies are received, all the lower layers are operating properly. If less than all the replies are received, an internetwork routing problem or a problem with the lower layers may exist. The following is an example of a basic **ping** command's output:

```
r2#ping 172.16.41.4

Type escape sequence to abort.
Sending 5, 100-byte ICMP Echos to 172.16.41.4,
 timeout is 2 seconds:
!!!!!
Success rate is 100 percent (5/5),
 round-trip min/avg/max = 4/4/4 ms
r2#
```

In this example, the exclamation points indicate that a successful echo reply was received. A period indicates a timeout condition and that the echo reply was not received.

Traceroute

When you need to know where data is traveling in a network, Traceroute is the perfect tool. Like the **ping** command, the **traceroute** command sends packets to the remote destination host and awaits replies. Traceroute tests each step along the network path. It sets the time-to-live (TTL) value (which is a hop-count value) to one for the three packets it sends to the first hop. When an intermediate router receives these packets, it decreases each packet's TTL value by one. The packets now have a TTL value of zero, which generates an error message. The intermediate router sends an error message to the source device for each packet it received. The source device increases the TTL value to two and sends three more packets out.

The first intermediate router receives the packets, decreases the TTL value by one, and forwards the packets. This process continues with each router that receives Traceroute packets, sending error messages back to the source router as the TTL value reaches zero. This way, not only can Traceroute determine response times from the error messages it receives, but it can also identify the last router along the network path that was reached successfully. Traceroute helps to answer the question, What route are my packets taking? As is the case with the **ping** command, if all the error messages are received (including messages from the remote destination host), the Network layer and all the lower layers are working well. If some of the error messages time out, you will be able to identify quickly where the problem is occurring. The following example lists output from the **traceroute** command:

```
r2#traceroute 172.16.50.4
r2#traceroute www.ce.mun.ca

Type escape sequence to abort.
Tracing the route to 172.16.50.4
```

```
1 172.16.41.4 4 msec 4 msec 4 msec
2 172.16.50.4 4 msec 5 msec 4 msec
r2#
```

In this output, "msec" indicates a successful Traceroute reply received, and an asterisk (*) indicates a timeout condition.

The **show interface** Command

The **show interface** command displays statistics for all the interfaces on the router or switch. This command helps to answer the question, Is my network link operating properly? Two aspects exist for each interface: a physical aspect and a logical aspect. The physical aspect includes the interface hardware and operates at the Physical layer. The logical aspect includes the interface software and operates at the Data Link layer. The hardware makes the actual network connection between devices, whereas the software transmits frames between devices. Therefore, two items must be verified when you're testing at the Physical and Data Link layers: the carrier detect signal and keepalive frames, respectively. A carrier detect signal triggers a line status that you can verify using the **show interface** command. The transmission of keepalive frames triggers the line protocol and can also be verified using the **show interface** command. The following example demonstrates the **show interface** command's output:

```
r2#show interface ethernet 0
Ethernet0 is up, line protocol is up
 Hardware is Lance, address is 00e0.1e68.4011
(bia 00e0.1e68.4011)
—More—
r2#
```

In this example, the line status is "up" (the interface hardware is currently active), and the line protocol is "up" (the software processes that handle the line protocol believe the interface is usable). In other words, interface Ethernet0 is up/up, and the carrier detect signal and keepalive frames are being communicated. However, this status only verifies that layers 1 and 2 are working properly; it does not indicate that any of the layers above them are working properly. Table 5.1 lists the different line status/line protocol combinations you may encounter.

You will often see an interface that reports "administratively down, line protocol is down" in the **show interface** output. This means that the interface was manually shut down or was disabled purposely.

Table 5.1 Line status and line protocol combinations.	
Line Status/Line Protocol Combination	**Description**
Ethernet0 is up, line protocol is up	The interface is operational.
Ethernet0 is up, line protocol is down	A network connection problem exists.
Ethernet0 is down, line protocol is down	A physical interface problem exists.
Ethernet0 is administratively down, line protocol is down	The interface has been disabled or shut down.

Trivial File Transfer Protocol

The Trivial File Transfer Protocol (TFTP) is a network protocol that has fewer capabilities than the File Transfer Protocol (FTP) but can allow for the sending and receiving of files across a network. In Cisco's world, TFTP is great for backing up the router or switch's IOS. Many network administrators even use TFTP to boot up a router or switch. Also, the boot sequence of a router will determine the location of the IOS, meaning the TFTP can be used as an alternative for booting in the event that the current IOS is not functional or simply does not work. This section looks at commands that will allow an administrator to copy Flash memory and an IOS to and from a TFTP host.

When setting the boot sequence on the router, you can use the following commands (assuming that the boot sequence will be Flash, TFTP, and ROM):

```
r2#config t
r2(config)# boot system flash ios_filename
r2(config)# boot system TFTP ios_filename TFTP_Address
r2(config)# boot system ROM
CTRL-Z
r2# copy running-config startup config
```

When you want to back up the Cisco IOS, the first thing you should do is to make sure the TFTP server has network connectivity. In order to do this, you can use the **ping** command, as shown here:

```
r2#ping 172.16.41.4

Type escape sequence to abort.
Sending 5, 100-byte ICMP Echos to 172.16.41.4,
 timeout is 2 seconds:
!!!!!
Success rate is 100 percent (5/5), round-trip
min/avg/max = 4/4/4 ms
```

Great! Now that you know you have connectivity to the TFTP server, you can now proceed to back up the IOS file to the server, as shown in the following command sequence:

```
r2#copy flash tftp
IP address of remote host [255.255.255.255]? 172.16.41.4
Filename to write on tftp host? Backup
Writing Backup !!!!!!!!!!!!!!!!!!!!!!!!!!!!!!!!!!!!!!!!!!!!!!!!!!!
Successful tftp write
r2#
```

Now let's try the reverse of that. Suppose you want to upgrade the IOS from a TFTP server. How would you do that? It is quite simple if you know how to perform the backup. Examine the following commands to complete the restoration or upgrade:

```
r2#copy tftp flash
IP address or name of  remote host [255.255.255.255]? 172.16.41.4
Name of TFTP filename to copy into flash[]? Backup
Copy backup from 172.16.41.4 into flash memory?
 [confirm] <return>
XXXXXXXXX bytes available for writing without erasure.
Erase flash before writing? [confirm] <return>
Clearing and initializing flash memory [please wait] ####.##
Loading from 172.16.41.4: !!!!!!!!!!!!!!!!!!!!!!!!!!!!!!!!!!!!
Verifying checksum…
VVVVVVVVVVVVVVVVVVVVVVVVVVVVVVVVVVVVVVVVV {text omitted}
Flash verification successful. Length = 180000,
  checksum = 0xA5C3
```

Other possible scenarios for the use of the TFTP server are to copy the current configuration there and use that configuration as a backup that can be restored at a later time. To copy the configuration file to a TFTP host, follow these commands:

```
r2#copy run tftp
address or name of remote host []? 172.16.41.4
destination filename [router-config]? SheldonB-config
!!
399 Bytes copied in 14.55 seconds (33 bytes/sec)
r2#
```

The reverse of the preceding example is to restore that same configuration file from a TFTP server into the router. The command sequence shown here will

allow you to successfully copy a configuration file from a TFTP server into a
router's memory:

```
r2#copy tftp run
address or name of remote host []? 172.16.41.4
source filename []? SheldonB-config
destination filename [running-config]? <return>
accessing tftp://172.16.41.4 (via ethernet1):
!!
[OK - 399/3099 bytes]
399 bytes copied in 6.32 seconds (77 bytes/sec)
r2#
```

The ability to use the full capabilities of TFTP from an administrator's perspective is crucial. Although the TFTP software itself is relatively scaled down and simple, its purpose is far reaching.

Practice Questions

Question 1

The CDP operates at which layer?

○ a. Transport

○ b. Network

○ c. Data Link

○ d. Physical

The correct answer is c. The CDP operates at the Data Link layer. Although the CDP can communicate over a variety of physical media, it does not operate at the Physical layer. Therefore, answer d is incorrect. The CDP allows a network device to exchange frames with other directly connected network devices. It enables those network devices (which may support different Network layer protocols) to discover each other's protocols as well as address information and capabilities. However, the CDP does not operate at the Network layer. Therefore, answer b is incorrect. Answer a is incorrect because the CDP does not operate at the Transport layer and is not concerned with end-to-end connectivity like other Transport layer protocols.

Question 2

Which command, when executed successfully, does not verify that two routers are routing packets between them successfully?

○ a. **ping**

○ b. **show interface**

○ c. **traceroute**

○ d. **telnet**

The correct answer is b. Although the **show interface** command displays the status of the interfaces on a router, it does not indicate whether packets are reaching their destination. The **ping** and **traceroute** commands verify routing by sending and receiving packets across the network. Therefore, answers a and c are incorrect. In order for the **telnet** command to be successful, packets must be sent and received properly, so it also verifies routing. Therefore, answer d is incorrect.

Question 3

Which of the following messages to the user indicates that there is a physical problem with Ethernet0?

○ a. Ethernet0 is down, line protocol is up

○ b. Ethernet 0 is up, line protocol is down

○ c. Ethernet0 is down, line protocol is down

○ d. Ethernet0 is administratively down, line protocol is down

The correct answer is a. Ethernet0 is down; line protocol is up indicates a problem with the physical connectivity, so recheck cable connections. Answer b is incorrect because Ethernet0 is up, line protocol is down indicates an issue with the protocols. Answer c is incorrect because Ethernet0 is down, line protocol is down indicates that the interface is not turned on and answer d is incorrect because a message of administratively down indicates that the interface has never been activated.

Question 4

Which of the following indicate that Ethernet port 0 has been manually disabled?

○ a. Ethernet0 is up, line protocol is up

○ b. Ethernet 0 is up, line protocol is down

○ c. Ethernet0 is down, line protocol is down

○ d. Ethernet0 is administratively down, line protocol is down

The correct answer is d. Answers a, b, and c all indicate that the interface is not fully operational. However, answers b and c are incorrect because they both indicate connectivity problems, whereas the correct answer, d, indicates the interface is down on purpose. Answer a is incorrect because it states that the line is operational.

Question 5

> Which of the following commands will successfully copy the router's startup configuration file to a TFTP server?
>
> ○ a. **copy TFTP flash**
>
> ○ b. **copy flash TFTP**
>
> ○ c. **copy running TFTP**
>
> ○ d. **copy startup tftp**

The correct answer is d because the startup configuration is actually referred to as the startup configuration at the CLI. Answer a is incorrect because that command will copy a file from TFTP server to flash memory. Answer b is incorrect because that command will copy the IOS from the router to the server. Answer c is incorrect because that command will copy the running configuration file to the TFTP server.

Question 6

> Which of the following commands will copy the current router configuration file to a TFTP server? [Choose the two best answers]
>
> ❏ a. **copy run tftp**
>
> ❏ b. **copy startup tftp**
>
> ❏ c. **copy running-configuration tftp**
>
> ❏ d. **copy running-configuration tftp server**

The correct answers are a and c. They are correct syntax and are acceptable commands, a is abbreviated yet acceptable. Answer b is incorrect because it is copying the startup configuration and not the current configuration. Answer d is incorrect because TFTP server is not a valid command.

Question 7

Of the following router commands: traceroute, ping, telnet, and TFTP, which three are the most effective for troubleshooting? [Choose the two best answers]

❑ a. **ping**

❑ b. **tftp**

❑ c. **telnet**

❑ d. **traceroute**

The correct answers are a, c, and d. Ping is correct because the ping command will test network connectivity and is easy to use. Telnet is also correct because if you can telnet into a router, you have established connectivity and also communication with the router. Traceroute is also correct because that command will allow the administrator to test the paths that the router will use to send data on to its destination. Answer b is incorrect because the TFTP server is used primarily as an off site storage for configuration files and IOS.

Need to Know More?

 Cisco. *Router Products Configuration Guide.* Cisco Internetwork Operating System, Release 11.0. Customer Order Number DOC-RPCG 11.0. Text Part Number 78-2032-01.

Chapters 2 and 3 provide additional detail on the Cisco IOS user interface commands.

 McNutt, Shawn, Mark Poplar, Jason Waters, and David Stabenaw. *CCNA Routing and Switching Exam Prep.* The Coriolis Group. Scottsdale, AZ, 2000. ISBN 1-57610-440-0.

This book is a great complement to the *CCNA Exam Cram* book. It has expanded coverage and detailed information about CCNA exam topics.

 Syngress Media, with Richard D. Hornbaker, CCIE. *Cisco Certified Network Associate Study Guide.* Osborne/McGraw-Hill. Berkeley, CA, 1998. ISBN 0-07-882487-7.

 With Cisco's documentation CD-ROM, you can immediately access Cisco's entire library of end-user documentation, selected product news, bug databases, and related information. The documentation CD-ROM is produced monthly.

 www.cisco.com is the official Cisco documentation Web site. It contains a lot of helpful information. From the home page, search for telnet, ping, traceroute, show interface, and/or TFTP Server, and you'll be presented with several pages of detailed information.

Router Configuration and Software Management

Terms you'll need to understand:

✓ Running configuration file

✓ Startup configuration file

✓ Trivial File Transfer Protocol (TFTP)

✓ **enable secret** password command

✓ **service password-encryption** command

✓ Boot field

✓ Configuration register

Techniques you'll need to master:

✓ Managing configuration files from the EXEC privileged mode

✓ Copying and moving configuration files

✓ Setting up router passwords, identifications, and banners

✓ Identifying the main Cisco internetwork operating system (IOS) commands for router startup

✓ Performing the initial configuration using the **setup** command

✓ Loading software from various sources on Cisco routers

✓ Backing up and upgrading software on Cisco routers

✓ Configuring a router via the initial setup sequence

This chapter focuses on a number of very important and often-applied skills in networking. The ability to manage configuration files, to load and copy Cisco software, and to understand the impact of these types of commands is vital for success. More importantly, you need to master these crucial skills to avoid causing a disaster in your company's network. Understanding the many password types and security levels used on Cisco routers is important. Finally, this chapter describes and illustrates the steps required to set up a router via the initial setup sequence.

Router Elements

This section describes the various interface modes in which you may work on a router. It also provides an overview of the different components within a router and explains how to examine the status of each of those components.

Router Modes

Regardless of how you access a router (through the console port, a modem connection, or a router interface), you can place it in one of several modes. Other router modes exist beyond the user and privileged modes in previous chapters. Each router mode enables specific functions to be performed. The different types of router modes include user, privileged, setup, RXBOOT, global configuration, and other configuration modes, as shown in Table 6.1.

Table 6.1	Router modes.		
Mode	**Function**	**How Accessed**	**Prompt**
User	Limited display	Log in to the router	**Router>**
Privileged	Display, testing, debugging, configuration file manipulation	From user mode, enter the **enable** command	**Router#**
Setup	Create initial router configuration	During router startup, if the configuration file is missing from NVRAM (console access only)	Interactive dialog prompts
RXBOOT	Perform router recovery	Press the Break key during router startup (console access only)	**>**
Global	Perform simple configuration	From EXEC privileged mode, enter the **configure** command	**Router(config)#**
Others	Perform complex and multiline configuration	From within global configuration mode; the command entered varies	**Router(config-<mode>)#**

User Mode

As stated earlier, user mode provides a display-only environment. You can view limited information about the router but cannot change the configuration.

Privileged Mode

Privileged mode enables you to perform an extensive review of the router. This mode supports testing commands, debugging commands, and commands to manage the router configuration files.

Setup Mode

Setup mode is triggered on router startup when no configuration file resides in nonvolatile random access memory (NVRAM). This mode executes an interactive prompted dialog box to assist in creating an initial router configuration.

RXBOOT Mode

A router's maintenance mode is called *RXBOOT mode* or *ROM monitor mode*. This mode facilitates recovery functions when the router password is lost or the IOS file stored in Flash memory has been erased or is corrupt. Pressing the Break key (from a console terminal directly connected to the router) within the first 60 seconds of startup also allows you to place the router in this mode.

Global Configuration Mode

You perform simple configuration tasks in global configuration mode. For example, router names, router passwords, and router banners are configured in this mode.

Other Configuration Modes

You perform complex router-configuration tasks in several other configuration modes. You enter interface, subinterface, controller, and routing protocol configurations from within these other modes. Table 6.2 provides a summary of the syntax for each router mode.

Table 6.2 Router configuration summary.	
Configuration Mode	**Router Prompt**
Interface	**NFLD(config-if)#**
Subinterface	**NFLD(config-subif)#**
Router	**NFLD(config-router)#**
IPX-Router	**NFLD(config-ipx-router)#**
Line	**NFLD(config-line)#**
Controller	**NFLD(config-controller)#**
Map-List	**NFLD(config-map-list)#**
Router-Map	**NFLD(config-route-map)#**

Router Components

Every router contains several components that compose its configuration. These components are RAM, NVRAM, Flash memory, ROM, and interfaces.

RAM

RAM serves as a working storage area for the router and contains data such as routing tables, various types of cache and buffers, as well as input and output queues. RAM also provides storage for temporary memory for the router's active IOS and configuration file (the running configuration file). However, all the contents of RAM are lost if the router is powered down or restarted.

NVRAM

Unlike RAM, nonvolatile RAM (NVRAM) retains its contents when the router is powered down or restarted. NVRAM stores permanent information, such as the router's backup configuration file. The startup configuration file is retrieved from NVRAM during startup and loaded into RAM.

Flash

Flash memory stores the Cisco IOS image and associated microcode. Flash memory is erasable, electronically reprogrammable ROM that retains its contents when the router is powered down or restarted. Several copies or versions of an IOS image can be contained in Flash memory. Flash memory allows software to be upgraded without chips on the processor being added, removed, or replaced.

ROM

Like Flash memory, ROM contains a version of IOS—usually an older version with minimal functionality. It also stores the bootstrap program and power-on diagnostic programs. However, software upgrades can be performed only by replacing chips on the central processing unit (CPU).

Interfaces

Interfaces provide the network connections where packets move in and out of the router. Depending on the model of router, interfaces exist either on the motherboard or on separate, modular interface cards. Figure 6.1 shows the various router components and the router elements they contain.

Router Status

Routine administration of a router involves examining the status of the router. The **show** command enables you to view the status of the router's components. You can execute **show** from either user or privileged mode. However, the keywords used with the **show** command are different in the user and privileged modes.

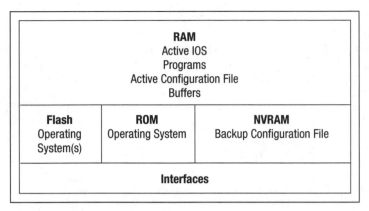

Figure 6.1 The router components.

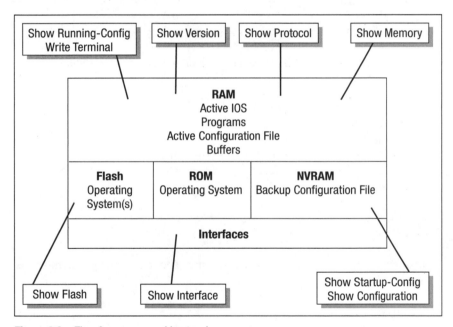

Figure 6.2 The **show** command keywords.

Figure 6.2 illustrates some of the more common **show** command keywords and the router components with which they are associated.

The **show version** command displays the hardware configuration, software version, boot images, and names and sources of configuration files, as shown here:

```
DALLAS#show version
Cisco Internetwork Operating System Software
IOS (tm) 2500 Software (C2500-IS-L), Version 11.3(7)T,
RELEASE SOFTWARE (fc1)
```

```
Copyright (c) 1986-1998 by cisco Systems, Inc.
Compiled Tue 01-Dec-98 12:21 by ccai
Image text-base: 0x0303A9D8, data-base: 0x00001000

ROM: System Bootstrap, Version 11.0(10c)XB1, PLATFORM SPECIFIC
RELEASE SOFTWARE
(fc1)
BOOTFLASH: 3000 Bootstrap Software (IGS-BOOT-R),
Version 11.0(10c)XB1, PLATFORM
SPECIFIC RELEASE SOFTWARE (fc1)

DALLAS uptime is 2 days, 7 hours, 17 minutes
System restarted by reload
System image file is "flash:c2500-is-l_113-7_T",
booted via flash

cisco 2500 (68030) processor (revision M) with
6144K/2048K bytes of memory.
Processor board ID 06972781, with hardware revision 00000000
Bridging software.
X.25 software, Version 3.0.0.
1 Ethernet/IEEE 802.3 interface(s)
1 Token Ring/IEEE 802.5 interface(s)
2 Serial network interface(s)
32K bytes of non-volatile configuration memory.
8192K bytes of processor board System flash (Read ONLY)

Configuration register is 0x2102

DALLAS#
```

The **show memory** command displays statistics about the router's memory, as shown here:

```
DALLAS#show memory
           Head Total(b) Used(b)  Free(b) Lowest(b) Largest(b)
Processor  87510 5733104  809476  4923628  4872780   4890708
     I/O 600000 2097152  488444  1608708  1476032   1532904


     Processor memory

Address Bytes Prev. Next Ref PrevF NextF Alloc PC What
87510   1068  0     87968 1         31A0B86 List Elements
87968   2868 87510 884C8 1         31A0B86 List Headers
884C8   3884 87968 89420 1         314B0E0 TTY data
89420   2000 884C8 89C1C 1         314D52E TTY Input Buf
```

```
89C1C     512 89420 89E48  1      314D55E TTY Output Buf
89E48    3000 89C1C 8AA2C  1      31B31BA Interrupt Stack
8AA2C      44 89E48 8AA84  1      36C16D8 *Init*
8AA84    1068 8AA2C 8AEDC  1      31A0B86 messages
8AEDC      88 8AA84 8AF60  1      31AFBAC Watched Boolean
8AF60      88 8AEDC 8AFE4  1      31AFBAC Watched Boolean
8AFE4      88 8AF60 8B068  1      31AFBAC Watched Boolean
8B068      88 8AFE4 8B0EC  1      31AFBAC Watched Boolean
8B0EC    1032 8B068 8B520  1      31B796A Process Array
8B520    1000 8B0EC 8B934  1      31B7D1C Process Stack
8B934     480 8B520 8BB40  1      31B7D2E Process
8BB40     128 8B934 8BBEC  1      31AFDBC Process Events
8BBEC      44 8BB40 8BC44  1      36C16D8 *Init*
8BC44    1068 8BBEC 8C09C  1      31A0B86 List Elements
--More--
```

The **show protocols** command displays the Network layer protocols and addresses that are configured on the router, as shown here:

```
DALLAS#show protocols
Global values:
 Internet Protocol routing is enabled
Ethernet0 is up, line protocol is up
 Internet address is 172.16.57.1/24
Serial0 is administratively down, line protocol is down
Serial1 is administratively down, line protocol is down
TokenRing0 is administratively down, line protocol is down
DALLAS#
```

The **show running-config** command displays the active configuration file. Use the **write terminal** command if the router's IOS version is 10.3 or earlier. The **write terminal** command is also supported in later versions of the IOS:

```
DALLAS#show running-config
Building configuration...
Current configuration:
!
version 11.3
service timestamps debug uptime
service timestamps log uptime
no service password-encryption
!
hostname DALLAS
!
interface Ethernet0
 description Engineering LAN Segment
```

```
 ip address 172.16.57.1 255.255.255.0
!
interface Serial0
 no ip address
 no ip mroute-cache
 shutdown
 no fair-queue
!
interface Serial1
 no ip address
 shutdown
!
interface TokenRing0
 no ip address
 shutdown
!
ip classless
!
!
line con 0
line aux 0
line vty 0 4
 login
!
end

DALLAS#
```

The **show startup-config** command displays the backup configuration file. Use the **show configuration** command if the router's IOS version is 10.3 or earlier. The **show configuration** command is also supported in later versions of the IOS:

```
DALLAS#show startup-config
Using 424 out of 32762 bytes
!
version 11.3
service timestamps debug uptime
service timestamps log uptime
no service password-encryption
!
hostname DALLAS
!
interface Ethernet0
 description Engineering LAN Segment
 ip address 172.16.57.1 255.255.255.0
!
```

```
interface Serial0
 no ip address
 no ip mroute-cache
 shutdown
 no fair-queue
!
interface Serial1
 no ip address
 shutdown
!
interface TokenRing0
 no ip address
 shutdown
!
ip classless
!
!
line con 0
line aux 0
line vty 0 4
 login
!
end

DALLAS#
```

The **show interface** command displays statistics for all the interfaces on the router or a specific interface:

```
DALLAS#show interface ethernet 0
Ethernet0 is up, line protocol is up
 Hardware is Lance, address is 00e0.1e60.9d9f
(bia 00e0.1e60.9d9f)
 Description: Engineering LAN Segment
 Internet address is 172.16.57.1/24
 MTU 1500 bytes, BW 10000 Kbit, DLY 1000 usec,
    reliability 255/255, txload 1/255, rxload 1/255
 Encapsulation ARPA, loopback not set, keepalive set (10 sec)
 ARP type: ARPA, ARP Timeout 04:00:00
 Last input 00:00:01, output 00:00:03, output hang never
 Last clearing of "show interface" counters never
 Queueing strategy: fifo
 Output queue 0/40, 0 drops; input queue 0/75, 0 drops
 5 minute input rate 0 bits/sec, 0 packets/sec
 5 minute output rate 0 bits/sec, 0 packets/sec
    42 packets input, 9697 bytes, 0 no buffer
    Received 42 broadcasts, 0 runts, 0 giants, 0 throttles
```

```
        0 input errors, 0 CRC, 0 frame, 0 overrun, 0 ignored, 0 abort
        0 input packets with dribble condition detected
        80 packets output, 16167 bytes, 0 underruns
        0 output errors, 0 collisions, 2 interface resets
        0 babbles, 0 late collision, 0 deferred
        0 lost carrier, 0 no carrier
        0 output buffer failures, 0 output buffers swapped out
DALLAS#
```

The **show flash** command displays information about the Flash memory device, as shown here:

```
DALLAS#show flash

System flash directory:
File Length  Name/status
 1   7181580 c2500-is-l_113-7_T
[7181644 bytes used, 1206964 available, 8388608 total]
8192K bytes of processor board System flash (Read ONLY)

DALLAS#
```

Managing Configuration Files

The process of managing configuration files is straightforward; however, it has been made difficult by the many different versions of Cisco software and the wide variety of architectures used in Cisco hardware. This section will bring light to these subjects, present an overview of the different types of configuration files and the commands used to move, display, and copy these files, and, finally, highlight some of the areas that can cause confusion when managing configuration files.

 The material presented in this chapter assumes the implementation of Cisco IOS release 11.0 or later, as does the CCNA exam.

Types of Configuration Files

Cisco IOS software uses and requires a configuration file to determine how a router is to function. Typically, network administrators enter the commands necessary for their environment into a router configuration file. Only two types of configuration files exist for the context of the CCNA exam:

➤ The running configuration file exists in RAM and contains the commands that Cisco IOS uses to drive the actions of the router.

Note: RAM is erased during power cycles or software reloads. Therefore, the running configuration file is erased as well.

➤ The startup configuration file exists in NVRAM and is the backup for the running configuration file.

 Startup configuration files reside in NVRAM; running configuration files exist in RAM.

The router will always use the running configuration file to execute. However, any time a router is restarted (cycling power or reloading the software), the running configuration file is erased and the startup configuration file is the only remaining configuration file. Therefore, during the boot sequence of a router, the router copies the startup configuration file to the running configuration file (NVRAM to RAM). Therefore, it is paramount that any time a change is made to a running configuration the change is also copied to the startup configuration. The many ways of preventing the loss of changes made are discussed in this chapter.

Displaying the Running and Startup Configuration Files

The purpose of displaying a running or startup configuration file is to determine the configuration commands being executed on a router. Use the **show running-config** and **show startup-config** commands to show the running configuration and startup configuration files, respectively. Displaying the running configuration file shows the commands being executed at the time that the **show** command is executed, as shown here:

```
Router#show running-config
Building configuration...
Current configuration:
Last configuration change at 03:25:38 UTC Sat Jan 1 2000
version 11.2
no service password-encryption
no service udp-small-servers
no service tcp-small-servers
hostname Router
enable secret 5 $1$2uUP$2I.LOxxD3wnX.7WDMHzb60
enable password cisco
no ip domain-lookup
```

```
interface Serial0
 ip address 138.144.2.2 255.255.255.0
 encapsulation frame-relay
 bandwidth 2000
 frame-relay lmi-type cisco

interface Serial1
 no ip address
 shutdown
!
interface TokenRing0
 ip address 138.144.3.1 255.255.255.0
 ring-speed 16
!
interface TokenRing1
 ip address 138.144.4.1 255.255.255.0
 ring-speed 16
!
router igrp 1
 network 138.144.0.0
!
no ip classless
!
snmp-server community public RO
!
line con 0
line aux 0
line vty 0 4
password cisco
login
!
end
```

*Note: The **Router#** prompt indicates that the command is initiated from the EXEC privileged (**enable**) command line. It is important to know in what mode a command should be executed.*

Configuring the Running and Startup Configuration Files

The running configuration file often requires changes while the router is functioning. Cisco IOS is designed to accept changes to a running or startup configuration file without restarting (reloading) or cycling the power of the router. The following commands are used to manipulate the configuration files:

➤ **Router# configure terminal**—Allows a user to add, change, or delete commands in the running configuration file while the router is executing

➤ **Router# configure memory**—Allows a user to add, change, or delete commands in the startup configuration file

 Making changes to the running configuration file will immediately affect the behavior of a router.

Backing Up and Restoring Configuration Files

Configuration files are copied and moved constantly in most networks. One common method of copying files is with the use of a Trivial File Transfer Protocol (TFTP) server. Most Unix machines have built-in TFTP support. Also, TFTP server programs are available for Windows-based PCs. Cisco makes a TFTP server program that is available on its Web site at the following Web address: **www.cisco.com/pcgi-bin/tablebuild.pl/tftp**. Cisco routers use a TFTP server to load IOS and to copy software and configuration files. To copy a file using TFTP, one device needs to be executing TFTP server software and the other device needs to be executing the client software. Cisco routers are equipped with both functions. Network administrators often need to back up a running or startup configuration file on a central server. The following command sequence accomplishes this goal:

```
Router# copy running-config TFTP
Remote host []? 172.15.12.2 (IP Address of TFTP Server)
Name of configuration file to write [router-confg]? <Return>
Write file Router-confg on host 172.15.12.2? [confirm] <Return>
Building configuration...
Writing Router-confg !!!!!!!!!!!!!!!!!!!![OK]
```

Note: Pay attention to the order and syntax of commands during the test. The function of a command can completely change, depending on the syntax.

The reverse process occurs when a configuration file is copied from a central server to an executing router. This process is most often used when a router has gone dead or someone has accidentally deleted the configuration file on the router. If the running configuration was backed up on a TFTP server, it is really simple to restore the configuration file. The first step for restoring the configuration file on a router is to determine Internet Protocol (IP) connectivity from the central server to the router. This might require the use of a ping test and/or the configuration of an IP address on the router. The following command sequence is used for restoring a running configuration file:

```
Router# copy TFTP running-config
Host or network configuration file [host]? <Return>
Address of remote host [255.255.255.255]? 172.15.12.2 (TFTP
Server)
Name of configuration file [Router-confg]?Router-confg  -
(File name)
Configure using Router-confg from 172.15.12.2? [confirm] <Return>
Loading Router-confg from 172.15.12.2 (via serial 1): !!!!!
[OK - 875/32723]
Router#
```

Exercise caution when performing configuration file changes across networks, especially to remote sites. Visit Cisco's Web site and utilize the search engine to identify anything you might need to be aware of while performing configuration file backups or restores in your network. Always be sure to find hardware-specific features before changing configuration files or Cisco IOS software.

Another method of backing up a running configuration is to save it to NVRAM. You should complete this process after every change to the running configuration file, unless a good reason exists to keep the startup configuration different. By copying the running configuration to NVRAM, you are ensuring that if the router is reloaded or the power is cycled, it will boot with the same configuration you are currently executing. The following command sequence is required for this process:

```
Router#copy running-config startup-config
Building configuration...
[OK]
```

The startup configuration file can also be copied into RAM, thereby overwriting the running configuration file, by performing the following command:

```
Router# Copy startup-config running-config
```

It is necessary to know all the backup and restore commands for the CCNA exam. Be sure to pay special attention to the syntax of these commands. It is easy to forget the sequence of words for the different commands.

Finally, the startup configuration file can be completely erased. When this occurs, the router boots into setup mode the next time it is reloaded:

```
Router#erase startup-config
```

Router Passwords

The router passwords on the Cisco router provide security against unwanted users; Cisco IOS passwords were never intended to resist a determined, intelligent attack. Many programs exist (Cisco is aware of these programs) that can crack the MD5 encryption algorithm Cisco IOS employs. Cisco always recommends that some type of user-authentication protocol be used to enhance the security of Cisco routers. RADIUS and TACACS are two of the more popular authentication methods that major corporations use today. Cisco routers utilize five different password types to provide security.

The **enable password** and **enable secret** Password Commands

The **enable password** and **enable secret** password commands are designed to provide an additional layer of security for passwords. Both commands allow you to establish an encrypted password that requires users to enter access enable mode. The **enable secret** command was developed to use an improved encryption algorithm. The **enable secret** password overrides the password for **enable password** when it is present. An **enable secret** password can be entered by issuing the following command:

```
Router(config)#enable secret NFLD
Router#
```

The **enable password** and **enable secret** commands also provide for security levels. These options are not part of the objectives set by the CCNA exam and are not, therefore, presented in this book.

The **console** and **auxiliary** Password Commands

The **console** and **auxiliary** password commands restrict user mode access via the console or auxiliary ports on the router:

```
Router(config)#line aux 0
Router(config-line)#login
Router(config-line)#password NFLD
```

The **login** command designates that you want users to have to enter their passwords every time they connect to the router via the auxiliary port. The **login** command can be added to the console port to require a password login as well. The **console** password is set with the same command format as the **aux** password, except that the keyword **aux** is changed to **con**.

The virtual terminal Password Command

The **virtual terminal** (or **vty**) password restricts user modes accessed via a Telnet session. The **virtual terminal** password must be set; otherwise, a user will not be able to log in to the router with a Telnet session. Multiple virtual terminal sessions can be engaged at one time. A separate password can be additionally specified for each virtual terminal session:

```
Router(config-line)#line vty 0 4
Router(config-line)#login
Router(config-line)#password NFLD
```

The Cisco IOS allows five simultaneous Telnet connections. Notice that the syntax is *line* then *line type* and *line number*. Cisco interface numbers always start with 0. For this example, we are specifying all five ports, numbers 0 through 4, to designate five virtual terminals that all use the password "NFLD."

Of the five different types of passwords, only the **enable secret** password is encrypted by default. For the remaining passwords, you must use the **service password-encryption** command. This command encrypts the **enable, console, auxiliary,** and **virtual terminal** passwords:

```
Router(config)#service password-encryption
```

Passwords that have already been set in the configuration file will not become encrypted; only passwords that are entered after the **service password-encryption** command has been entered will be encrypted. The **service password-encryption** command does not provide a high level of network security, but it helps to keep unauthorized individuals from viewing a password in a configuration file.

Router Identification and Banner

A router's name is referred to as the *hostname*. The default hostname for all Cisco routers is "Router." You can change the hostname of a router in global configuration mode by entering the **hostname** command. The hostname is changed with the following commands:

```
Router(config)#hostname NFLD
NFLD(config)#
```

Notice that the hostname changed from "Router" to "NFLD" immediately after executing the command.

The **banner motd** command allows you to display a message-of-the-day (MOTD) banner every time you log in to the router. Even though the banner message was designed to convey day-to-day messages, it is typically used for displaying security messages for legal reasons:

```
NFLD(config)#banner motd * Authorized Access Only,
 All Violations Will Be Prosecuted *
NFLD(config)#
```

Note: The asterisk (*) before the word "Authorized" and after the word "Prosecuted" represents the start and finish of the text to be displayed as the banner.

In this scenario, the next time you Telnet into the router, the MOTD banner will display the following message:

```
Authorized Access Only, All Violations Will Be Prosecuted.
User Access Verification
Password:
```

A description can be added to every interface using the **description** command. Typically, an interface description, which is limited to 80 characters, is used to describe the function of the interface:

```
NFLD(config)#interface s0
NFLD(config-line)#description 56K between NFLD and San Diego
NFLD(config-line)#
```

The next time someone views the running configuration file, he or she will see the following description:

```
interface Serial0
description 56K connection between NFLD and San Diego
ip address 138.144.2.2 255.255.255.0
encapsulation frame-relay
bandwidth 2000
frame-relay lmi-type cisco
```

Initial Configuration of a Cisco Router

The first time a Cisco router is powered on, the startup configuration file is blank, so it will boot into the initial configuration dialog. This dialog is designed to walk a novice through the basic steps and requirements of configuring a Cisco router.

The initial configuration dialog is a menu-driven command-and-response query designed to configure a router with a bare-bones configuration. The dialog will start anytime a configuration file is not found in NVRAM during the boot sequence, as described previously. The two instances in which a configuration file will not exist in NVRAM are when the router is powered on for the first time and when the router is reloaded subsequent to the startup configuration file being erased.

The following code is a sample initial router configuration phase:

```
Would you like to enter the initial configuration
dialog? [yes] <Return>
First, would you like to see the current interface
summary? [yes] <Return>
Any interface listed with OK? Value "NO" does not have a
valid configuration
Interface    IP-Address   OK?   Method     Status    Protocol
Serial 0     unassigned   NO    not set    up        down
Serial 1     unassigned   NO    not set    up        down
Ethernet 1   unassigned   NO    not set    up        down
Ethernet 2   unassigned   NO    not set    up        down
Configuring global parameters:
```

Notice that in the configuration dialog, many of the questions have answers in brackets following them. These are the default values or answers for the questions. To accept a default value, simply press Enter and move on to the next question. If you don't want to use the default value, simply enter your own. Also, if at any time you are stumped as to the proper syntax to use, you can always type "?" at the prompt for help or press the Tab key, which will finish your syntax for you.

The preceding interface summary indicates that the router has two serial and two Ethernet interfaces. In this example, we will configure both serial interfaces and neither of the Ethernet interfaces. None of the four interfaces has been assigned an IP address, which is indicated by the "unassigned" designation, listed under the IP-Address column. The status of the interface is set to "up" because this is the default value. We must manually shut down the interface to turn it off. However, the protocol is listed as "down" because no active connections are on the interface. After the interface summary is displayed, the next step in the initial configuration dialog is to configure the hostname, passwords, routing protocols, and IP addressing, as shown here:

```
Enter host name [Router] NFLD
The enable secret is a one-way cryptographic secret used instead
 of the enable password when it exists.
Enter enable secret: NFLD
The enable password is used when no enable secret exists and when
Using older software and some boot images.
Enter enable password: Cisco
```

```
Enter the virtual terminal password: Telnet
Configure SNMP Network Management? [yes]: no
Configure IP? [yes]<Return>
      Configure IGRP Routing? [yes]: no
      Configure RIP Routing? [yes]: no
Configure Interfaces:
      Configuring interface Ethernet 0:
      Is this interface in use? [yes] no
      Configuring interface Ethernet 1:
      Is this interface in use? [yes] no
      Configuring interface Serial 0:
      Is this interface in use? [yes] <Return>
      Configure IP on this interface? [yes] <Return>
      Configure IP unnumbered on this interface? [no] : <Return>
      IP Address for this interface: 172.29.3.4
      Number of bits in subnet field [8]: <Return>
      Class B network is 172.29.0.0, 8 subnet bits; mask is
255.255.255.0
      Configuring interface Serial 1:
      Is this interface in use? [yes] <Return>
      Configure IP on this interface? [yes] <Return>
      Configure IP unnumbered on interface? [no] : <Return>
      IP Address for this interface: 172.29.4.3
      Number of bits in subnet field [8]: <Return>
      Class B network is 172.29.0.0, 8 subnet bits; mask is
255.255.255.0
```

Now we have configured the two serial interfaces, set up our passwords, and chosen any routing protocols we want to utilize. For the sake of simplicity, however, we did not turn on either the Routing Information Protocol (RIP) or the Interior Gateway Routing Protocol (IGRP). The router will then show us the configuration that we created:

```
The following configuration command script was created:
Hostname NFLD
Enable secret 5 09371034073401823
Enable password Cisco
Line vty 0 4
Password Telnet
No snmp-server
!
ip routing
!
interface Ethernet 0
Shutdown
No ip address
```

```
Interface Ethernet 1
Shutdown
No ip address
Interface Serial 0
Ip address 172.29.3.4 255.255.255.0
Interface Serial 1
Ip address 172.29.4.3 255.255.255.0
!
end
Use this configuration? [yes/no]: yes
```

We have now completed the initial configuration dialog and successfully configured the NFLD router with IP addressing.

Upgrading Cisco IOS Software

Cisco IOS is constantly being revised to add new features or to fix bugs in previous versions. The process of upgrading software on a Cisco router can be broken
down into three main steps:

1. Back up the current Cisco IOS.

2. Copy the new Cisco IOS to the router.

3. Reload the Cisco router and verify the new IOS.

Backing Up the Current IOS

The first part of backing up the current IOS involves determining what version
of IOS is running on the router and the file name of the software image. It is also
necessary to note the size available in Flash memory. The new version of IOS
must not be larger than the total Flash memory on the router. The **show version**
command displays this information, as shown here:

```
NFLD#sh vers
Cisco Internetwork Operating System Software
IOS (tm) 2500 Software (C2500-J-L), Version 11.2(13),
RELEASE SOFTWARE (fc1)
Copyright (c) 1986-1998 by cisco Systems, Inc.
Compiled Tue 31-Mar-98 12:27 by tlane
Image text-base: 0x0303F1E4, data-base: 0x00001000
ROM: System Bootstrap, Version 11.0(10c)XB1,
PLATFORM SPECIFIC RELEASE SOFTWARE (fc1)
BOOTFLASH: 3000 Bootstrap Software (IGS-BOOT-R),
 Version 11.0(10c)XB1,
PLATFORM SPECIFIC RELEASE SOFTWARE (fc1)
```

```
NFLD uptime is 7 minutes
System restarted by reload
System image file is "flash:11-2-13.img", booted via flash

cisco 2500 (68030) processor (revision L)
with 2048K/2048K bytes of memory.
Processor board ID 07112268, with hardware revision 00000000
Bridging software.
SuperLAT software copyright 1990 by Meridian Technology Corp.
X.25 software, Version 2.0, NET2, BFE and GOSIP compliant.
TN3270 Emulation software.
2 Ethernet/IEEE 802.3 interface(s)
2 Serial network interface(s)
32K bytes of non-volatile configuration memory.
16384K bytes of processor board System flash (Read ONLY)
Configuration register is 0x2102
```

From the preceding command listing, we can determine that we have 16,384KB of Flash memory available. Therefore, we can copy any software image less than or equal to 16,384KB to this device. The name of the file is provided as "11-2-13.img." After the memory requirements and the file name have been determined, we need to copy the old image to a TFTP server. This step gives us a fallback procedure in case the new software image is corrupt:

```
NFLD#copy flash TFTP
System flash directory:
File Length  Name/status
 1   7969232 11-2-13.img
[7969296 bytes used, 8807920 available, 16777216 total]
Address or name of remote host [255.255.255.255]? 172.16.24.134
Source file name? 11-2-13.img
Destination file name [11-2-13.img]? <Return>
Verifying checksum for '11-2-13.img' (file # 1)... OK
Copy '11-2-13.img' from Flash to server
 as '11-2-13.img'? [yes/no]y
!!!!!!!!!!!!!!!!!!!!!!!!!!!!!!!!!!!!!!!!!!!!!!!!!!!!!!!!!!!!!!!!!!!!!!!!
!!!!!!!!!!!!!!!!!!!!!!!!!!!!!!!!!!!!!!!!!!!!!!!!!!!!!!!!!!!!!!!!!!!!!!!!
!!!!!!!!!!!!!!!!!!!!!!!!!!!!!!!!!!!!!!!!!!!!!!!!!!!!!!!!!!!!!!!!!!!!!!!!
!!!!!!!!!!!!!!!!!!!!!!!!!!!!!!!!!!!!!!!!!!!!!!!!!!!!!!!!!!!!!!!!!!!!!!!!
!!!!!!!!!!!!!!!!!!!!!!!!!!!!!!!!!!!!!!!!!!!!!!!!!!!!!!!!!!!!!!!!!!!!!!!!
!!!!!!!!!!!!!!!!!!!!!!!!!!!!!!!!!!!!!!!!!!!!!!!!!!!!!!!!!!!!!!!!!!!!!!!!
!!!!!!!!!!!!!!!!!!!!!!!!!!!!!!!!!!!!!!!!!!!!!!!!!!!!!!!!!!!!!!!!!!!!!!!!
!!!!!!!!!!!!!!!!!!!!!!!!!!!!!!!!!!!!!!!!!!!!!!!!!!!!!!!!!!!!!!!!!!!!!!!!
!!!!!!!!!!!!!!!!!!!!!!!!!!!!!!!!!!!!!!!!!!!!!!!!!!!!!!!!!!!!!!!!!!!!!!!!
!!!!!!!!!!!!..!!!!!!!!!!!!!!!!!!!!!!!!!!!!!!!!!!!!!!!!!!!!!!!!!!!!!!!!!!
!!!!!!!!!!!!!!!!!!!!!!!!!!!!!!!!!!!!!!!!!!!!!!!!!!!!!!!!!!!!!!!!!!!!!!!!
!!!!!!!!!!!!!!!!!!!!!!!!!!!!
```

```
Upload to server done
Flash copy took 00:04:36 [hh:mm:ss]
```

Upgrading the IOS

After the current IOS has been backed up to a TFTP server and the available memory on the router has been checked, we can proceed with the upgrade of the IOS. The new IOS must reside on the TFTP server, as shown here:

```
NFLD#copy TFTP flash
Proceed? [confirm]<Return>

System flash directory:
File Length  Name/status
 1  7969232 11-2-14.img
[7969296 bytes used, 8807920 available, 16777216 total]
Address or name of remote host [172.16.24.134]?<RETURN>
Source file name? 11-2-14.img
Destination file name [11-2-14.img]?
Accessing file '11-2-14.img' on 172.16.24.134...
Loading 11-2-14.img from 172.16.24.134 (via Ethernet1): ! [OK]

Erase flash device before writing? [confirm]
Flash contains files. Are you sure you want to erase? [confirm]

System configuration has been modified. Save? [yes/no]:
% Please answer 'yes' or 'no'.

System configuration has been modified. Save? [yes/no]: y
Building configuration...
[OK]

Copy '11-2-14.img' from server
 as '11-2-14.img' into Flash WITH erase? [yes/no]y

%SYS-5-RELOAD: Reload requested
%SYS-4-CONFIG_NEWER: Configurations from version 11.2 may not be
correctly understood.
%FLH: 11-2-14.img from 172.16.24.134 to flash ...

System flash directory:
File Length  Name/status
 1  7969232 11-2-14.img
[7969296 bytes used, 8807920 available, 16777216 total]
Accessing file '11-2-14.img' on 172.16.24.134...
Loading 11-2-14.img from 172.16.24.134 (via Ethernet1): ! [OK]
Erasing device... eeeeeeeeeeeeeeeeeeeeeeeeeeeeeeeeeeeeeeeeeeeeeeeeeeeee
  ...erased
```

```
Loading 11-2-14.img from 172.16.24.134 (via Ethernet1): !!!!!!!!!
!!!!!!!!!!!!!!!!!!!!!!!!!!!!!!!!!!!!!!!!!!!!!!!!!!!!!!!!!!!!!!!!!!!!
!!!!!!!!!!!!!!!!!!!!!!!!!!!!!!!!!!!!!!!!!!!!!!!!!!!!!!!!!!!!!!!!!!!!
!!!!!!!!!!!!!!!!!!!!!!!!!!!!!!!!!!!!!!!!!!!!!!!!!!!!!!!!!!!!!!!!!!!!
!!!!!!!!!!!!!!!!!!!!!!!!!!!!!!!!!!!!!!!!!!!!!!!!!!!!!!!!!!!!!!!!!!!!
!!!!!!!!!!!!!!!!!!!!!!!!!!!!!!!!!!!!!!!!!!!!!!!!!!!!!!!!!!!!!!!!!!!!
!!!!!!!!!!!!!!!!!!!!!!!!!!!!!!!!!!!!!!!!!!!!!!!!!!!!!!!!!!!!!!!!!!!!
!!!!!!!!!!!!!!!!!!!!!!!!!!!!!!!!!!!!!!!!!!!!!!!!!!!!!!!!!!!!!!!!!!!
[OK - 7969232/16777216 bytes]
Verifying checksum... OK (0xF865)
Flash copy took 0:07:00 [hh:mm:ss]
```

Reloading the Router

Depending on what type of router mode we have, when we copy a new version of software to the router, the router will either reload itself or return with the **Router#** prompt. If the router returns with a prompt, we use the **Router# reload** command to restart the router and load the new software. The router **reload** command is as follows:

```
Router# reload
```

Practice Questions

Question 1

> Which of the following commands will allow you to review the contents of NVRAM? [Choose the two best answers]
>
> ❏ a. **show configuration**
>
> ❏ b. **show protocols**
>
> ❏ c. **show version**
>
> ❏ d. **show running-config**
>
> ❏ e. **show startup-config**

The correct answers are a and e. The **show configuration** and **show startup-config** commands display the router's backup configuration file from NVRAM. The **show protocols, show version,** and **show running-config** commands will allow you to review the contents of RAM, not NVRAM. Therefore, answers b, c, and d are incorrect.

Question 2

> Which of the following router components contains the router's IOS image?
>
> ○ a. Flash memory
>
> ○ b. NVRAM
>
> ○ c. RAM
>
> ○ d. Interfaces

The correct answer is a. Flash memory contains the IOS images used by the router. If no image resides in Flash memory, the image in ROM will be used. NVRAM and RAM contain the backup configuration and active configuration files, respectively. Therefore, answers b and c are incorrect. Interfaces provide the network connections for the router. Therefore, answer d is incorrect.

Question 3

Which of the following router components contain versions of the router's configuration file? [Choose the two best answers]

❑ a. Flash memory

❑ b. NVRAM

❑ c. RAM

❑ d. ROM

The correct answers are b and c. NVRAM contains the backup configuration file for the router, whereas RAM contains the router's active configuration file. Flash memory and ROM do not contain a configuration file; they contain the router's IOS image files. Therefore, answers a and d are incorrect.

Question 4

Which of the following commands will allow you to review the contents of RAM? [Choose the three best answers]

❑ a. **show configuration**

❑ b. **show protocols**

❑ c. **show version**

❑ d. **show running-config**

❑ e. **show startup-config**

The correct answers are b, c, and d. The **show protocols**, **show version**, and **show running-config** commands allow you to review the contents of RAM. The **show configuration** and **show startup-config** commands allow you to review the router's backup configuration file from NVRAM, not RAM. Therefore, answers a and e are incorrect.

Question 5

> Which command would allow you to add, modify, or delete commands in the startup configuration file?
>
> ○ a. **show startup-config**
>
> ○ b. **show running-config**
>
> ○ c. **configure terminal**
>
> ○ d. **configure memory**

The correct answer is d. The **configure memory** command allows you to enter commands into the startup configuration file stored in NVRAM. Answers a and b are incorrect because they only allow you to view the startup and running configuration files, respectively. Answer c is incorrect because it allows you to add, modify, or delete commands in the running configuration file, not in the startup configuration file.

Question 6

> Which command would be used to restore a configuration file to RAM on a Cisco router?
>
> ○ a. **router#copy TFTP running-config**
>
> ○ b. **router>copy TFTP running-config**
>
> ○ c. **router#copy TFTP startup-config**
>
> ○ d. **router>copy TFTP startup-config**

The correct answer is a. To restore a configuration file, the file must be copied from a TFTP server to the Cisco router. This is a trick question, because you must be in EXEC privileged mode to perform this function. Answers b and d are incorrect because the question implies that the command is initiated from EXEC mode; you can determine this by the > symbol (versus the # symbol) at the end of the word "router" in answers b and d. Answer c is incorrect because the startup configuration file is not in RAM, and the question requires that you copy to the running configuration file, which is in RAM.

Question 7

Which of the following commands will display the running configuration file to a console terminal?

○ a. **router>show running-config**

○ b. **router#show startup-config**

○ c. **router#show flash**

○ d. **router>show version**

○ e. None of the above

The correct answer is a. The command to display a running configuration file to a console terminal is **show running-config**. Answer b displays the startup configuration file to the console monitor and is therefore incorrect. Answer c is incorrect because it displays any IOS images or configuration files stored in Flash memory. Answer d displays the software version and hardware on this router and is therefore incorrect.

Question 8

If you need to copy the currently executing configuration file into NVRAM, which command would accomplish this goal?

○ a. **router#copy startup-config running-config**

○ b. **router#copy startup-config TFTP**

○ c. **router#copy running-config startup-config**

○ d. **router>copy startup-config running-config**

The correct answer is c. The startup configuration file exists in NVRAM. So, to copy a configuration file to NVRAM, the current startup configuration file must be overwritten. Answer a is incorrect because the startup configuration file is not the currently executing image, and this command is attempting to write the configuration file to RAM. Answer b is incorrect because the startup configuration file is not the currently executing configuration file, and TFTP does not exist in NVRAM. Answer d is incorrect because the startup configuration file is not the currently executing image and because the command is being executed from EXEC mode.

Question 9

> Which of the following commands would not set a password on a Cisco router?
>
> ○ a. **router(config)#enable secret**
>
> ○ b. **router(config-line)#password NFLD**
>
> ○ c. **router(config)#service encryption password**
>
> ○ d. **router(config)#enable password**

The correct answer is c. The **service encryption password** command is used to encrypt passwords in configuration files. Answer a is incorrect because it is used to set the "enable secret password". Answer d is incorrect because it is used to set the "enable password". Answer b is incorrect because this command is used to set the Telnet, auxiliary, or console password, depending on which line configuration mode the router is in when the command is executed.

Question 10

> In which of the following scenarios would a router boot into the initial configuration dialog after its power has been cycled? [Choose the two best answers]
>
> ❑ a. When someone copies the startup configuration file to a TFTP server.
>
> ❑ b. When the running configuration file is copied to the startup configuration file.
>
> ❑ c. When the router is powered on for the first time.
>
> ❑ d. When the **write erase** command is executed immediately before the router is powered down.

The correct answers are c and d. The initial configuration dialog starts anytime a configuration file cannot be found in NVRAM. This occurs when a **write erase** command is performed on the startup configuration file or when the router is being powered on for the first time. Answer a is incorrect because copying a startup configuration file to a TFTP server will not cause a router to boot into the initial configuration dialog. Copying the running configuration file to the startup configuration file will not cause the router to boot into the initial configuration dialog. Therefore, answer b is incorrect.

Question 11

> Which of the following configuration register values would force a router to boot from ROM?
>
> ○ a. 0x2103
>
> ○ b. 0x210F
>
> ○ c. 0x2101
>
> ○ d. 0x2104

The correct answer is c. A configuration register with the value 0x2101 forces a router to boot from ROM. Only when the boot field has a value of 1 or 0 will the router boot from ROM. Answers a, b, and d are incorrect because all these values would cause the router to look at the boot commands in the configuration file to determine what IOS to load.

Question 12

> Where does the running configuration file exist in a Cisco router?
>
> ○ a. NVRAM
>
> ○ b. ROM
>
> ○ c. RAM
>
> ○ d. Flash memory

The correct answer is c. The running configuration file exists in RAM. This file is erased when a router is reloaded or its power is cycled. Answer b cannot be correct because ROM is a read-only device, and configuration files are constantly being updated. Answer a is incorrect because NVRAM is used to maintain the startup configuration file, not the running configuration file. Answer d is incorrect because Flash memory stores a copy of the IOS software, not the running configuration files.

Question 13

> Which is the correct command to back up Cisco IOS software?
>
> ○ a. **router#copy running-config startup-config**
>
> ○ b. **router(config)#copy TFTP flash**
>
> ○ c. **router#copy flash TFTP**
>
> ○ d. **router#copy flash NVRAM**

The correct answer is c. To back up Cisco IOS software, you must copy it to a TFTP server or another storage device. Answer a is incorrect because this command deals with configuration files, not Cisco IOS software. Answer b is incorrect because this command would be used to restore the Cisco IOS to a router. Answer d is incorrect because **copy flash NVRAM** is not a valid command.

Question 14

> Which of the following is not a valid Cisco command?
>
> ○ a. **router>show version**
>
> ○ b. **router#show running-config**
>
> ○ c. **router#show startup-config**
>
> ○ d. **router#show RAM**

The correct answer is d. **show RAM** is not a Cisco IOS command. Answers a, b, and c are incorrect because they are Cisco commands.

Need to Know More?

 Chappell, Laura. *Introduction to Cisco Router Configuration.* Cisco Systems Inc., Macmillan Computer Publishing. Indianapolis, IN, 1998. ISBN 0-7645-3186-7. This is a great introduction to Cisco router configuration.

 Lammle, Todd, Donald Porter, and James Chellis. *CCNA Cisco Certified Network Associate.* Sybex Network Press. Alameda, CA, 1999. ISBN 0-7821-2381-3. This book is full of helpful information.

 McNutt, Shawn, Mark Poplar, Jason Waters, and David Stabenaw. *CCNA Routing and Switching Exam Prep.* The Coriolis Group. Scottsdale, AZ, 2000. ISBN 1-57610-440-0. This book is a great complement to *CCNA Exam Cram.* Several chapters have expanded information about router configuration, including instructions on setting up and configuring a test lab.

 Syngress Media, with Richard D. Hornbaker, CCIE. *Cisco Certified Network Associate Study Guide.* Osborne/McGraw-Hill. Berkeley, CA, 1998. ISBN 0-07-882487-7. This book is a great study tool.

 The Cisco Web page, **www.cisco.com**, also provides some helpful information. Use the search engine to search for the following topics: password configuration, 2500 software upgrade, and managing configuration files.

IP Addressing and Routing

Terms you'll need to understand:

✓ IP addressing

✓ Subnetting

✓ Routing protocol

Techniques you'll need to master:

✓ Subnetting techniques

✓ Converting from binary to decimal

✓ Configuring a router

This chapter is the "big dog" of all the chapters. There are many concepts in this chapter that are extremely important to the CCNA exam and to your career. The chapter focuses on explaining the fundamentals of IP addressing and IP routing. We will explain IP in its binary and decimal forms. The ability to understand IP in both forms is expected of beginning engineers. In addition, this chapter explains and identifies the differences among the various classes of IP addresses. After providing a foundation, we'll introduce and explain the concept of subnetting. We will also cover the steps required to configure, verify, and monitor IP on a Cisco router. Because the path determination and switching functions of a router rely on routing protocols, we'll discuss the goals and types of routing algorithms and protocols. We'll review the strengths and weaknesses of two popular routing algorithms, and I'll highlight techniques to mitigate the weaknesses. In addition, we will list router configuration commands to enable routing protocols.

IP Addressing

The purpose of an IP address is to identify uniquely a device to the rest of an IP network. IP addresses have two parts: a network ID and a host ID. Each plays an important role in uniquely identifying a device.

The purpose of having two distinct parts of an address is to simplify the process of finding any individual host in a sea of networks. Computers use the network ID to route data to the gateway device of the network quickly. The gateway device of that network then uses the host ID part of the IP address to identify a device on that network. The division of the IP address into two parts allows for a quick and accurate method of isolating a host's network and then identifying the host. The concepts of *classful addressing* and *subnetting* increase the complexities of IP addressing a little; nevertheless, they are interesting topics that are staples of networking. Before these topics are tackled, however, it is important that you understand the format of an IP address in more detail.

Dotted Decimal Notation

IP addresses are typically shown in *dotted decimal notation*, which was developed so that people could easily read and write IP addresses. An IP address in its native form is binary. It is composed of 32 bits that have been divided into 8-bit groups, referred to as *octets* or *bytes*. An IP address in dotted decimal notation specifies the decimal value of each of the four octets, separated by dots. An example of a dotted decimal IP address is 134.153.178.50. An IP address under IP Version 4 (IPv4). To take the concept a little further, IP Version 6 is coming up and that version is written in hex.

Each octet can have a decimal value between 0 and 255. Why? The total number of possible values for a binary number with 8 bits can be written mathematically as 2^8. Although 2^8 has a total value of 256, IP addresses begin with the number 0; therefore, the decimal range starts at 0 and ends with 255, for a total of 256 possible values.

The ability to convert IP addresses to both binary and decimal values is essential to using IP addressing effectively. The difference between the decimal and binary number systems involves the number of digits they use. The decimal system uses 10 digits: 0, 1, 2, 3, 4, 5, 6, 7, 8, and 9. In this case, "dec" in the word *decimal* refers to 10 digits. The binary number system uses two digits: 0 and 1. In this case, "bi" in the word *binary* refers to two digits.

When a decimal number is higher than 9, the proper procedure is to increase the number of digits used to represent the number. The first time you increase the number of digits, you indicate this by putting the number 1 to the left of the new number, 0.

The method used to increase a binary number is the same, except it uses only two values. When a binary value is higher than 1, the proper procedure is to increase the number of digits used to represent the number by one. The first time you increase the number of digits, you indicate this by putting the number 1 to the left of the new number, 0. Because this binary number equals the same number of increments as the decimal number 2, it is said to have a decimal value of 2.

Adding the decimal value of every bit in the octet derives the total decimal value of an octet. The total decimal value of an octet is displayed in an IP address in dotted decimal notation. Table 7.1 is a sample binary-to-decimal conversion table.

Now that you know the difference between dotted decimal and binary, let's see if you know the binary number for the IP address 134.153.178.50. If you answered 10000110.10011001.10110010.00110010, you are correct.

Note: For the CCNA exam, you should be able to perform conversions fairly quickly so that you can save time for the more difficult questions. Oh and by the way, no calculators allowed.

Table 7.1   Binary-to-decimal conversion.

Binary Value	Bit Conversion	Decimal Value
00000001	1	1
00000010	2 + 0	2
00000110	4 + 2 + 0	6
11110000	128 + 64 + 32 + 16 + 0 + 0 + 0 + 0	240
11111111	128 + 64 + 32 + 16 + 8 + 4 + 2 + 1	255

IP Classes

The number of bits assigned to the network ID and the host ID depends on the number of hosts required on a given network and the number of networks required in an environment. Before the idea of classful addressing was in place, it was the network administrator's responsibility to determine which bits in the 32-bit address to assign to the network ID and which bits to assign to the host ID. If the number of hosts required on a given network was enormous, the network administrator assigned a large portion of the 32 bits available to host IDs and used a small portion for network IDs. If a large number of networks were required with only a few hosts per network, the network administrator used a small portion of the bits for host IDs and a large number for network IDs.

This method of allocating address space was inefficient, often giving small organizations the right to a large number of IP address spaces. Therefore, IP address space was divided into three classes in the attempt to meet the needs of large and small organizations. (Actually, the IP address was divided into five classes; however, we will focus on the three main classes used by the Internet community.) With the class system, it is possible to assign a corporation address space based on the number of hosts and networks it requires. This system is referred to as *classful addressing*. Classful addressing divides the 4,294,967,296 (2^{32}) possible IP addresses into five different classes.

A class A, B, C, or D IP address can be determined by looking at the first three bits of the address. Table 7.2 illustrates the relationship between the first three bits of an IP address and its class. Also, note the range in the decimal value for each class. When you understand IP addressing, you will only need to look at the first octet of an IP address in decimal format to determine its class. The class of an IP address governs the number of bits that can be used for network IDs and the number of bits that can be used for host IDs. For example, an organization that is allocated a class B address must use 16 bits to identify its network ID and 16 bits to identify its host ID. It is important to note that this strict rule can be avoided, and most often is, through a process known as *subnetting*.

Class A

Class A addresses are typically assigned to very large organizations, universities, and the military. It is extremely difficult—if not impossible—to get a class A address today. These addresses are identified in binary by the first bit having a value of 0 or in decimal by having a value between 1 and 126. Class A addresses use the first 8 bits to specify the network ID and the last 24 bits to designate the host ID, as shown in Table 7.2.

Class A addresses have a maximum of 126 network IDs. This value is arrived at by taking the number of bits used for the network ID to the power of 2. In this

Table 7.2	Class addressing.		
IP Class	**Network/Node Portion**	**Range**	**Example**
A	Network.Node.Node.Node	0–127	55.48.108.69
B	Network.Network.Node.Node	128–191	134.153.178.80
C	Network.Network.Network.Node	192–223	210.12.88.100
D	Multicast	224–239	224.178.88.100
E	Research		

case, 2^7 equals a total of 128. However, the network ID 0.0.0.0 is reserved for the default route, and the network ID 127.0.0.0 is reserved for the loopback function. Therefore, the range of possible class A network IDs in decimal is 1 to 126.

Each class A network ID can support a total of 16,777,214 (2^{24}–2) host IDs. The purpose of subtracting 2 from the possible number of hosts is to remove two special host IDs. Any time every bit in the host ID portion of an IP address has a value of 1, it is considered a *broadcast IP address*, meaning that all hosts should read a message sent to this address. Obviously, no device should have an address that is used for broadcasting information. The second consideration is when every bit in the host ID's binary value is 0. This value is used to denote a network ID number.

Class B

Class B addresses are typically assigned to medium and large organizations. These addresses are identified in binary by the first two bits having a value of 10 or in decimal by having a value between 128 and 191. Class B addresses use the first 16 bits to specify the network ID and the last 16 bits to designate the host IDs. Because the first two bits of all class B addresses are always 10, however, only 14 bits are available to be used for network IDs. This allows a total of 16,384 (2^{14}) class B network addresses. Each network ID supports a total of 65,534 (2^{16}–2) host IDs.

Class C

Class C addresses are typically assigned to small and medium organizations. These addresses are identified in binary by the first three bits having a value of 110 or in decimal by having a value between 192 and 223. Class C addresses use the first 24 bits to specify the network ID and the last 8 bits to designate the host IDs. Because the first 3 bits of a class C address are 110, however, only 21 bits are available to be used for network IDs. This allows a total of 2,097,152 (2^{21}) class C network addresses. Each network ID supports a total of 254 (2^8–2) host IDs.

Note: It is important to be able to identify the class of an IP address quickly by looking at its decimal or binary value.

Other Classes

Two other classes of addresses are available in the IPv4 address space. These classes are not used as public address space, but have been reserved for specific functions. Class D addresses are identified in binary by the first 4 bits having a value of 1110 or in decimal by having a value between 224 and 239. Class D addresses have been reserved to support IP *multicasting*, which is the process of using one address to send a message to a group of people. The main benefit of sending a chunk of data headed for multiple destinations is that it has to be sent between the transit routers only once and hence a ton of bandwidth is conserved. Class E addresses are identified in binary by the first 4 bits having a value of 1111 or in decimal by having a value between 240 and 247. Class E addresses have been reserved for experimental or research use.

Subnetting

Subnetting creates multiple IP networks from a single allocated class A, B, or C IP network. Subnetting divides a single class A, B, or C network into smaller subnetworks. One of the major goals of allocating IP addresses to organizations based on their size is to allocate only one class A, B, or C address to any given organization. Therefore, only one routing entry needs to be maintained per organization. However, organizations have the need for multiple subnetworks within their networks. Subnetting allows organizations to have multiple networks and the InterNIC to allocate single class A, B, or C networks.

Internet routers need to maintain only one classful network entry per organization, because each organization is assigned only one class A, B, or C IP address. (Organizations are typically assigned only one class address; however, this is not always true, thanks to subnetting.) Even though organizations divide their IP addresses into multiple networks, they still look like single class A, B, or C IP addresses to the rest of the world. Organizations accomplish this by performing route summarization at the boundaries of their networks and any other networks.

Default Mask

A *default mask* is a 32-bit number divided into four octets, just like an IP address. A default mask indicates the number of bits used to identify the network ID, and it's implied with all class A, B, and C addresses. Class A addresses imply an 8-bit default mask because the first 8 bits in these addresses designate the network ID. Therefore, the default mask (the number of bits that indicate the network ID) can be represented in decimal format as 255.0.0.0. Table 7.3 illustrates the default masks for class A, B, and C addresses in binary and decimal format. Note that the default mask represents the number of bits used to identify the network ID.

After viewing Table 7.3, it is easy to see that a default mask indicates which bits are used to identify the network ID versus the host ID. Why do we need a default

Table 7.3	Default masks of class A, B, and C addresses.	
Class	**Binary Notation**	**Dotted Decimal Notation**
A	11111111.00000000.00000000.00000000	255.0.0.0
B	11111111.11111111.00000000.00000000	255.255.0.0
C	11111111.11111111.11111111.00000000	255.255.255.0

mask if we can already determine this by the class of the IP address? As mentioned previously, organizations often have the need to increase the number of networks in their intranet. However, when an organization has only one block of IP addresses it can advertise to the Internet but wishes to have many subnetworks in its environment, the organization can indicate that it has used some of the host ID bits as network ID bits by providing a subnet mask.

Subnet Mask

A *subnet mask* is an extension to the default mask. It indicates the number of bits in addition to the default mask that should be used to identify network IDs. What does this do for an organization? It increases the number of networks an organization can create from one class A, B, or C network ID.

For example, if an organization has a registered class C address and needs to create two networks, it must somehow get more network IDs. The organization can accomplish this by using some of the bits designated as host IDs as network IDs. However, the organization must indicate that this class C address is no longer using the default 24 bits as a network ID. The organization can indicate this by applying a subnet mask to represent the additional bits that are to be used as network IDs versus host IDs. The subnet mask can be represented in various ways; in this chapter, we will refer to the subnet mask as the default mask plus any additional bits used for network IDs.

Logical ANDing

How should the subnet mask be used to determine what the network ID is for an IP address? To determine the network ID and the host ID for an IP address, it is necessary to perform a process known as *logical ANDing*. When information is sent to a router and is destined for a remote location, the router cares only about which network to send the information to. The router knows the subnet mask and the destination IP, so the ANDing process is used with these two addresses to determine the remote network to send the information to. This indicates which bits to use as network bits and which bits to use as host bits when the IP address is deciphered. When the subnet mask is applied to an IP address, each bit starting from the most significant bit to the least significant bit is compared between the IP address and the subnet mask. For example, the first bit of the first octet of the

IP address is compared with the first bit of the first octet of the subnet mask. The resulting value from this bit-by-bit comparison is the network ID. The rule set to apply is listed as follows:

➤ If the subnet mask and the IP address both have values of 1, the resulting network ID bit is 1.

➤ If the subnet mask has a value of 1 and the IP address has a value of 0, the resulting network ID bit is 0.

➤ If the subnet mask has a value of 0, the resulting network ID bit is 0.

Table 7.4 illustrates the logical ANDing process. Note that, in Table 7.4, the only difference between the dotted decimal IP address and the dotted decimal network ID is in the last two octets. The difference between the values in the octet is due to the commingling of network and host bits in the same octet. The logical ANDing process drops the entire host IDs and retains the network IDs. Therefore, in Table 7.4, we determine that the host 129.253.235.252 is actually part of the network 129.253.232.0.

Table 7.5 illustrates another example of the logical ANDing process using a class C address. Note that with a class C address, the only difference in the IP address occurs in the last octet. The reason that the difference is isolated to the last octet is that in a class C address, only the last octet contains bits assigned to host IDs, so only these bits are available for subnetting.

So far, you have learned that IP addresses are divided into classes to allocate the IP address space to varying sizes of organizations efficiently. Efficient allocation of address space also minimizes the number of entries that need to be maintained in the routing tables of Internet routers. Because organizations required more networks than the InterNIC believed reasonable to assign due to wasted IP address

Table 7.4   The logical ANDing process.

Binary IP Address	Dotted Decimal IP Address
10000001.11111101.11101011.11111010	129.253.235.250
11111111.11111111.11111000.00000000	255.255.248.0
10000001.11111101.11101000.00000000	129.253.232.0

Table 7.5   The logical ANDing process for a class C address.

Binary IP Address	Dotted Decimal IP Address
11000001.11011101.10110001.11101000	193.221.177.58
11111111.11111111.11111111.11100000	255.255.255.224
11000001.11011101.10110001.00100000	193.221.177.32

space, a subnet mask was created, giving organizations a tool for increasing the number of networks they had by borrowing bits from the host IDs of their assigned IP address space. A subnet mask uses the logical AND process to distinguish between the network ID and the host ID of an IP address.

Next, we'll discuss some of the items to consider when determining the number of bits to use for the subnet mask. A bad decision on a subnet mask can place constraints on an organization's future addressing choices.

Subnetting Consideration

Remember that the purpose of the subnet mask is to give an organization the flexibility to increase the number of networks in its environment. So, you might think that an organization should give itself the maximum number of networks possible with its assigned IP address space. Any time a bit is added to the network ID, however, a bit is removed from the host ID. Therefore, if the number of networks is increased, the number of host IDs available per network is decreased. Table 7.6 illustrates this fact by presenting the number of network and host IDs for class B IP addresses with different subnet masks.

Organizations need to determine the happy medium between sufficient host IDs and network IDs for their specific needs. The cost of changing the subnet mask on thousands of computers because of a scaling issue is not a welcome thought for network administrators. Here are some of the questions that must be asked before a subnet addressing scheme is developed:

➤ What is the total number of network IDs the organization needs today?

➤ What is the total number of host IDs the largest network requires today?

➤ What is the total number of network IDs the organization will need in the future?

➤ What is the total number of host IDs the largest network will require in the future?

Table 7.6   Class B networks with various subnet masks.

Subnet Mask	Bits in Subnet Mask	Network IDs	Host IDs
255.255.255.0	24	$2^8-2 = 254$	$2^8-2 = 254$
255.255.255.128	25	$2^9-2 = 510$	$2^7-2 = 126$
255.255.255.192	26	$2^{10}-2 = 1,022$	$2^6-2 = 62$
255.255.255.224	27	$2^{11}-2 = 2,046$	$2^5-2 = 30$
255.255.255.240	28	$2^{12}-2 = 4,094$	$2^4-2 = 14$
255.255.255.248	29	$2^{13}-2 = 8,190$	$2^3-2 = 6$

The answers to these questions will determine how an organization subnets its assigned IP address space. The purpose of asking about current and future requirements is to get an understanding of what is absolutely needed today and what should be planned for the future. To illustrate the process of classful IP addressing, subnetting, and logical ANDing as well as IP addressing considerations, examples using class A and B addresses are provided in the following sections.

Class A Network Example

This example uses a fictitious company named DGR to illustrate the process of determining the proper subnetting for an organization. DGR has been allocated the class A IP address 114.0.0.0 by the InterNIC. DGR must determine the proper way to use this IP address space to support its current and future needs. To determine these needs, we must answer the four questions suggested previously. These questions are repeated here, along with DGR's responses to them:

➤ What is the total number of network IDs DGR needs today? Answer: 5,000.

➤ What is the total number of network IDs DGR will need in the future? Answer: 9,000.

➤ What is the total number of host IDs DGR requires on its largest network today? Answer: 1,000.

➤ What is the total number of host IDs DGR will require on its largest network in the future? Answer: 2,000.

DGR has been assigned only one network; however, it needs several more to support its current and future requirements. DGR plans to use subnetting to create more network IDs. As mentioned previously, by default, 24 bits are allocated for host IDs with a class A IP address space. We know that DGR requires 5,000 networks today and 9,000 in the future. Therefore, to create enough network IDs, we have to take bits from the host IDs and use them for network IDs. How many bits have to be taken from the host ID bits to provide 5,000 network IDs?

DGR requires a total of 13 bits to provide 5,000 network IDs. The number of bits required can be determined by taking 2^{13} (for a total of 8,192 possible networks). A subnet mask of 255.255.248.0 is used to represent the 13 bits of subnetting. However, 13 bits provide only 8,192 total possible networks, which is not enough to support DGR's expected growth. A total of 14 bits is required to ensure that 9,000+ networks can be supported in the future. If DGR uses 14 bits as the subnet mask (a subnet mask of 255.255.252.0), it has a total of 16,384 (2^{14}) possible network IDs. DGR would prefer to use 14 bits of the host ID to subnet the current 114.0.0.0 class A address; however, taking 13 bits from the host ID would provide a sufficient number of network IDs (subnets) to provide for today's needs. Table 7.7 illustrates the number of bits required to provide 5,000 and 9,000+ network IDs.

DGR must determine whether enough bits still remain to provide an adequate number of host IDs. DGR requires 1,000 host IDs today and expects to need 2,000 host IDs in the future. How many bits are required to provide 1,000 host IDs? How many bits are required to provide 2,000 host IDs? How many bits are still available to be used as host IDs?

The number of bits required for 1,000 host IDs is 10, which provides a total combination of 1,022 (2^{10}–2). Remember that we subtract 2 to represent the broadcast (all 1s) and the zero (all 0s) value in each network. However, DGR requires 11 bits to provide sufficient host IDs to support its future requirement of 2,000 hosts.

DGR has only 24 bits of host IDs in its class A 114.0.0.0 IP address to use for both hosts and networks. To get enough host IDs for 2,000 users per network and 9,000+ network IDs, however, it would take 14 network ID bits and 11 host ID bits, for a total of 25 bits. DGR is short one bit, so it has to decide whether to limit the number of hosts or networks to have in the future. In this case, DGR would probably opt to use only 13 bits (8,192 networks) for network IDs and 11 bits for host IDs (2,046 host IDs per network). The decision can become more difficult, however, when an organization doesn't have the luxury of owning an entire class A IP address.

Class C Network Example

In this example, we will define the actual subnets and host IDs. If an organization named CMN has been assigned the IP address space 210.14.12.0, it has been assigned a class C address with a default mask of 255.255.255.0. This organization requires five networks today and expects to need eight in the future. In addition, CMN expects the largest number of hosts on a given network now and in the future to be 30 users.

CMN requires more networks and must subnet the 8 bits allocated to host IDs to provide these networks. To do so, CMN must subnet 3 bits to provide eight more networks (2^3). The subnet mask of this IP address is now 255.255.255.224. The value of the last octet has changed to represent the 3 bits (128 + 64 + 32 = 224) that are now used to identify networks instead of hosts. However, CMN

Table 7.7	The number of bits required for 5,000 and 9,000+ network IDs.		
IP Address	**Subnet Mask**	**Network IDs**	**Host IDs**
114.0.0.0	255.255.248.0	$2^{13} = 8192$	$2^{11} - 2 = 2046$
114.0.0.0	255.255.252.0	$2^{14} = 16384$	$2^{10} - 2 = 1022$

must make sure that it will have enough host IDs left to identify all 30 devices on its largest network. CMN has 5 bits remaining for host IDs, giving it a total of 30 (2^5-2) host IDs per network.

CMN has a total of eight subnets; these are listed in Table 7.8, along with the range of host IDs available for each subnet. A total of 30 host IDs exist for each subnet because the "all 0s" and "all 1s" host IDs have not been included. The "all 1s" host ID is reserved for the broadcast of information. For example, for subnet 210.14.12.64, host ID 210.14.12.95 is the broadcast address, because every bit used for determining the host ID is set to 1.

Summary of Subnetting

You have seen that flexibility has been built into IP addressing via a process known as *subnetting*, which allows organizations to divide up classful network IDs into a number of other networks. Any device can determine how an IP address is divided by looking at the IP address's subnet mask. This mask indicates which bits have been used for subnetting and which bits are still being used to identify hosts. Of course, each class of IP address has a default mask. Furthermore, we identified some important questions to consider when setting up an addressing scheme. Specifically, you need to know the number of hosts and networks an organization requires in the present and the future.

 The ability to decipher subnet masks and classes of IP addresses for the CCNA exam is crucial. The good news is that this ability is also crucial to being proficient at networking in general. Therefore, feel good about spending a significant amount of time practicing the art of subnetting.

Table 7.8 Subnets and host IDs for IP address 210.14.12.0.				
Subnet	Lowest Host ID	Highest Host ID	"All 1s" Host ID	"All 0s" Host ID
210.14.12.0	210.14.12.1	210.14.12.30	210.14.12.31	210.14.12.0
210.14.12.32	210.14.12.33	210.14.12.62	210.14.12.63	210.14.12.32
210.14.12.64	210.14.12.65	210.14.12.94	210.14.12.95	210.14.12.64
210.14.12.96	210.14.12.97	210.14.12.126	210.14.12.127	210.14.12.96
210.14.12.128	210.14.12.129	210.14.12.158	210.14.12.159	210.14.12.128
210.14.12.160	210.14.12.161	210.14.12.190	210.14.12.191	210.14.12.160
210.14.12.192	210.14.12.193	210.14.12.222	210.14.12.223	210.14.12.192
210.14.12.224	210.14.12.225	210.14.12.254	210.14.12.255	210.14.12.224

Configuring and Verifying IP Addresses

We have spent a significant amount of time covering IP addressing and have focused on topics such as classful addressing and subnetting. Because of the volume of information presented in these areas, you might think that it is extremely difficult to configure a Cisco router with an IP address. Wrong. The process of configuring a Cisco router with an IP address and subnet mask is very simple. When you have determined your IP addressing scheme, the actual process of configuring the router takes only a few moments. Enter the IP address at the configuration mode of the interface that is being addressed. The actual commands are shown in Listing 7.1.

Listing 7.1   Configuring an Ethernet interface with an IP address.

```
Router#configure terminal
Router(config)#interface ethernet 0
Router(config-if)#IP Address 172.16.24.12 255.255.255.0
Router(config-if)#exit
Router(config)#
```

In this example, Ethernet interface 0 was configured with the class B address 172.16.24.12. A subnet mask of 8 bits was used, as indicated by the mask 255.255.255.0.

IP Host Names

With Cisco routers, it is possible to map a literal hostname to a numeric IP address. This can often make it easier to navigate around a complex network. For example, if we wanted to map the hostname "Coriolis" with the IP address 172.16.30.12, we would perform the following set of commands:

```
Router(config)#ip host coriolis 172.16.30.12
Router(config)#exit
```

Now an administrator can use the literal "Coriolis" in place of the numeric IP address when configuring the router and navigating around the network.

Verifying IP Addresses

The process of verifying IP addresses is one that you will perform countless times during your career as a network professional. Knowing how to use the many different tools for verifying IP addresses will save you an enormous amount of time in the long run. The three tools that are vital to know for the CCNA exam are **Ping**, Telnet, and **Traceroute**.

Ping

The Ping test is used to test IP connectivity between two devices. *IP connectivity* means that both devices have the ability to send IP packets to each other. Ping tests layer 3 connectivity between two devices. The **ping** command sends Internet Control Message Protocol (ICMP) echo packets to the destination device. The destination device responds with ICMP echo reply packets if it receives the message. If the message does not reach its destination, the last hop sends an ICMP "host unreachable" packet back to the sending device. An example of a **ping** between two devices on different networks is shown in Listing 7.2.

Listing 7.2   Pinging between two devices.

```
Router>ping 172.16.29.3
Type escape sequence to abort.
Sending 5, 100-byte ICMP echos to 172.16.29.3,
Timeout is 5 seconds
!!!!!
Success rate is 100%, round-trip min/avg/max = 2/4/8 ms
Router>
```

These messages indicate that five ICMP echo requests were sent to host 172.16.29.3. If these messages did not reach their destination in 5 seconds, they would be dropped. An exclamation point (!) is written to the screen each time an ICMP echo reply packet is received by the sending device. Therefore, the sending device received all five ICMP echo requests. A number of variations to the Ping test allow the user to extract more detailed information. We encourage you to explore this tool.

Telnet

The Telnet application can be used to test Application layer connectivity between two hosts. The Telnet application is used to gain remote access to a host device; therefore, it must travel across all layers of the Open Systems Interconnection (OSI) model to reach its destination. The fact that Telnet passes through all seven layers of both the source and destination devices makes it an effective tool. If you can open a Telnet session, you know that all layers of the OSI model are functioning properly.

Traceroute

The **traceroute** command is used to determine the actual path a packet takes between its source and destination. The **traceroute** command uses ICMP and the time-to-live (TTL) field in the IP header to map the typical course a packet would take between two destinations. The TTL field's original purpose was to identify transient packets caught in routing loops. This is accomplished by setting the TTL field to some value (usually 255) and subtracting 1 from the value each time the packet reaches a router. When the TTL field reaches a value of 0, a router drops the packet. The Traceroute program capitalizes on the fact that routers drop IP packets with a value of 0. Whenever a router decreases a TTL packet to a value of 0, it sends an ICMP "TTL exceeded" message back to the sending device. It is this ICMP message that the Traceroute program uses to gather information about each hop between two devices.

An example of a **traceroute** between two devices is shown in Listing 7.3.

Listing 7.3   Traceroute between two devices.

```
Router#traceroute 172.16.19.2
Type escape sequence to abort.
Tracing the route to 172.16.19.2

1 172.16.14.254 100 msec 10 msec 4 msec
2 172.16.13.254 100 msec 10 msec 5 msec
3 172.16.63.250 110 msec 12 msec 8 msec
4 172.16.19.2 140 msec *
```

Monitoring IP

The functioning of IP in a router can be monitored in many ways. Three of the best and most useful commands are the **show ip protocol, show ip interface**, and **show ip route** commands. Although these three commands do not provide a 100-percent comprehensive view of IP, they will provide enough information for the majority of inquiries.

The **show ip interface** Command

The **show ip interface** command contains a vast amount of information about any interface using the IP protocol. An example of the **show ip interface** command is provided in Listing 7.4. The first line of the command output distinguishes whether the interface has data-link connectivity and is administratively active. From an IP perspective, the command output illustrates that the IP interface is using an IP address of 172.16.52.10 with a 24-bit default mask. In addition, the maximum transmission unit (MTU) size of all IP packets has been set to 1,500 bytes. Executing this command provides a wealth of information. I encourage you to explore this command and identify key information that can be retrieved with it.

Listing 7.4   The **show ip interface** command.

```
Router#sh ip int e0
Ethernet0 is up, line protocol is up
```

```
Internet address is 172.16.52.10/24
Broadcast address is 255.255.255.255
Address determined by non-volatile memory
MTU is 1500 bytes
Helper address is not set
Directed broadcast forwarding is enabled
Outgoing access list is not set
Inbound access list is not set
Proxy ARP is enabled
Security level is default
Split horizon is enabled
ICMP redirects are always sent
ICMP unreachables are always sent
ICMP mask replies are never sent
IP fast switching is enabled
IP fast switching on the same interface is disabled
IP multicast fast switching is enabled
Router Discovery is disabled
IP output packet accounting is disabled
IP access violation accounting is disabled
TCP/IP header compression is disabled
Probe proxy name replies are disabled
Gateway Discovery is disabled
Policy routing is disabled
Network address translation is disabled
```

The **show ip protocol** Command

The **show ip protocol** command is used to determine which protocols are performing routing for IP. The command identifies the IP networks that routing is being performed on and displays the protocol name, frequency of protocol updates, and gateways. An example of the **show ip protocol** command is provided in Listing 7.5.

Listing 7.5   The **show ip protocol** command.

```
Router#sh ip prot
Routing Protocol is "eigrp 33"
 Outgoing update filter list for all interfaces is not set
 Incoming update filter list for all interfaces is not set
 Default networks flagged in outgoing updates
 Default networks accepted from incoming updates
 EIGRP metric weight K1=1, K2=0, K3=1, K4=0, K5=0
 EIGRP maximum hop count 100
 EIGRP maximum metric variance 1
 Redistributing: static, eigrp 33
 Automatic network summarization is in effect
```

```
Routing for Networks:
 172.16.25.0
Passive Interface(s):
 Serial0
 Serial1
 Serial2
 Serial3
 Serial4
 Serial5
 Serial6
 Serial7
Routing Information Sources:
 Gateway          Distance   Last Update
 Gateway          Distance   Last Update
 148.171.63.2     90         0:00:00
 148.171.63.3     90         0:00:02
 148.171.63.4     90         0:00:02
 148.171.63.11    90         0:00:02
 148.171.63.126   90         0:00:00
Distance: internal 90 external 170
```

The **show ip route** Command

The **show ip route** command displays the routing table that the router uses to forward packets. The command also displays through which method it learned of the route, such as static, connected, Interior Gateway Routing Protocol (IGRP), and so forth. This command can be used to understand why a packet follows a certain path when traveling between two devices. An example of the **show ip route** command is provided in Listing 7.6.

Listing 7.6   The **show ip route** command.

```
Router#sh ip route
Codes: C - connected, S - static, I - IGRP, R - RIP, M - mobile,
    B - BGP
    D - EIGRP, EX - EIGRP external, O - OSPF,
    IA - OSPF inter area
    N1 - OSPF NSSA external type 1, N2 - OSPF NSSA
    external type 2
    E1 - OSPF external type 1, E2 - OSPF external type 2,
    E - EGP
    i - IS-IS, L1 - IS-IS level-1, L2 - IS-IS level-2,
    * - candidate default
    U - per-user static route, o - ODR

Gateway of last resort is 172.16.50.1 to network 0.0.0.0
```

```
C    172.16.50.0 is directly connected, Ethernet0
C    172.16.51.0 is directly connected, Ethernet1
S    140.71.0.0/16 [1/0] via 172.16.50.3
S*   0.0.0.0/0 [1/0] via 172.16.50.1
E    172.16.29.0/16 via 172.16.50.1
```

Routing Activities

Now that you know how the IP addressing and subnetting take place, let's shift gears yet again to explore the wonderful world of routing. Routing occurs within the Network layer (layer 3) of the OSI model. By sending packets from source network to destination network, the Network layer gives its best effort in the delivery of end-to-end services. Getting packets to their next hop requires a router to perform two basic activities: path determination and packet switching.

Path determination involves reviewing all available paths to a destination network and choosing the optimal route on which to send a packet. Network topology information used to determine optimal routes is collected and stored in routing tables, which contain information such as the destination network, the next hop, and an associated metric (the cost of sending packets to that next hop).

Packet switching involves changing a packet's physical destination address to that of the next hop. However, the packet's destination logical address remains constant during the packet switching process.

Routing Algorithms and Protocols

Routers choose the optimal or best route based on the available route information. A *routing algorithm* aids in the collection of route information and the determination of the best path. These algorithms may vary in several aspects. They may differ based on the goals they were designed to achieve within an internetwork. In addition, several types of routing algorithms exist to suit specific internetwork requirements. The metrics used by different routing algorithms also vary.

A *routing protocol* is a standard method of implementing a particular routing algorithm. For the purpose of our discussions, *routing protocols* mean the routing algorithms or the protocols that implement them.

Goals of Routing Protocols

As the needs of internetworks changed, new routing protocols were created to meet those needs. For example, a routing protocol that functioned well in a small internetwork five years ago may certainly experience problems in the large internetworks in use today.

Routing protocols have been designed to meet one or more of the following design goals:

> ➤ Flexibility

> ➤ Optimality

> ➤ Rapid convergence

> ➤ Robustness

> ➤ Simplicity

Flexibility

A routing protocol should be flexible. It should be able to adapt quickly to its ever-changing network environment. If a network segment goes down, a flexible routing protocol is able to detect that event and determine the next best path to use while the segment is down. When the network segment becomes available, the routing protocol should also update its route table to reflect that event. Flexible routing protocols can also adapt to changes in network variables, such as network bandwidth and delay.

Optimality

The optimality of a routing protocol gauges its ability to choose the best route correctly. The metrics used by the protocol affect its optimality. For example, one protocol may heavily weight number of hops as its metric, whereas another may use a combination of number of hops and network delay.

Rapid Convergence

Convergence occurs when all routers within an internetwork agree on the optimal routes through the internetwork. Network events such as routes going down or becoming available cause routers to recalculate optimal paths and distribute update messages about network routes. These messages permeate the entire network until all routes converge and agree on optimal routes. Slow convergence of the routing protocol can cause problems, such as a routing loop.

A *routing loop* occurs when two or more routers have not yet converged and are broadcasting their inaccurate route tables. In addition, they are most likely still switching packets based on their inaccurate route tables. Figure 7.1 illustrates this case. An event has just occurred within the network—router A lost its path to network 5. While router A is updating its route table, it receives an update from router B that says network 5 is one hop away.

Router A increases the counter by 1 and adds this new information to its route tables. In turn, router A broadcasts its updated route table to router C, which

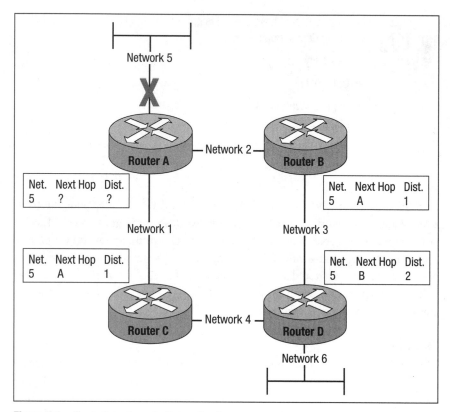

Figure 7.1 Illustration of a potential routing loop.

updates its table and broadcasts the erroneous information to router D. Router D updates its table and propagates the misinformation to router B.

This cycle will continue ad infinitum. If packets traversing the network are destined for network 5, they will loop between router A and router B until the packet becomes too old and is discarded. Figure 7.2 illustrates this situation.

Robustness

Robust and stable routing protocols perform correctly during unusual and unpredictable network events. High utilization, hardware failures, and incorrect configurations can create significant problems within a network. A robust routing protocol is stable during a variety of network situations.

Simplicity

The simplicity of a routing protocol refers to its ability to operate efficiently. Because routing protocols collect and store route information, a protocol is

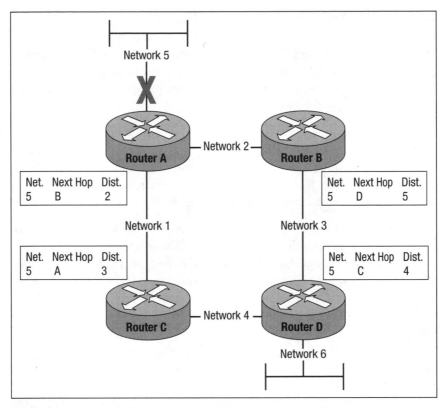

Figure 7.2   Illustration of of the end result of a routing loop.

competing for the router's limited physical resources. A routing protocol must perform its functions with minimal administrative overhead.

Types of Routing Protocols

Routing protocols can also be categorized by type. The type of routing protocol deployed within an internetwork should be based on the organizational requirements.

Types of routing protocols include:

➤ Static or dynamic

➤ Single path or multipath

➤ Flat or hierarchical

➤ Interior or exterior

➤ Distance vector or link state

Static or Dynamic

A network administrator configures static routes manually. When defining a *static route*, the administrator configures the destination network, next hop, and appropriate metrics. The route does not change until the network administrator changes it. Static routes function well in environments where the network is simple and network traffic is predictable.

Dynamic routes adjust to changes within the internetwork environment automatically. When network changes occur, routers begin to converge by recalculating routes and distributing route updates. The route-update messages permeate the network, which causes more routers to recalculate their routes. This route-update process continues until all routers have converged.

Occasionally, static routes augment dynamic routes. In a dynamically routed environment, a router discards a packet if the destination network does not appear in the route table. However, a static route can be configured to handle this situation. A *default route* (which points to a router) can be established to receive and attempt to process all packets for which no route appears in the routing table.

Single Path or Multipath

When calculating the optimal path for a particular network, some routing protocols simply choose the best *single path* to a destination network. Others allow more than one optimal path if the paths have equal metric values. A *multipath protocol* enables traffic load-balancing using the multiple paths and offers additional advantages over single-path protocols, such as reliability.

Flat or Hierarchical

A routing environment is considered *flat* if all routers are peers to each other. Routers that use a flat routing protocol may communicate with any other router in the network as directly as possible. Like static routing, a flat routing protocol functions well in simple and predictable network environments.

Alternatively, a *hierarchical* routing environment contains several routers that compose a backbone. Most traffic from non-backbone routers usually traverses the backbone routers (or at least travels to the backbone) in order to reach another non-backbone router. Within a hierarchical routing environment, autonomous systems (sometimes referred to as *domains* or *areas*) can be established. Being part of the same autonomous system enables a group of routers to share network topology information with each other, but that same information is not shared outside the group. Although several layers or tiers may exist within the hierarchy, the routers at the highest level comprise the backbone. Cisco, as of publication of this book, is eager to promote a three-tier system. Cisco has a backbone, distribution, and access layer, and equipment is being manufactured and marketed according to these layers. Backbone must provide the fastest throughput possible, without making any routing decisions or as little as possible. Those are high-end expensive and complex routers and switches. Distribution level is where most of the routing is happening. Those are mid-level boxes. Access level is where hosts are connected to the network, and they are mostly 2000 series of switches and routers. While it is not very important to know the model numbers for the CCNA exam, the three-level architecture that Cisco has is a must to know when working in any network environment. Typically, the network backbone comprises its own autonomous system or domain.

Interior or Exterior

An *interior* routing protocol operates within a single autonomous system or domain. These protocols are typically implemented within an organization's private network. Routers that are running interior routing protocols are considered *intradomain routers*; they only need to know about other routers within their domain. Conversely, an *exterior* routing protocol conveys routing information between domains. Exterior routing protocols are in use within the Internet. *Interdomain routers* need to know how to route traffic between autonomous systems and can protect against errors or problems with one domain affecting another.

Distance Vector or Link State

Distance vector protocols require each router to send all or a large part of its route table to its neighboring routers. *Link state protocols* require each router to send the state of its own interfaces to every router in the internetwork. Distance vector protocols are simple and straightforward, but they converge slowly and consume a significant amount of bandwidth because they have to send updates every set amount of time and entire tables as opposed to the updated entries, which can cause routing loops. Link state protocols converge quickly, but they require more of the router's central processing unit (CPU) and memory resources.

Each routed protocol can be implemented in one or more routing protocols. The routing protocols (or standard set of rules) actually enable the router to determine the best path. Common routing protocols include:

➤ Routing Information Protocol (RIP)

➤ Interior Gateway Routing Protocol (IGRP)

➤ Open Shortest Path First (OSPF)

➤ Enhanced Interior Gateway Routing Protocol (EIGRP)

➤ Border Gateway Protocol (BGP)

➤ Exterior Gateway Protocol (EGP)

Table 7.9	Interior routing protocols.				
Routing Protocol	Static or Dynamic	Single Path or Multipath	Flat or Hierarchical	Interior or Exterior	Distance Vector or Link State
RIP	Dynamic	Single path	Flat	Interior	Distance vector
IGRP	Dynamic	Multipath	Flat	Interior	Distance vector
OSPF	Dynamic	Multipath	Hierarchical	Interior	Link state
EIGRP	Dynamic	Multipath	Flat	Interior	Advanced distance vector

RIP and IGRP are the two types of routing protocols that will be covered in detail in this book. Table 7.9 lists the common interior routing protocols and their characteristics.

Note: IGRP and EIGRP are Cisco proprietary routing protocols. They are only supported on Cisco routers.

Routing Metrics

Routing protocols use many different metrics to determine the optimal route. These variables can be used individually or in combination with one another to create the metric defined within a given routing protocol.

Metrics used in routing protocols include:

➤ Bandwidth

➤ Delay

➤ Load

➤ Path length

➤ Reliability

Bandwidth

The available capacity of a network link is known as its *bandwidth*. Typically, a 10Mbps Ethernet link is preferable to a 56Kbps Frame Relay link. However, if other metrics such as delay are considered, the Ethernet link may not be the optimal path.

Delay

Network delay refers to the amount of time necessary to move a packet through the internetwork from source to destination. Delay is a conglomeration of several other variables, including physical distance between source and destination, bandwidth and congestion of intermediate links, and port queues of intermediate routers.

Load

Load is an indication of how busy a network resource is. CPU utilization and packets processed per second are two valuable factors when calculating the load.

Path Length

In some routing protocols, *path length* refers to the sum of the costs of each link traversed up to the destination network. Other routing protocols refer to path length as the *hop count*, which is the number of passes through a router that a packet makes on its way to the destination network.

Reliability

This metric allows the network administrator to assign a numeric value arbitrarily to indicate a reliability factor for the link. Some network links go down more than others do; some are easily repaired and become available relatively quickly. The reliability metric is simply a method used to capture an administrator's experience with a given network link.

A routed protocol such as IP or IPX is concerned with the movement of user traffic. A routing protocol such as RIP or OSPF is concerned with maintaining route tables.

Distance Vector vs. Link State

This section highlights the similarities and differences between two types of widely used routing protocols: distance vector and link state.

Distance Vector Overview

A distance vector routing protocol sends all or part of its route table across the network, but only to its neighbors. The route table contains the distance and direction to any network within its domain. Figure 7.3 provides an overview of the distance vector process.

Periodically, router A broadcasts its entire route table to its neighbors, router B and router C. Router B updates the route information it received by increasing the metric value, which is usually the hop count, by 1. Router B then compares the route information it just received and updated with the existing route information from its route table. Router B replaces existing route information with an updated entry only if the updated route information has a lower calculated metric. Router B then broadcasts its route table to its direct neighbors, router D and

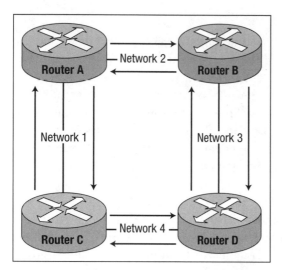

Figure 7.3 Illustration of the Distance Vector Process.

router A. This process occurs regularly and in all directions for all directly connected neighbors. Although this process enables routers to accumulate network distance information, the routers do not know the network's exact topology.

Note: The default value for RIP updates to occur is every 30 seconds.

Link State Overview

A *link state* routing protocol (sometimes referred to as *shortest path first*) sends only the state of its own network links across the network, but it sends this information to every router within its domain. This process enables routers to learn and maintain full knowledge of the network's exact topology and how it is interconnected. Figure 7.4 provides an overview of the link state process.

Link state routing protocols rely on several components to acquire and maintain knowledge of the network:

➤ Router C broadcasts and receives link state packets to and from other routers via the network. Link state packets contain the status of a router's links or network interfaces.

➤ Router C builds a topology database of the network.

➤ Router C runs a Shortest Path First (SPF) algorithm against the database and generates an SPF tree of the network, with router C as the root of the tree.

➤ Router C populates its route table with optimal paths and ports to transmit data through to reach each network.

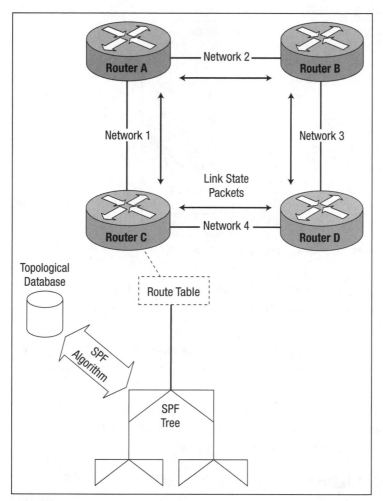

Figure 7.4   Illustration of the Link State Process.

Network Discovery

When a router starts up, it must undergo a *network discovery* process, which enables the router to begin communicating with other routers on the network. Figure 7.5 illustrates the network discovery process for distance vector protocols. Router A has just started up and is configured to run a distance vector.

Router A begins the discovery process by identifying its neighbor, router B. Router A begins populating its route table with its directly connected networks, networks 1 and 2, which receive a metric of 0. It passes its route table to router B and receives router B's entire route table. Router A increases the distances of each entry by one hop. After the distances have been updated, router A will already

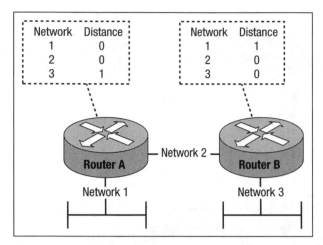

Figure 7.5   Illustration of the Network Discovery Process.

have better routes to networks 1 and 2, but not network 3. Router A increases the distance to network 3 by one hop and stores this in its route table.

The network discovery process for link state protocols is similar to that of distance vector protocols. Instead of route tables, routers exchange link state packets and use that information to build their topology databases, SPF trees, and route tables.

Regardless of whether a router uses a distance vector or link state routing protocol, the router dynamically discovers its network environment. It can then use its route table to perform the packet-switching function.

Topology Changes

After the router has discovered the network, it must also keep up with network topology changes. Depending on the protocol used, a router transmits route information periodically or when a network event occurs. Routers detect changes in the network topology via these updates.

Most distance vector protocols handle topology changes through regularly scheduled updates. After a specified interval, a router broadcasts its route table to its neighbor. Route recalculation occurs, if necessary, and updates in the network topology are broadcast. The route distribution timers are not synchronized across routers.

Link state protocols rely on network events to address topology changes. If a router detects a network event (such as one of its neighbors is no longer reachable or a new neighbor appears), it triggers an update. The router broadcasts the state of its links to all other routers within the domain. Upon receiving the update, other routers update their topology database and broadcast the state of their links also. When all updates have been received, each router updates its SPF tree and route tables accordingly. At this point, the network has converged. Event-triggered updates have a ripple effect within a network.

Distance Vector Problems

The fact that route updates with a distance vector protocol occur after a specified interval can become problematic. With RIP, route updates are broadcast every 30 seconds by default. As a result, distance vector protocols converge slowly. Routing loops and the problems they create were discussed previously in this chapter. Routing loops create a condition known as *counting to infinity*, where the distance metric is continually increased because the network has not fully converged.

Distance Vector Remedies

One technique to remedy a count-to-infinity situation involves a maximum hop count. Although this count will not prevent a routing loop, it does reduce the time that the routing loop exists. A maximum hop count, when reached, forces a router to mark a network unreachable rather than increase the distance metric.

Routing loops also occur when information that contradicts information sent previously is broadcast back to a router. Router A sends information about network 5 to router B. *Split horizon* prevents a router from sending information it received about a network back to the neighbor that originally sent the information. For example, split horizon prohibits router B and router C from sending any information about network 5 back to router A.

Route poisoning occurs when a router detects that a network is down and immediately marks it as unreachable. This route update is broadcast throughout the network. While the other routers slowly converge, the router maintains this poisoned route in its route table and ignores updates from other routers about better routes to the network. The poisoned route is removed after several update cycles. Route poisoning works well with hold-down timers.

A *hold-down timer* indicates that no updates to a particular route should be accepted until the timer expires. A hold-down condition is triggered when a router receives an update from its neighbor indicating that a reachable network has just gone down. The router marks the network as unreachable and starts its hold-down timer. While the timer is active, updates from any other router are ignored. Updates about the unreachable network are accepted only from the neighboring router that initially indicated the unreachable network while the timer is active. If the neighboring router indicates that the network is reachable again, the router stops the hold-down timer and updates its route table. When the hold-down timer expires, the router marks the network reachable and receives updates from any router.

The following techniques help to stabilize distance vector protocols:

➤ Maximum hop count

➤ Split horizon

➤ Route poisoning

➤ Hold-down timers

Link State Problems

Because link state routing protocols have knowledge of the entire network and converge quickly, they do not suffer from the same problems as distance vector protocols. One problem that affects link state protocols is the significant memory and processor resources required from the router itself when acquiring and maintaining full knowledge of large networks. As updates move through the network, each router must receive the update, recalculate its information, and send its own link information. Of course, this type of overhead affects the ability of the router to move user data packets through the network.

A second shortcoming of link state protocols is the amount of network bandwidth that can be consumed while the network converges. Routers flood updates about the state of their links to every other router in the network, so the amount of bandwidth consumed is significant. As routers collect link information from each other, the amount of bandwidth available for end-user communications is reduced. This high level of bandwidth utilization typically occurs on initialization of the network or when several routers start up simultaneously.

Additional problems can occur during the link state update process itself. It is imperative that each router receives all the packets in a timely manner and that the updates are synchronized. For example, if one part of the network receives route information before another part, convergence may take longer, or SPF trees and route tables may store inaccurate information. Additionally, as routers attempt to move link state packets through the network, they may be doing so without fully constructed SPF trees or route tables.

The following problems may occur within networks using link state protocols:

➤ Router resource usage

➤ Network bandwidth consumption

➤ Update synchronization

Link State Remedies

One remedy for link state problems involves minimizing the resources required to build and maintain route tables. The time between periodic updates can be lengthened to reduce the processing resources required. Also, routers can be identified to serve as border routers. The border routers can then exchange route summaries with other border routers and each core router to reduce the bandwidth consumed during the update process and to isolate update processes to hierarchical areas. The border router then passes updates to the routers within its area.

Another technique involves coordinating link state updates. Timestamps and sequence numbers can be attached to the link state packet. Routers then realize when they receive inaccurate or old link state packets.

 The following techniques help to stabilize link state protocols:

➤ Minimize router resource usage by lengthening the update frequency or exchanging route summaries.

➤ Coordinate updates with timestamps or sequence numbers.

Both distance vector and link state routing protocols have demonstrated their worth over time. Each has advantages that may suit a particular network design perfectly. Several factors must be considered when choosing a routing protocol, including business policies and operational issues. Table 7.10 provides a quick comparison of distance vector and link state routing protocols.

Routing Protocol Configuration and Review

This section highlights the basic router commands necessary to add the RIP and IGRP to a router configuration.

RIP

Table 7.11 lists the configuration commands necessary to enable RIP on a router.

Table 7.10 Distance vector versus link state routing protocols.	
Distance Vector	**Link State**
Sees the network from its neighbor's perspective.	Sees the entire network from its own perspective.
Distance metrics accumulate from router to router.	Calculates shortest path to other routers.
Route updates occur periodically.	Route updates are event-triggered.
Convergence is slow.	Convergence is fast.
Broadcasts the entire route table to neighbors.	Broadcasts link status information to all other routers.

Table 7.11	RIP configuration commands.
Task	**Router Command**
Enter global configuration mode	RouterA#; **configure terminal**
Enter RIP configuration mode	RouterA (config); **#router rip**
Configure network 172.16.0.0 to be advertised	RouterA (config-router)#; **network 172.16.0.0**
Exit configuration mode	RouterA (config-router)#; **Ctrl+Z**

The **show IP protocol** command displays detailed information about each IP routing protocol that has been configured on the router.

The output shown in Listing 7.7 displays the results of the **show IP protocol** command after RIP has been configured.

Listing 7.7 RIP configuration display.

```
RouterA#
RouterA#show ip protocol <Return>
Routing Protocol is "rip"
  Sending updates every 30 seconds, next due in 2 seconds
  Invalid after 180 seconds, hold down 180, flushed after 240
  Outgoing update filter list for all interfaces is not set
  Incoming update filter list for all interfaces is not set
  Redistributing: rip
  Default version control: send version 1, receive any version
    Interface       Send  Recv  Key-chain
    Ethernet0        1     1     2
    Loopback0        1     1     2
    Serial0          1     1     2
  Routing for Networks:
    172.16.0.0
  Routing Information Sources:
    Gateway         Distance      Last Update
    172.16.24.252      120        00:00:12
  Distance: (default is 120)

RouterA#
```

Note: By default, RIP sends updates every 30 seconds. Also, the RIP hold-down timer is set to 180 seconds, and a neighbor router has an IP address of 172.16.24.252.

IGRP

Table 7.12 lists the configuration commands necessary to enable IGRP on a router.

The output shown in Listing 7.8 displays the results of the **show IP protocol** command after IGRP has been configured.

Listing 7.8   IGRP configuration display.

```
RouterA#
RouterA#show ip protocol <Return>
Routing Protocol is "igrp 1"
  Sending updates every 90 seconds, next due in 7 seconds
  Invalid after 270 seconds, hold down 280, flushed after 630
  Outgoing update filter list for all interfaces is not set
  Incoming update filter list for all interfaces is not set
  Default networks flagged in outgoing updates
  Default networks accepted from incoming updates
  IGRP metric weight K1=1, K2=0, K3=1, K4=0, K5=0
  IGRP maximum hopcount 100
  IGRP maximum metric variance 1
  Redistributing: igrp 1
  Routing for Networks:
    172.16.0.0
  Routing Information Sources:
    Gateway          Distance        Last Update
    172.16.24.252        100         00:00:15
  Distance: (default is 100)
RouterA#
```

Note: By default, IGRP sends updates every 90 seconds. Also, the IGRP maximum hop count is set to 100, and a neighbor router has an IP address of 172.16.24.252.

Table 7.12 IGRP configuration commands.	
Task	**Router Syntax**
Enter global configuration mode	RouterA#**configure terminal**
Enter IGRP routing protocol configuration mode for autonomous system 1	RouterA(config); #**router igrp 1**
Configure network 172.16.0.0 to be advertised	RouterA(config-router)#; **network 172.16.0.0**
Exit configuration mode	RouterA (config-router)#; **Ctrl+Z**

Practice Questions

Question 1

> The following IP address is listed in dotted decimal format. What is the corresponding binary value of this IP address?
>
> 112.14.12.8
>
> ○ a. 01100000.00110000.01101111.10110111
>
> ○ b. 0.11.0.11
>
> ○ c. 01110000.00001110.00001100.00001000
>
> ○ d. 01110000.00001110.11000000.00110011

The correct answer is c. The conversion of these binary bits yields a decimal value of 112.14.12.8. Answer a can be identified quickly as incorrect by noting that the fourth octet begins with 1, but its value is not greater than 128. Answer b can be eliminated immediately because it is not in the format of a binary IP address. Answer d can be judged to be incorrect by determining the decimal value of either the third or fourth octet. It is important to note that it is not necessary to convert each one of the possible answers into decimal format. It is much quicker to eliminate the obviously wrong answers (such as b) and then isolate reasons to remove other answers before converting any values.

Question 2

> Which of the following statements is not true concerning the deciphering of a subnet ID from an IP address and subnet mask using the ANDing process?
>
> ○ a. If the subnet mask and the IP address both have values of 1, the resulting network ID bit is 1.
>
> ○ b. If the subnet mask has a value of 1 and the IP address has a value of 1, the resulting network ID bit is 0.
>
> ○ c. If the subnet mask has a value of 1 and the IP address has a value of 0, the resulting network ID bit is 0.
>
> ○ d. If the subnet mask has a value of 0, the resulting network ID bit is 0.

The correct answer is b. It specifies that a network ID bit of 0 is the result when comparing a subnet mask bit with a value of 1 and an IP address with a value of

1. This is *not* one of the rules used to decipher network IDs. Therefore, answer b is the correct answer. Answers a, c, and d are the three rules presented in this chapter for deciphering network IDs from an IP address with a subnet mask. Therefore, these answers are incorrect.

Question 3

> Which of the following tools can be utilized to test IP connectivity between two devices? [Choose the three best answers]
>
> ❑ a. **Ping**
>
> ❑ b. **Telnet**
>
> ❑ c. **Traceroute**
>
> ❑ d. **show ip interface**
>
> ❑ e. **show ip protocol**

The correct answers are a, b, and c. Ping, Telnet, and Traceroute are all tools mentioned in this chapter for testing IP connectivity between two devices. Answers d and e are incorrect because **show ip interface** and **show ip protocol** are used to monitor IP addresses and the functioning of IP within a local router.

Question 4

> Which of the following tools will identify the address of intermediate hops between two destinations?
>
> ○ a. **Traceroute**
>
> ○ b. **Telnet**
>
> ○ c. **Ping**
>
> ○ d. **Rlogin**
>
> ○ e. TCP

The correct answer is a. The **traceroute** command can be used to identify the address of every intermediate hop between two locations. Answer b is incorrect because the **telnet** command is used to obtain remote control of a destination device. Answer c is incorrect because the **ping** command only tells users whether they have IP connectivity. Answer d is incorrect because **rlogin** is a command used for remote access on Unix machines. Finally, answer e is incorrect because TCP is a layer 4 protocol, and it is not used for testing IP connectivity.

Question 5

> Which of the following commands will show the MTU size used by the interface?
>
> ○ a. **show ip route**
>
> ○ b. **show ip interface**
>
> ○ c. **show ip protocol**

The correct answer is b. The **show ip interface** command displays a wealth of information regarding the interface specified, including the MTU size. Answers a and c are incorrect because neither of these commands displays information regarding the MTU size of an interface.

Question 6

> Which of the following is the default mask of a class A IP address?
>
> ○ a. 255.0.0.255
>
> ○ b. 255.255.0.0
>
> ○ c. 255.0.0.0
>
> ○ d. 255.255.255.0

The correct answer is c. Class A addresses have a default mask of 8 bits or 255.0.0.0. Answer a is incorrect because all default masks are contiguous bits. Answer b is incorrect because 255.255.0.0 is the default mask of a class B IP address, not a class A IP address. Answer d is incorrect because 255.255.255.0 is the default mask of a class C IP address, not a class A IP address.

Question 7

> Which of the following are basic functions of a router? [Choose the two best answers]
>
> ❑ a. Packet switching
>
> ❑ b. Packet filtering
>
> ❑ c. Path determination
>
> ❑ d. Rapid convergence

The correct answers are a and c. Routers packet-switch when they have determined the best path. Path determination is the process of choosing the best network path from all available network paths. Packet filtering is a technique used to control inbound and/or outbound packets to or from a router. Therefore, answer b is incorrect. Rapid convergence is a design goal of some routing protocols. Therefore, answer d is incorrect.

Question 8

Network routing information distributed among routers is stored in which of the following?

O a. Flash memory

O b. Route table

O c. Metric table

O d. NVRAM

The correct answer is b. Route tables contain information about destination networks and the next hop along the optimal path to get there. Flash memory contains the operating system images used by the router. Therefore, answer a is incorrect. Metric information is contained within a router's route table. Therefore, answer c is incorrect. NVRAM contains the router's active configuration files. Therefore, answer d is incorrect.

Question 9

Which of the following conditions is a problem experienced by distance vector routing protocols?

O a. Split horizon

O b. Route poisoning

O c. Counting to infinity

O d. Maximum hop count

O e. Hold-down timers

The correct answer is c. Counting to infinity can result from the slow convergence inherent in distance vector protocols. Split horizon, route poisoning, maximum hop count, and hold-down timers are techniques/items used to reduce the occurrence and impact of the counting-to-infinity situation. Therefore, answers a, b, d, and e are incorrect.

Question 10

> What router command will display the routing protocol settings (such as timers and neighbors) configured on a router?
>
> O a. **show protocol**
>
> O b. **show routing protocol**
>
> O c. **show ip protocol**
>
> O d. **show running-config**

The correct answer is c. The **show ip protocol** command displays all routing protocols that are active on the router. In addition, it displays other values such as timers, neighbors, and when the next update will be sent. The **show protocol** command displays information about routed protocols such as IP and IPX. Therefore, answer a is incorrect. The **show routing protocol** command is invalid. Therefore, answer b is incorrect. The **show running-config** command displays some routing protocol information, such as the networks that are being advertised to other routers. Therefore, answer d is incorrect.

Question 11

> Which of the following help to mitigate the shortcomings of link state protocols? [Choose the two best answers]
>
> ❑ a. Maximum hop count
>
> ❑ b. Minimize router resource usage
>
> ❑ c. Coordinate updates
>
> ❑ d. Route poisoning

The correct answers are b and c. Lengthening the update frequency or exchanging router summaries at specific border routers helps to minimize router resource usage. Therefore, answer b is correct. Also, attaching timestamps or sequence numbers on link state packets helps to coordinate update information between routers. Therefore, answer c is correct. A maximum hop count and route poisoning address problems with distance vector protocols. Therefore, answers a and d are incorrect.

Question 12

Which router commands, if executed from the global configuration prompt, enable RIP routing for network 172.16.0.0?

○ a. **router rip 1** and **network 172.16.0.0**

○ b. **router rip all**

○ c. **router rip** and **network 172.16.0.0**

○ d. **network 172.16.0.0**

The correct answer is c. The **router rip 1** command enables RIP routing, and the **network 172.16.0.0** command enables the router to advertise that network to other routers. Answers a and b are incorrect because the **router rip 1** command requires no additional parameters. Answer d is incorrect because you must first enter routing protocol configuration mode before configuring a network to be advertised.

Question 13

Which of the following conditions are problems experienced by link state routing protocols? [Choose the two best answers]

❑ a. Split horizon

❑ b. High router resource usage

❑ c. High network bandwidth consumption

❑ d. Unsynchronized updates

❑ e. Hold-down timers

The correct answers are b and d. Problems with high router resource usage and high network bandwidth can occur during convergence as link state packets flood the network. Also, if link state packet updates are not synchronized, inaccurate SPF trees and route tables may result, and convergence may take longer. Split horizon and hold-down timers are techniques used to reduce problems in distance vector routing protocols. Lastly, high network bandwidth consumption is not an issue because it takes less bandwidth to send event-triggered updates rather than broadcasting entire tables every 30 seconds. Therefore, answers a, c, and e are incorrect.

Need to Know More?

 McNutt, Shawn, Mark Poplar, Jason Waters, and David Stabenaw: *CCNA Routing and Switching Exam Prep*. The Coriolis Group. Scottsdale, AZ, 2000. ISBN 1-57610-440-0.

This book is a great complement to the *CCNA Exam Cram* book.

 Moy, John T. *OSPF: Anatomy of an Internet Routing Protocol*. Addison-Wesley Publishing Company. Reading, MA, 1998. ISBN 0-20163-472-4.

This book gives detailed information about various Internet routing protocols and then focuses specifically on OSPF.

 Parkhurst, William R. *Cisco Router OSPF: Design and Implementation Guide*. McGraw-Hill. New York, 1998. ISBN 0-07048-626-3.

This book reviews routing protocol configuration commands and also discusses advanced topics, such as route redistribution between routing protocols.

 www.cisco.com/public.technotes/tech_protocol.shtml, the official Cisco documentation Web site, discusses the routing protocol Web pages for IGRP/EIGRP and OSPF. You can also review more information about exterior routing protocols such as BGP and EGP.

Internet Package Exchange (IPX)

Terms you'll need to understand:

- ✓ NetWare
- ✓ Internet Packet Exchange (IPX)
- ✓ Network Operating System (NOS)
- ✓ Network Basic Input/Output System (NetBIOS)
- ✓ Routing Information Protocol (RIP)
- ✓ Service Advertisement Protocol (SAP)
- ✓ NetWare Core Protocol (NCP)
- ✓ Sequence Packet Exchange (SPX)
- ✓ Network interface card (NIC)
- ✓ Encapsulation
- ✓ Ticks
- ✓ Hop count
- ✓ NetWare Link State Protocol (NLSP)
- ✓ NetWare shell

Techniques you'll need to master:

- ✓ Describing the two parts of network addressing
- ✓ Identifying the parts of network addressing in specific protocol address examples
- ✓ Listing the required IPX address and encapsulation type
- ✓ Adding the RIP routing protocol to your configuration

This chapter introduces NetWare and the IPX protocol. Like Internet Protocol (IP), IPX resides at the Network layer of the Open Systems Interconnection (OSI) model. This chapter describes how the NetWare protocol suite maps to the OSI model and covers IPX addressing, encapsulation, and SAPs. IPX commands for configuring, monitoring, and troubleshooting IPX are also listed.

In the early 1980s, Novell created a proprietary suite of protocols for local area networks (LANs) called *NetWare*. Derived from Xerox Network Systems, NetWare defined protocols for the upper five layers of the OSI model. It is considered a network operating system (NOS) and provides support for file sharing, printing, database access, and various applications. Like other NOSs, NetWare is based on a client/server architecture, where clients (such as PCs) request services from different servers (such as printer servers).

NetWare Protocol Suite

Table 8.1 shows the relationship between the OSI model and the NetWare protocol suite.

Upper Layers

NetWare supports many applications, such as email and other industry-standard protocols. For example, NetWare includes emulation software that supports NetBIOS application interfaces. NetBIOS is a common Session layer interface specification from IBM and Microsoft. Other protocols are as follows:

➤ *Routing Information Protocol (RIP)*—RIP is a distance vector routing protocol primarily used to determine routes through IPX networks. It uses tick and hop counts to base this determination on. A server will build its routing table information based on updates from other servers it is directly connected to. The updates are sent every 60 seconds and are sent to all IPX-enabled interfaces.

Table 8.1 A comparison of the OSI model and the NetWare protocol suite.	
OSI Reference Model	**Novell Netware Protocols**
Application	RIP, SAP, NCP, NetBIOS, NLSP, and applications
Presentation	RIP, SAP, NCP, NetBIOS, and applications
Session	RIP, SAP, NCP, NetBIOS, and applications
Transport	RIP, SAP, NCP, NetBIOS, IPX, and applications
Network	RIP, SAP, NCP, NetBIOS, IPX, and SPX
Data Link	IPX and Open Data Link (ODL)
Physical	Media Access Protocols (Ethernet, Token Ring, and so on)

➤ *Service Advertising Protocol (SAP)*—SAP is generally used for the request and advertising of services. A NetWare server would advertise its services while the client uses it to locate services on the network. A SAP broadcast is sent out every 60 seconds to advertise services. Keep in mind that the broadcast contains information on all services offered by other servers as well. Here's how it works: A SAP advertisement is sent out, and the server that receives the advertisement stores it in its SAP table. That same server then sends out updates, which include the newly learned information. At some point, all the servers will have information on all services offered.

➤ *NetWare Core Protocol (NCP)*—NCP is a protocol that enables clients to have access to network security, printing, and files.

➤ *Sequenced Packet Exchange (SPX)*—SPX is a connection-oriented protocol that ensures data delivery between communicating nodes. An ID is added to the SPX header that creates virtual circuits between devices. Similar to other transport protocols, SPX provides reliable, connection-oriented services that supplement NetWare's Network layer protocol.

Network Layer

NetWare uses IPX as its Network layer protocol. Like other network protocols, IPX supports the routing of information from a source network, through any intermediate networks, to the destination network. Also, IPX is connectionless. That is, it does not require acknowledgment of each packet it transmits; SPX provides that capability. IPX relies on RIP to exchange network routing information.

Data Link and Physical Layers

NetWare supports several different Media Access Protocols and physical media types. NetWare can run over an Ethernet or Token Ring LAN. It can also operate in several wide area network (WAN) environments, including Integrated Services Digital Network (ISDN), Point-to-Point Protocol (PPP), and Frame Relay.

IPX Addressing

Similar to addresses within an IP network, an IPX logical address contains a network number and a node number. Although an IPX logical address can contain up to 80 bits (network and node portions, similar to an IP address), a network administrator defines the IPX network number, which can contain a maximum of 32 bits. The node number is provided by the Media Access Control (MAC) address of the network interface card (NIC) and can be up to a maximum of 48 bits. Because MAC addresses are unique, it is impossible for two devices within the same network to possess the same node number. Also, using the MAC address as the node's logical address eliminates the need for the Address Resolution Protocol (ARP) to determine the physical address.

Note: An IPX address consists of a network number and a node number that is usually the node's MAC address and is often written in hex. In the IPX address 00009A60.0000.6606.45B8, the first eight hex digits (00009A60) represent the network portion, whereas the last 12 hex digits (0000.6606.45B8) represent the node portion.

IPX Encapsulation

Novell's IPX supports various encapsulation types; several of these types can be configured on a single router interface. As IPX packets are passed to the Data Link layer, the packets are encapsulated into one of several framing types supported by NetWare. However, you need to assign each encapsulation type to a unique network number on the router's interface. (The encapsulation type you select depends on the router's interface.) Table 8.2 lists the four Ethernet encapsulation types and the corresponding Cisco internetwork operating system (IOS) names you will need to use when configuring the router.

Even though a single interface can support multiple encapsulation types, clients and servers that use different encapsulation types cannot communicate directly. Instead, they communicate via the router.

 The default encapsulation types for Cisco routers are:

➤ Ethernet: NOVELL-ETHER

➤ Token Ring: SAP

➤ Fiber Distributed Data Interface (FDDI): SNAP

IPX Routing

RIP, the routing protocol used by IPX, is a distance vector routing protocol that relies on ticks and hop counts as its metrics. A *tick* is a measure of delay time,

Table 8.2 Ethernet encapsulation framing types.		
IPX Name	**Cisco IOS Name**	**Usage**
Ethernet II	ARPA	With TCP/IP and DECnet
Ethernet 802.2	SAP	With NetWare version 4.x and OSI routing
Ethernet SNAP	SNAP	With TCP/IP, IPX, and AppleTalk
Ethernet 802.3	NOVELL-ETHER	With NetWare versions 2.x and 3.x

about 1/18th of a second. In RIP version 2, ticks serve as the primary value used in determining the best path. If two or more network paths have the same tick value, RIP then uses the hop count (the number of routers the packet must traverse) to break the tie. If multiple network paths have equal tick values and hop counts, RIP either uses a user-defined tiebreaker or load-balances across the paths.

Note: Although IPX uses RIP as its default, two other routing protocol choices exist: Novell's Netware Link Services Protocol (NLSP) and Cisco's Enhanced Interior Gateway Routing Protocol (EIGRP).

IPX Service Advertisement

In an IPX network, servers advertise across the network (that is, they broadcast the services they offer and their addresses). These advertisements are defined within the SAP and are supported by all versions of NetWare. Clients learn of services that are being provided by issuing SAP broadcast queries and receiving SAP responses. SAP broadcasts traverse the network on a regular basis (every 60 seconds, by default). Routers also receive SAP broadcasts, learn of services offered, and store the information in SAP tables. However, routers do not forward SAP broadcasts; they share SAP table information with other routers. Like SAP broadcasts, SAP table information is forwarded every 60 seconds, by default.

A unique hexadecimal number identifies the services within a SAP broadcast. Table 8.3 lists some common SAP services.

One example of a SAP broadcast involves a Get Nearest Server (GNS) request. A client workstation typically issues this type of request when it needs to log in to the network server. The client broadcasts the GNS request across the network, and both the NetWare file server and the router receive the request. If a file server resides on the network, it replies with a GNS SAP. If no file server responds and the router knows of another file server, the router responds with information from its SAP table.

Here are the key features of IPX:

➤ The logical address is 80 bits (network.node).

➤ The interface MAC address is the node address.

➤ A router interface can support multiple encapsulation protocols.

➤ RIP is the default routing protocol.

➤ Servers advertise their services in SAP packets.

Table 8.3   Common SAP services.

Hex Number	SAP Description
0004	NetWare file server
0007	Print server
0024	Router

Configuring IPX

Configuring Novell IPX on a router requires that both global and interface parameters be set. Global configuration includes starting the IPX routing process and enabling load balancing, if appropriate for your network. Interface configuration includes assigning unique network numbers to each interface and defining encapsulation settings, if different from the default.

Note: Multiple network numbers can be assigned to an interface, setting the stage for support of multiple encapsulation types.

Table 8.4 lists the global configuration commands necessary to enable IPX routing. These commands must be executed from the global configuration prompt.

The following output lists the interface configuration command required for IPX routing on an interface (you must configure this command for each interface connected to an IPX network):

```
DALLAS(config-if)#ipx network 12 encapsulation SAP
```

Here, **12** indicates a unique IPX network number, and **encapsulation SAP** is optional and indicates the framing that will be used (sap, snap, and so forth).

To further illustrate, the IPX network configuration depicted below would require the following commands to be executed:

```
DALLAS#config t
DALLAS(config)#
DALLAS(config)# ipx routing
DALLAS(config)# ipx maximum-paths 2
DALLAS(config)# int e0
```

Table 8.4   IPX global configuration commands.

Command	Description
ipx routing [node]	Enables Novell IPX routing
ipx maximum-paths [paths]	Enables round-robin load balancing across multiple equal metric paths

```
DALLAS(config-if)# ipx network 10 encapsulation sap
DALLAS(config-if)# exit
DALLAS(config)# interface s1
DALLAS(config-if)# ipx network 11 encapsulation snap
DALLAS(config-if)# exit
DALLAS(config)# interface e1
DALLAS(config-if)# ipx network 12 encapsulation sap
DALLAS(config-if)# exit
DALLAS(config)# interface s0
DALLAS(config-if)# ipx network 13 encapsulation snap
DALLAS(config-if)# exit
DALLAS(config)#
```

The method above shows commands to configure a primary encapsulation on an interface. Below a subinterface is configured to support multiple networks.

```
DALLAS#config t
DALLAS(config)#int s1.22
DALLAS(config)# ipx network 22a encap sap
DALLAS(config-if)# exit
DALLAS(config)#
```

Monitoring IPX

After you configure IPX on the router, the commands listed in this section enable you to monitor IPX activity.

The **show ipx interface** command displays IPX status and parameters configured on each interface. Sample output from this command is shown in Listing 8.1.

Listing 8.1   The **show ipx interface** command.

```
Ethernet0 is up, line protocol is up
  IPX address is 1A.00e0.b055.28e1,SAP [up] line-up,
      RIPPQ:0,SAPPQ:0
  Delay of this IPX network,
      in ticks is 1 throughput 0 link delay 0
  IPXWAN processing not enabled on this interface.
  IPX SAP update interval is 1 minute(s)
  IPX type 20 propagation packet forwarding is disabled
  Outgoing access list is not set
  IPX Helper access list is not set
  SAP GNS processing enabled, delay 0 ms,
  output filter list not set
  SAP Input filter list is not set
  SAP Output filter list is not set
```

```
SAP Router filter list is not set
Input filter list is not set
Output filter list is not set
Router filter list is not set
Netbios Input host access list is not set
Netbios Input bytes access list is not set
Netbios Output host access list is not set
Netbios Output bytes access list is not set
Updates each 60 seconds, aging multiples RIP: 3 SAP: 3
SAP interpacket delay is 5 ms, maximum size is 480 bytes
RIP interpacket delay is 5 ms, maximum size is 432 bytes
IPX accounting is disabled
IPX fast switching is configured (enabled)
RIP packets received 25913, RIP packets sent 4
SAP packets received 122226, SAP packets sent 3
```

This interface has been configured for IPX network 1a with encapsulation type "sap". It sends SAP broadcasts every 60 seconds.

Listing 8.2 shows the **show ipx route** command output. This command displays the contents of the IPX routing table entries.

Listing 8.2 The **show ipx route** command.

```
Codes:C-Connected primary network,c-Connected secondary network
      S-Static,F-Floating static,L-Local (internal),W-IPXWAN
      R-RIP,E-EIGRP,N-NLSP,X-External,s-seconds,u-uses

4 Total IPX routes. Up to 2 parallel paths and 16 hops allowed.

No default route known.

C   1A (SAP),            Et0
R      1002 [02/01] via 1A.00aa.0047.5aa6,   45s, Et0
R   361FB7A0 [02/01] via 1A.0080.5f65.abbd,   51s, Et0
R   5F78776E [21/01] via 1A.0080.5f78.776e,    1s, Et0
```

This router can reach four IPX networks. It is directly connected to network 1a and has learned (via RIP) of three other IPX networks that it can reach via its Ethernet 0 interface.

The **show ipx servers** command displays the contents stored in the SAP table. Sample output from this command is shown in Listing 8.3.

Listing 8.3 The **show ipx servers** command.

```
Codes: S - Static, P - Periodic, E - EIGRP, N - NLSP,
       H - Holddown, + = detail
```

```
22 Total IPX Servers
Table ordering is based on routing and server info
  Type Name               Net        Address      Port Route Hops Itf
P    4 HOUSTON_FS_01      361FB7A0.0000.0000.0001:0451  2/01 1   Et0
P    7 HOUSTON_PS_01      10008022.0080.c780.d9c7:0451  2/01 1   Et0
P   2C BKUPEXECv7_01      361FB7A0.0000.0000.0001:400D  2/01 1   Et0
P  107 HOUSTON_FS_01      361FB7A0.0000.0000.0001:8104  2/01 1   Et0
P  23F HOUSTON_FS_01      361FB7A0.0000.0000.0001:907B  2/01 1   Et0
P  26B HOUSTON_____    361FB7A0.0000.0000.0001:0005  2/01 1   Et0
P  278 HOUSTON_____    361FB7A0.0000.0000.0001:4006  2/01 1   Et0
P  30C 0060B00294C400CG   10008022.0060.b002.94c4:400C  1/00 1   Et0
P  30C 0060B096AB7910C4   10008022.0060.b096.ab79:400C  1/00 1   Et0
P  30C 0060B096AB7920C4   10008022.0060.b096.ab79:401C  1/00 1   Et0
P  30C 0060B096AB79B0C4   10008022.0060.b096.ab79:402C  1/00 1   Et0
P  30C 0060B0CC836B10C4   10008022.0060.b0cc.836b:400C  1/00 1   Et0
P  30C 0060B0CC836BA0C4   10008022.0060.b0cc.836b:401C  1/00 1   Et0
P  30C 0060B0CC836BB0C4   10008022.0060.b0cc.836b:402C  1/00 1   Et0
P  30C 0800098A09E400CE   10008022.0800.098a.09e4:400C  1/00 1   Et0
P  355 00202055777_APPS   10008022.00a0.c959.91d2:6000  1/00 1   Et0
P  39B 002020HOUSTONNOT   10008022.0080.5f78.776e:6000  1/00 1   Et0
P  535 PS_CLR_03          10008022.0800.1104.175a:5005  1/00 1   Et0
P  640 IWEARPOLLY         10008022.0080.c780.e9c1:E885  1/00 1   Et0
P  640 HOUSTON_APPS_01    10008022.00a0.c959.91d2:E885  1/00 1   Et0
P  64E HOUSTON_APPS_01A   10008022.00a0.c959.91d2:4068  1/00 1   Et0
P  82B HOUSTON_FS_01      361FB7A0.0000.0000.0001:400D  2/01 1   Et0
```

This router has received SAPs from several different types of servers.

Listing 8.4 provides the **show ipx traffic** command output. This command displays summary information on the number and type of IPX packets transmitted and received by the router.

Listing 8.4   The **show ipx traffic** command.

```
System Traffic for 0.0000.0000.0001 System-Name: RouterA
Rcvd:    165726 total, 37463 format errors,
         0 checksum errors, 0 bad hop count,
         15539 packets pitched, 155441 local destination,
         0 multicast
Bcast:   155405 received, 6 sent
Sent:    7 generated, 0 forwarded
         0 encapsulation failed, 0 no route
SAP:     17409 SAP requests, 0 SAP replies, 22 servers
         104725 SAP advertisements received, 0 sent
         0 SAP flash updates sent, 112 SAP format errors,
         last seen from 0.0000.0
         000.0000
```

```
RIP:     8284 RIP requests, 1 RIP replies, 4 routes
         17633 RIP advertisements received, 0 sent
         0 RIP flash updates sent, 0 RIP format errors
Echo:    Rcvd 0 requests, 0 replies
         Sent 0 requests, 0 replies
         2024 unknown: 0 no socket, 0 filtered, 2024 no helper
         0 SAPs throttled, freed NDB len 0
Watchdog:
         0 packets received, 0 replies spoofed
Queue lengths:
         IPX input: 0, SAP 0, RIP 0, GNS 0
         SAP throttling length: 0/(no limit),
         0 nets pending lost route reply
         Delayed process creation: 0
EIGRP:   Total received 0, sent 0
         Updates received 0, sent 0
         Queries received 0, sent 0
         Replies received 0, sent 0
         SAPs received 0, sent 0
NLSP:    Level-1 Hellos received 0, sent 0
         PTP Hello received 0, sent 0
         Level-1 LSPs received 0, sent 0
         LSP Retransmissions: 0
         LSP checksum errors received: 0
         LSP HT=0 checksum errors received: 0
         Level-1 CSNPs received 0, sent 0
         Level-1 PSNPs received 0, sent 0
         Level-1 DR Elections: 0
         Level-1 SPF Calculations: 0
         Level-1 Partial Route Calculations: 0
```

This router has received more than 100,000 SAP advertisements from various servers.

Note: Given the high number of SAP advertisements that are broadcast through an IPX network, IPX is considered "chatty."

Troubleshooting IPX

The commands listed in this section provide information to assist you in diagnosing problems with IPX.

You must be connected to the router's console or configure log messages to be displayed to your terminal session before you will be able to view any debug messages. As with any **debug** command, be aware that it is network intensive.

The **debug ipx routing activity** command displays information on IPX routing updates. Here's an example:

```
DALLAS#debug ipx routingact(ivity)
IPX routing debugging is on
```

The **debug ipx sap activity** command displays IPX SAP packet information that's sent and received on the router. Here's an example:

```
DALLAS#debug ipx sap activity
```

The **no debug all** command quickly turns off any debug commands that are active.

 You can use the following commands to monitor and troubleshoot IPX activity:

➤ **show ipx interface**

➤ **show ipx route**

➤ **show ipx server**

➤ **show ipx traffic**

➤ **debug ipx routing activity**

➤ **debug ipx sap activity**

Practice Questions

Question 1

Which of the following protocols is used within the Transport layer of the NetWare protocol suite?

○ a. Ethernet

○ b. UDP

○ c. SPX

○ d. ARP

The correct answer is c. SPX is the Transport layer protocol used within NetWare's protocol suite. Answer a is incorrect because Ethernet is a Data Link layer protocol that supports NetWare. UDP is a Transport layer protocol, but it is used within the TCP/IP suite. Therefore, answer b is incorrect. Answer d is incorrect because ARP resides at the Network layer within the TCP/IP suite.

Question 2

Which of the following is a valid and complete IPX address?

○ a. 0080.c747.b122

○ b. 1a.0080.c747.b122

○ c. 1a.172.16.101.123

○ d. 1a

The correct answer is b. It is a complete IPX logical address for network 1a and node 0080.c747.b122. Answer a is incorrect because it is a node address (MAC address) and is incomplete. Answer c contains an IPX network number (1a) but also includes an IP address. Therefore, answer c is incorrect. Answer d is only an IPX network number. Therefore, answer d is incorrect.

Question 3

Which of the following is the default routing protocol within an IPX network?

○ a. RIP

○ b. NLSP

○ c. EIGRP

○ d. IGRP

The correct answer is a. RIP is the default routing protocol within an IPX network. Although either NLSP or EIGRP can be used as the routing protocol for IPX, neither is the default. Therefore, answers b and c are incorrect. IGRP is not supported within IPX. Therefore, answer d is incorrect.

Question 4

IPX RIP version 2 uses which of the following metrics to determine the best path? [Choose the two best answers]

❑ a. Bandwidth

❑ b. Hop count

❑ c. Load

❑ d. Ticks

The correct answers are b and d. Hop count and ticks (delay) are the two metrics used within IPX RIP version 2. Bandwidth and load are not used in RIP but rather in more sophisticated routing protocols such as EIGRP and OSPF. Therefore, answers a and c are incorrect.

Question 5

> Which of the following are Cisco names for standard IPX encapsulation types?
> [Choose the five best answers]
>
> ❏ a. arpa
>
> ❏ b. sap
>
> ❏ c. ethernet
>
> ❏ d. token ring
>
> ❏ e. snap
>
> ❏ f. novell-ether
>
> ❏ g. novell

The correct answers are a, b, d, e, and f. Cisco's encapsulation name for Ethernet II is arpa; for Ethernet_802.2, it's sap; for Ethernet_SNAP and Token Ring_SNAP, it's snap; for Ethernet_802.3, it's novell-ether; and for Token-Ring, it's sap. Answers c and g are incorrect because ethernet and novell are not IPX encapsulation types.

Question 6

> Which configuration command must be executed for each interface supporting IPX?
>
> ○ a. **ipx routing**
>
> ○ b. **ipx protocol**
>
> ○ c. **ipx interface**
>
> ○ d. **ipx network**

The correct answer is d. The **ipx network** command assigns a network number to a router interface. This command must be repeated for each IPX network that the router must support. The **ipx routing** command enables IPX routing within the router. Therefore, answer a is incorrect. Answers b and c are also incorrect because **ipx protocol** and **ipx interface** are not valid commands.

Question 7

Which of the following statements represent a feature of an IPX environment? [Choose the answers that best apply]

- ❏ a. A logical address is 80 bits (network.node).
- ❏ b. The interface MAC address is the node address.
- ❏ c. A router interface can support multiple encapsulation protocols.
- ❏ d. RIP is the default routing protocol.

The correct answers are a, b, c, and d. They are all features of an IPX environment.

Question 8

Which router command displays the contents of the router's SAP table?

- ○ a. **show ipx traffic**
- ○ b. **show ipx route**
- ○ c. **show ipx server**
- ○ d. **show ipx interface**

The correct answer is c. The **show ipx server** command displays the information learned through SAP advertisements. Answer a is incorrect because the **show ipx traffic** command displays the number and type of IPX packets transmitted and received by the router. The **show ipx route** command displays the contents of the IPX routing table. Therefore, answer b is incorrect. The **show ipx interface** command displays IPX status and parameters configured on each interface. Therefore, answer d is incorrect.

Question 9

The IPX encapsulation type "novell_ether" is the default for which type of LAN interface?

- ○ a. Ethernet
- ○ b. Token Ring
- ○ c. FDDI
- ○ d. Serial

The correct answer is a. The default encapsulation type for FDDI is snap. The default encapsulation type for Ethernet is novell-ether, and for Token Ring, sap is the default. Therefore, answer b is incorrect. Because a serial interface is a WAN interface, it does not have a default encapsulation type. Therefore, answer d is incorrect.

Question 10

Which of the following reside within the upper layers of the NetWare protocol suite? [Choose the three best answers]

❑ a. NCP

❑ b. NetBIOS emulation

❑ c. NOS

❑ d. NetWare shell

The correct answers are a, b, and d. NCP is a collection of server routines that interfaces with other applications. NetBIOS is a common Session layer interface specification from IBM and Microsoft. A NetWare shell determines whether application calls require network services. Answer c is incorrect because NetWare itself is considered an NOS and cannot be a protocol within NetWare.

Need to Know More?

 Chappell, Laura. *Novell's Guide to LAN/WAN Analysis: IPX/SPX*. IDG Books Worldwide. Foster City, CA, 1998. ISBN 0-76454-508-6.

This book provides additional information about IPX, SPX, RIP, and NCP. It also introduces techniques for performing network analysis, troubleshooting, and optimization within a NetWare environment. The book includes a CD-ROM that contains a demonstration version of LAN analyzer software.

 Cisco Systems. *Cisco IOS Solutions for Network Protocols, IPX, APP Vol. 2*. ISBN 1-57870-050-7.

This book provides exhaustive information about implementing and troubleshooting IPX within a network utilizing Cisco IOS.

 McNutt, Shawn, Mark Poplar, Jason Waters, and David Stabenaw. *CCNA Routing and Switching Exam Prep*. The Coriolis Group. Scottsdale, AZ, 2000. ISBN 1-57610-440-0.

This book is a great complement to the *CCNA Exam Cram*. Chapter 8 covers IPX.

 Using Cisco's documentation CD-ROM, you can immediately access Cisco's entire library of end-user documentation, selected product news, bug databases, and related information. The documentation CD-ROM is produced monthly.

 www.cisco.com, the official Cisco Web site, contains several Cisco white papers on topics such as connecting Novell LANs to the Internet and NLSP route aggregation when you search for "Novell IPX."

Router Access Lists

Terms you'll need to understand:

✓ IP extended access list

✓ Service Advertisement Protocol (SAP)

✓ IPX standard access list

✓ IPX extended access list

✓ IPX SAP filter

Techniques you'll need to master:

✓ Configuring extended access lists for IP

✓ Configuring standard access lists for IPX

✓ Configuring extended access lists for IPX

✓ Configuring IPX SAP filters

✓ Monitoring access list operations on the router

✓ Verifying access list operations on the router

This chapter covers access lists for IP and IPX traffic. *Access lists* allow network administrators to restrict access to certain networks, devices, and services. They provide an effective means of applying security within an organization; they also permit or deny specific types of traffic to pass through an interface. The types of IP traffic they filter can be based on source or destination address or address range, protocol, precedence, type of service, icmp-type, icmp-code, icmp-message, igmp-type, port, or state of the TCP connection. These filtered types can also be based on the source or destination address, sockets, protocol number, and SAP type. In addition, other IPX access lists restrict other types of traffic; however, these additional categories are not covered because they are beyond the scope of the CCNA exam. A full list of access lists is provided in Table 9.1.

Access lists provide a powerful set of tools that can deny and permit users to access specific applications or hosts. The tradeoff for using access lists, however, is that they require processing power to compare packets entering or exiting an interface with the entries in the list.

A wide variety of access lists can be applied to a router interface. This chapter focuses only on the IP standard and extended access lists, IPX SAP access lists, and IPX standard and extended access lists.

IP Access Lists

IP access lists are used to deny or permit specific traffic into or out of an interface on a router. They filter IP source and destination addresses and protocol- or service-specific traffic. IP access lists are of two types: standard and extended. The difference between the two is the precision by which each can filter IP traffic.

Table 9.1   Types of access lists.

Numeric Range	Description
1 through 99	IP standard access list
100 through 199	IP extended access list
200 through 299	Protocol type-code access list
300 through 399	DECnet access list
600 through 699	AppleTalk access list
700 through 799	48-bit Media Access Control (MAC) address access list
800 through 899	IPX standard access list
900 through 999	IPX extended access list
1,000 through 1,099	SAP access list

IP Standard Access Lists

IP standard access lists filter traffic based on the source IP address or address range. Therefore, administrators can use this tool to restrict access to specific users and allow access to others. The lists are applied to the interface of a router where traffic is to be filtered, and they restrict access into or out of the interface. The direction in which traffic is restricted is determined by the Cisco command used to apply the access list to the interface.

IP Standard Access List Commands

Creating and applying an access list to an interface consists of two steps, both of which are performed in the configuration mode of a router. First, the access list must be created. A single access list can consist of many access list *statements*. An access list *number* identifies an individual access group, which can consist of many access list *entries*. In addition, the order in which access list entries are created plays an important role in the behavior of the access list. When traffic passes through the interface, it is compared with each access list entry in the order in which the entries were created. If the traffic matches an access list entry, the indicated function (permit or deny) of the access list entry is performed on the traffic. When a packet is permitted entry, the router caches the entry, and any subsequent packets in this session are granted access without being applied against the access list. All access lists have an implicit **deny all** statement at the end. Therefore, if the traffic does not match any entry, it is denied access into or out of the interface. The command to create an access list is as follows:

```
Access-list access-list-number {deny|permit} source
[source-wildcard]
```

The format of the preceding command is typical of Cisco commands. The command can be interpreted as follows. The nonitalicized words should be written exactly as shown. In this case, the pipe symbol (|) indicates that either **deny** or **permit** should be written, but not both. The italicized words indicate that a character string must be written in this field. In this case, the character string would be a number. The square brackets indicate that a field is optional. A brief description of each field is provided in Table 9.2.

The **source-wildcard** field, referred to as a *wildcard mask*, is used to identify bits in an IP address that have meaning and bits that can be ignored. In this case, the wildcard mask is referred to as a *source-wildcard*, indicating that it is a wildcard mask of the source IP address. A source-wildcard mask is applied to a source IP address to determine a range of addresses to permit or deny.

Table 9.2	IP standard access list command field descriptions.
Identifier	**Description**
access-list-number	A dotted decimal number between 1 and 99
deny	Denies access if the condition is matched
permit	Permits access if the condition is matched
source	The number of the network or host from which the packet is being sent
source-wildcard	Wildcard bits to be applied to the source

At first, the best way to learn wildcard masks is to convert them from decimal to binary format. The wildcard mask is applied by comparing the IP address bits with the corresponding IP wildcard bits. A 1 bit in the wildcard mask indicates that the corresponding bit in the IP address can be ignored. Therefore, the IP address bit can be either 1 or 0. A 0 in the wildcard mask indicates that the corresponding bit in the IP address must be strictly followed. Therefore, the value must be exactly the same as specified in the IP address. Tables 9.3 and 9.4 illustrate how to apply a source-wildcard mask to a source address to determine a range of addresses.

Tables 9.3 and 9.4 illustrate that the first three octets must be strictly followed; therefore, the values of these octets must be 172.16.16 to be a match. The 1 bits in the fourth octet, however, indicate that any value between 0 and 255 will result in a match. Therefore, any host with the IP address of 172.16.16.0 through 172.16.16.255 is a match for this source IP address and source-wildcard mask.

Table 9.3	Applying a source-wildcard mask to a source IP address in binary format.
Source Address in Bits	**Binary**
Source address	10101100.00010000.00010000.00000000
Source-wildcard	00000000.00000000.00000000.11111111
Result	10101100.00010000.00010000.any

Table 9.4	Applying a source-wildcard mask to a source IP address in decimal format.
Source Address in Bits	**Decimal**
Source address	172.16.16.0
Source-wildcard	0.0.0.255
Result	172.16.16.any

The next step is to apply the access list to an interface. The syntax for doing so is as follows:

```
DALLAS(config-if)#ip access-group access-list-number {in|out}
```

Here, **access-list-number** is the number used to identify the access list. This number must be the same as the one specified in the **access-list** command used to create the previously shown entries. The **in|out** option indicates whether this list is to filter on inbound or outbound traffic through the interface. It is important to remember that the access list is being applied to a specific interface on a router, rather than to all the interfaces on the router.

Creating and Applying an IP Standard Access List

The network shown in Figure 9.1 is used to illustrate IP standard access lists further.

In this example, suppose you want to permit the following devices to have access to network 172.16.4.0:

➤ Any device on network 172.16.14.0

➤ Any device on network 172.16.3.0 except 172.16.3.5

➤ Only the device with the IP address of 172.16.12.4 on network 172.16.12.0

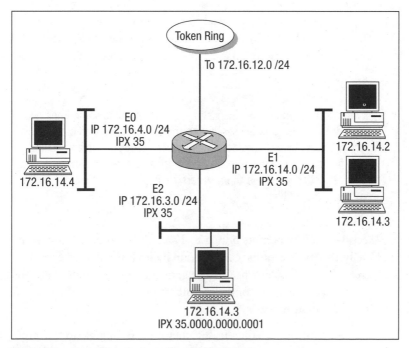

Figure 9.1   Illustration of a network using access lists.

Applying an IP standard access list to a router interface involves two steps. The first step is to create the access list to indicate all the source addresses that are permitted or denied access. The second step is to apply the access list to the interface on which you are restricting either outbound or inbound traffic. By applying the **access-group** command to interface Ethernet 0, you can restrict access to network 172.16.4.0. The commands to create this access list are as follows:

```
DALLAS#configure terminal
DALLAS(config)#access-list 5 permit 172.16.14.0 0.0.0.255
DALLAS(config)#access-list 5 deny 172.16.3.5 0.0.0.0
DALLAS(config)#access-list 5 permit 172.16.3.0 0.0.0.255
DALLAS(config)#access-list 5 permit 172.16.12.4 0.0.0.0
DALLAS(config)#access-list 5 deny 0.0.0.0 255.255.255.255
```

These commands restrict and permit the traffic detailed in the requirements. The first **access-list** entry permits access to all users from network 172.16.14.0 to pass through the access list on Ethernet 0. Note that the source-wildcard of 0.0.0.255 indicates that every host ID in the last octet can be ignored, thus allowing all IP addresses between 172.16.14.0 and 172.16.14.255 access. The second **access-list** command denies host ID 172.16.3.5 to pass through the access list. Note that the source-wildcard of 0.0.0.0 indicates that only the source address specified (172.16.3.5) is denied access. The third **access-list** command permits all users on network 172.16.3.0 to pass through the access list. Note that host ID 172.16.3.5 will still not be allowed to pass through the access list, because any traffic from this host was dropped by the previous **deny** command. The order in which a **permit** or **deny** command is placed in an access list is extremely important.

When adding new entries to existing access lists, it is sometimes necessary to reorder the access list so that it will filter traffic correctly. Often, the best way to reorder the entries is to copy all the entries into a text file, add or remove the required entries, and reorder them in that text file. After you have them ordered correctly, add them all to the router configuration.

The fourth **access-list** entry permits only user 172.16.12.4 to pass through the access list. Finally, the last **access-list** command in italics is implicit whenever an access list is created; therefore, any packet not generated by the router with the access list that does not match one of the permit entries is dropped. You do not have to configure this **deny** entry.

Before these access list entries can filter traffic, they must be applied to the interface as an access group. The access lists are going to be applied to outbound packets on Ethernet 0. Therefore, any packet attempting to travel out interface Ethernet 0 must match one of the entries in access group 5. The steps to configure an outbound access list on Ethernet 0 are as follows:

```
DALLAS#config t
Enter configuration commands, one per line. End with CNTL/Z.
DALLAS(config)#interface ethernet 0
DALLAS(config-if)#ip access-group 5 out
```

Here, **access-group 5** has been applied to the outbound Ethernet 0 interface. Now, every packet that is sent out the Ethernet 0 interface will be checked to see if it matches. More complicated scenarios for restricting access through an interface exist. Sometimes a network administrator wants to permit only a range of IP addresses through an access list. However, it is more complicated to permit access to a range of IP addresses that do not fall exactly on octet bit boundaries. A second example follows to illustrate this scenario.

Continue to use the network provided in Figure 9.1; however, in this case, you want to allow devices to have access only to network 172.16.4.0. Therefore, you want to permit access to any device with the IP address between 172.16.3.32 and 172.16.3.39.

For this scenario, you must determine the proper source-wildcard mask to apply to allow access to devices in the IP address range 172.16.3.32 through 172.16.3.39. Start with the IP address 172.16.3.32 to create this access list. Next, apply a network mask that allows eight incremental bits in the fourth octet. Table 9.5 illustrates the proper source IP address and source-wildcard mask in binary and decimal format for this example.

Table 9.5 illustrates that by applying the source-wildcard mask of 0.0.0.7, a range of IP addresses that do not fall on an octet boundary has been allowed. Each permitted address is determined by taking the bits indicated as ignored bits by the source-wildcard mask and listing the possible permutations. Here are a few good rules to know:

➤ When you're grouping IP addresses, the group size is always a power of 2 (2, 4, 8, 16, and so forth).

➤ Any time IP addresses are grouped together, the first IP address in the group is divisible by the size of the group. For example, a group of eight IP addresses can start only on multiples of eight (8, 16, 24, and so forth).

➤ The wildcard mask is always one less than the group size. For example, a group of eight has a wildcard mask of seven. A group of 64 has a wildcard mask of 63.

Table 9.5	Applying a source-wildcard mask to a source IP address in binary format. The address is shown in binary and decimal for clarification.	
Source Address in Bits	**Binary**	**Decimal**
Source address	10101100.00010000.00000011.00100000	172.16.3.32
Source-wildcard	00000000.00000000.00000000.00000111	0.0.0.7
Permitted address 1	10101100.00010000.00010000.00100000	172.16.3.32
Permitted address 2	10101100.00010000.00010000.00100001	172.16.3.33
Permitted address 3	10101100.00010000.00010000.00100010	172.16.3.34
Permitted address 4	10101100.00010000.00010000.00100011	172.16.3.35
Permitted address 5	10101100.00010000.00010000.00100100	172.16.3.36
Permitted address 6	10101100.00010000.00010000.00100101	172.16.3.37
Permitted address 7	10101100.00010000.00010000.00100110	172.16.3.38
Permitted address 8	10101100.00010000.00010000.00100111	172.16.3.39

Although IP standard access lists provide a powerful set of tools for restricting access, they can only restrict access based on the source IP address. IP extended access lists increase the variables that can be used to restrict access through an interface.

IP Extended Access Lists

IP standard access lists filter traffic based on the source IP address only; therefore, administrators can use this tool to restrict access to specific users only. Because administrators wanted more control of the traffic that could travel through interfaces, Cisco responded with IP extended access lists, which perform the same basic function as standard access lists (permitting and denying IP packets through an interface) but extend the types of IP traffic that can be filtered. Consequently, IP extended access lists allow for more precise filtering of IP traffic. Whereas IP standard access lists allow only source IP address filtering, IP extended access lists provide source and destination IP address filtering. In addition, IP extended access lists filter on layer 4 protocols, such as Transmission Control Protocol (TCP) and User Datagram Protocol (UDP), look into the TCP or UDP header, and allow filtering on TCP/UDP port numbers. Table 9.6 provides a list of some of the most common layer 4 protocols and TCP port numbers that are filtered using IP extended access lists.

Knowing these TCP and UDP port numbers is a good move for the CCNA exam. Although there are many other port numbers, these port numbers are the most important for the exam.

Table 9.6	Common port numbers filtered using IP extended access lists.	
Protocol	**Port Number**	**Protocol Name**
TCP	21	File Transfer Protocol (FTP)
	23	Telnet
	25	Simple Mail Transfer Protocol (SMTP)
UDP	53	Domain Name System (DNS)
	69	Trivial File Transfer Protocol (TFTP)
	80	Hypertext Transfer Protocol (HTTP)
	161, 162	Simple Network Management Protocol (SNMP)

In addition, IP extended access lists allow filtering based on the IP precedence field, TOS field, icmp-type, icmp-code, icmp-message, igmp-type, and TCP-established connections. This book covers only source and destination address, IP protocol, and TCP/UDP port numbers.

IP Extended Access List Commands

The steps taken to create and apply an IP extended access list are the same as those used for an IP standard access list. First, create the access list entries. Second, apply the access list group to the interface where you want to filter traffic.

 It is important to enter IP extended access list entries in the correct order. Also, an implicit **deny all** traffic entry is at the end of every IP extended access list.

The command to create an IP extended access list is very similar to the command used to create an IP standard access list. However, the additional filtering capabilities require some additional fields in the command. The command to create an access list is as follows:

```
access-list access-list-number {deny|permit} protocol source
source-wildcard [operator port [port]]  destination [destination-
wildcard] [operator port [port]]
```

Because how to read the command list was covered in the IP standard access list section, only the additional fields are discussed here. The first noticeable difference is the addition of the **protocol** field. This field is typically filled with TCP or UDP (other possibilities exist, but these are beyond the scope of this book and the CCNA exam). The **operator port [port]** field is used to indicate the TCP/UDP port or range of ports for the **source** and **source-wildcard** fields. In addition, the **destination** and **destination-wildcard** fields are added with their corresponding **operator port [port]** field. Basically, the fields necessary to filter traffic on source and destination addresses, the IP protocol (TCP or UDP), and port numbers have been added. In addition, the **access-list-number** field must now be a number between 100 and 199, as indicated in Table 9.1. A complete list of all of the fields in the IP extended access list command is provided in Table 9.7.

To apply an IP extended access list, use the same IP access group command that is used for standard access lists. Simply apply the access list to the interface where you want to filter traffic.

Creating and Applying an IP Extended Access List

To illustrate the use of the IP extended access list functionality, continue to use the network shown in Figure 9.1. In this example, you want to extend the types of traffic being filtered. Suppose you want to permit the following traffic to pass through your access list:

Table 9.7   Access list command field descriptions.

Access List Command	Description
access list-number	Identifies the access list for which the number belongs
deny	Denies access if the condition is matched
permit	Permits access if the condition is matched
protocol	The name or number of the IP protocol
source	The number of the network or host from which the packet is being sent
source-wildcard	Wildcard bits to be applied to the source
destination	The number of the network or host from which the packet originated
destination-wildcard	Wildcard bits to be applied to the destination
precedence	Filters packets by precedence level
tos	Filters packets by type of service
icmp-type	Filters packets by icmp-type
icmp-code	Filters packets by icmp-code
icmp-message	Filters packets by icmp-message
igmp-type	Filters packets by igmp-type
operator	Compares source or destination ports
port	A decimal value or name of a TCP or UDP port
established	Indicates an established connection
log	Causes an information logging entry

➤ Any device on network 172.16.14.0 is permitted to communicate with any device on network 172.16.4.0 using IP, TCP, and port number 23 (Telnet).

➤ Device 172.16.14.2 is permitted to communicate with device 172.16.4.4 using IP, UDP, and UDP port number 69 (TFTP).

➤ Device 172.16.14.3 is permitted to communicate with any device on any network using IP and TCP for any port number.

The following commands create this access list:

```
DALLAS#configure terminal
DALLAS(config)#access-list 105 permit tcp 172.16.14.0 0.0.0.255
172.16.4.0 0.0.0.255 eq 23
DALLAS(config)#access-list 105 permit udp host 172.16.14.2
host 172.16.4.4 eq 69
DALLAS(config)#access-list 105 permit tcp host 172.16.14.3 any
any
DALLAS(config)#access-list 105 deny any any
```

Let's discuss these access list entries. The first entry performs the extended functionality by indicating that only TCP traffic from any device on network 172.16.14.0 (indicated by the source-wildcard mask of 0.0.0.255) is permitted to communicate with 172.16.4.0 (indicated by the destination-wildcard of 0.0.0.255) using the TCP port number (indicated by the operator **eq** and the port number 23). The operator **eq** stands for "equal to." A subset of the different possible operators is supplied in Table 9.8.

The second entry introduces the word "host" into the command; this is a short way of indicating the wildcard mask 0.0.0.0. However, the "host" word precedes the IP address, versus the traditional trailing wildcard mask. So, in this entry, only the device with the IP address 172.16.14.2 has been allowed to communicate with device 172.16.4.4 using the UDP for the port number 69 (TFTP).

The third entry introduces the word "any" into the command. Similar to the word "host" in the preceding condition, the "any" word is a short way of indicating any source or destination address with the wildcard mask 255.255.255.255.

Table 9.8	Extended access list command field descriptions.
Operator	**Meaning**
eq	Match only packets on a given port number
lt	Match only packets with a lower port number
gt	Match only packets with a greater port number
range	Match only packets in the range of port numbers

This mask indicates that all IP addresses are being described; therefore, it does not matter what source or destination IP address is specified. In this case, all destination addresses have been described. So, in this entry, the device with IP address 172.16.14.3 has been allowed to communicate with any device using the TCP for any port number.

The last entry in italics is the implicit **deny all** statement. It is not necessary to add this entry, because it is always there.

The second step is applying the access list to the interface that you are restricting. Specify whether you are filtering outbound or inbound traffic by adding the keyword "out" or "in" to the end of the command. In this example, apply the access list to Ethernet 1 to illustrate the ability of IP extended access lists to filter traffic based on destination address as well as source address. The command to apply the access group to the interface is as follows:

```
DALLAS#config t
Enter configuration commands, one per line. End with CNTL/Z.
DALLAS(config)#interface ethernet 1
DALLAS(config-if)#ip access-group 105 in
```

In summary, extended access lists are used to increase the preciseness of your filtering. The steps performed to create and apply access lists do not change.

IPX Access Lists

The basic concepts that applied to IP standard and extended access lists apply also to IPX access lists. The main difference is that these lists filter IPX addresses or other IPX-related items. The four types of IPX access lists are listed in Table 9.9.

This book does not cover IPX NetBIOS access lists because they are beyond the scope of the CCNA exam. Before proceeding, refer to Table 9.1 to know the access list number ranges for these IPX access lists.

Table 9.9 Types of IPX access lists.	
Name	**Function**
IPX standard access list	Restricts access based on IPX source and destination address
IPX extended access list	Restricts access based on IPX source and destination address, IPX protocol, and source and destination sockets
SAP access list	Restricts access based on IPX SAP
IPX NetBIOS access list	Restricts IPX Network Basic Input/Output System (NetBIOS) traffic based on NetBIOS names

It is vital that you know the numbers associated with each type of access list. This will save you time on the CCNA exam, because you will be able to rule out incorrect answers quickly.

IPX Standard Access Lists

The IPX standard access lists follow the same rules as IP access lists. The general rules to remember are:

➤ The order in which access list entries are configured determines the order in which traffic is checked.

➤ The implicit **deny all** statement exists at the bottom of every IPX access list.

The **access-list** command is used to create a standard IPX access list. Because this is the same command used to create the IP standard access list, the router uses the access list number to differentiate between IP and IPX standard access lists. The command format is as follows:

```
access-list access-list-number {deny|permit} source-
network[.source-node [source-node-mask]] [destination-
network[.destination-node [destination-node-mask]]]
```

To illustrate IPX access lists, we'll use the network shown in Figure 9.1.

Creating and Applying an IPX Standard Access List

In this example, you are going to deny IPX network 25 access to IPX network aa but allow IPX network 35 to access IPX network aa. The first step is to create the access lists:

```
DALLAS#configure terminal
DALLAS(config)#access-list 805 deny 25 aa
DALLAS(config)#access-list 805 permit 35 aa
```

In the preceding example, the **deny** statement is not actually required because of the implicit **deny all** at the end of all access lists; it is provided here to illustrate the example. Although they were not shown in this example, source- and destination-wildcard masks could have been used to specify ranges of addresses. Refer to the IP standard and extended access lists shown previously for the steps to apply wildcard masks.

The next step is to apply the access list to an interface. This step is the same for IP standard and extended access lists; simply pick the appropriate interface where you want to filter the traffic and assign the access list to that interface. The command to perform this step is as follows:

```
DALLAS#config t
Enter configuration commands, one per line. End with CNTL/Z.
DALLAS(config)#interface ethernet 0
DALLAS(config-if)#ipx access-group 805 out
```

Note that the command changed from **ip access-group** to **ipx access-group**; otherwise, it is exactly the same command.

Spend most of your time understanding IP access lists thoroughly. After you have mastered this skill, understanding IPX access lists is trivial, because the only real difference is the type of logical address being used.

The concept of using the word "any" to represent all addresses was introduced during the discussion of IP standard and extended access lists. IPX standard and extended access lists use the number -1 to perform the same function. For example, suppose you want to allow any network address except IPX network 25 to access IPX network aa. The access list entries would be created as follows:

```
DALLAS#configure terminal
DALLAS(config)#access-list 805 deny 25 aa
DALLAS(config)#access-list 805 permit -1 -1
```

In this example, IPX network 25 was denied access to IPX network aa first. This command must be performed first, because all traffic is compared with the access list in the order in which the entries are configured. Therefore, any traffic from IPX network 25 is denied based on the first entry, and all other IPX network traffic is allowed to pass through, because it matches the second entry.

IPX Extended Access Lists

IPX extended access lists increase the preciseness with which IPX traffic can be filtered. IPX extended access lists allow filtering on source and destination addresses, the IPX protocol, and source and destination sockets. The command format for an IPX extended access list is as follows:

```
access-list access-list-number {deny|permit} protocol source
[source-wildcard] source-socket destination [destination-
wildcard] destination-socket
```

The preceding command extends the IPX standard access list functionality by adding the **protocol** and the **source** and **destination socket** fields. The **protocol** field is used to describe IPX protocols, such as Sequenced Packet Exchange (SPX) and SAP. The **socket** field is similar to the **port** field used with IP extended access lists. It uses a number to identify a specific service.

Continue to use the sample network in Figure 9.1 to illustrate IPX extended access lists. Suppose you want to allow all IPX networks except 35 to use all IPX protocols and sockets to use the services of network 15. The commands to configure this scenario would be as follows:

```
DALLAS#configure terminal
DALLAS(config)#access-list 905 deny -1 35 0 15 0 0
DALLAS(config)#access-list 905 permit -1 -1 0 0 15 0 0
```

Note that all IPX protocols (indicated by -1) and all IPX sockets (indicated by the 0) are indicated in both entries; however, it is explicitly identified in the first entry that IPX network 35 cannot access IPX network 15. In the second entry, all networks are identified as being allowed to use all services on the destination network, 15. The IPX access list can be applied to interface Ethernet 0 as follows:

```
DALLAS#config t
Enter configuration commands, one per line. End with CNTL/Z.
DALLAS(config)#interface ethernet 0
DALLAS(config-if)#ipx access-group 905 out
```

IPX SAP Filters

As explained in this chapter, SAP messages are a common source of traffic on IPX networks. Typically, Novell servers generate SAP advertisements to communicate the different services that they offer. Administrators often want to filter what advertisements are delivered to specific networks, so they create IPX SAP filters and apply them to the appropriate interfaces. The command to create an IPX SAP filter is as follows:

```
access-list access-list-number {deny|permit} source [source-
wildcard] [service-type [server-name]]
```

To illustrate the use of an IPX SAP filter, suppose you want to filter all SAP type 4 (file server) messages from IPX server 35.0000.0000.0001 from reaching IPX network aa. First, create the access list entry using the following commands:

```
DALLAS#configure terminal
DALLAS(config)#access-list 1005 deny 35.0000.0000.0001 4
DALLAS(config)#access-list 1005 permit -1
```

In the preceding example, the specific server, 35.0000.0000.0001, is denied from sending SAP type 4 messages and permitted every other address to send any SAP type. Remember that an implicit **deny all** is on every access list.

Second, apply the access list to an interface using the following commands:

```
ipx output-sap-filter access-list number
ipx input-sap-filter access-list number
ipx router-sap-filter access-list-number
```

IPX allows you to designate the direction of traffic to filter by using the keyword "output," "input," or "router" in the command. This is different from an IP access list, where you designate the direction in which to filter traffic by adding the word "out" or "in" to the end of the command. Therefore, to apply the example to an interface, simply perform the following command:

```
DALLAS#config t
Enter configuration commands, one per line. End with CNTL/Z.
DALLAS(config)#interface ethernet 0
DALLAS(config-if)#ipx output-sap-filter 1005
```

Monitoring and Verifying Access Lists

After you have configured all your access lists, it is important that you review your entries and determine whether you are filtering traffic in the manner intended. Many different methods exist to monitor and verify access lists. For the scope of this book and the CCNA exam, we will illustrate only two of the more basic methods. Refer to the *Cisco Command Reference* to identify some of the other methods used to monitor access lists. To determine which access lists you have applied to specific interfaces, use the **show ip interface** command as follows:

```
DALLAS# show ip interface
Ethernet 0 is up, line protocol is up
     Internet address is 172.16.4.4, subnet mask is 255.255.255.0
     Broadcast address is 255.255.255.255
     Address determined by non-volatile memory
     No helper address
     No secondary address
     Outgoing access list 5 is set
     Inbound access list is not set
     Proxy ARP is enabled
     Security level is default
     Split horizon is enabled
     ICMP redirects are always sent
     ICMP unreachables are always sent
```

```
      ICMP mask replies are never sent
      IP fast switching is enabled
      Gateway Discovery is disabled
      IP accounting is disabled
      TCP/IP header compression is disabled
DALLAS#
```

The entry identifying the outbound access list is highlighted. To get a more detailed look at the type of access lists you have applied, use the **show access-lists** command as follows:

```
DALLAS>show access-lists
Standard IP access list 5
permit 172.16.14.0, wildcard bits 0.0.0.255
deny 172.16.3.5, wildcard bits 0.0.0.0
permit 172.16.4.0, wildcard bits 0.0.0.255
permit 172.16.12.4, wildcard bits 0.0.0.0
Extended IP access list 105
permit tcp 172.16.14.0 0.0.0.255 172.16.4.0 eq 23
permit udp host 172.16.14.2 host 172.16.4.4 eq 69
permit tcp host 172.16.14.3 any any
deny 0.0.0.0 255.255.255.255
DALLAS>
```

Practice Questions

Question 1

Which of the following commands will apply an IP standard access list to an interface?

- ○ a. **ip access-group 204 in**
- ○ b. **ip access group 110**
- ○ c. **ip access-group 45 out**
- ○ d. **ip access-group 105 out**
- ○ e. **ipx access-group 805 in**

The correct answer is c. The command in answer c identifies an IP standard access list by the access list number 45, which is the proper numeric range for identifying an IP standard access list. Answer a is incorrect because it uses access list number 204, which is reserved for protocol-type access lists, not IP standard access lists. Answer b is incorrect because the command is not in the correct format. In addition, it should specify whether the access group is being applied against inbound or outbound packets with the "in" or "out" identifier. The command format should be **ip access-group**, not **ip access group**. Answer d is incorrect because it identifies an IP extended access list (access list number 105), not an IP standard access list. Answer e is incorrect because it identifies an IPX standard access list, not an IP extended access list.

Question 2

Which of the following can be used to permit or deny traffic with IP standard access lists? [Choose the two best answers]

- ❑ a. Source IP address
- ❑ b. A range of source IP addresses
- ❑ c. Destination IP address
- ❑ d. A range of destination IP addresses

The correct answers are a and b. IP standard access lists allow IP traffic to be filtered based on source IP addresses; they also allow both individual IP addresses and a range of IP addresses to be specified. Answers c and d are incorrect because

IP standard access lists do not filter traffic based on individual IP addresses or a range of destination IP addresses.

Question 3

For an IP standard access list, which source IP address and source-wildcard mask would indicate all IP addresses from IP network 172.16.23.0 /24?

○ a. 172.16.23.4 0.0.0.0

○ b. 172.16.23.0 0

○ c. 172.16.23.0 0.0.0.255

○ d. 172.16.23.0 0.0.255.0

The correct answer is c. It uses a wildcard mask of 0.0.0.255 to identify any bit combination in the fourth octet; therefore, any source IP address with the value of 172.16.23.0 through 172.16.23.255 is identified. Answer a is incorrect because it identifies only the IP address 172.16.23.4. All the bits in every octet must be strictly followed, as indicated by the source-wildcard mask of 0.0.0.0. Answer b is incorrect because it identifies only the source IP address of 172.16.23.0. Answer d is incorrect because the source-wildcard mask of 0.0.255.0 indicates that any combination of bits in the third octet is identified; however, the fourth octet must be strictly followed. This source IP address and source-wildcard mask combination indicates that the third octet can be any value, but the fourth must be 0.

Question 4

Which of the following commands will apply an IP extended access list to an interface?

○ a. **ip access-group 204 in**

○ b. **ip access group 110**

○ c. **ip access-group 115 out**

○ d. **ip access-group 95 out**

○ e. **ipx access-group 805 in**

The correct answer is c. The command in answer c identifies an IP extended access list by the correct numeric range (100 through 199) for IP extended access lists. Answer a is incorrect because it uses the access list number 204, which is reserved for protocol type access lists. Answer b is incorrect because the command is not in the correct format; it should be **ip access-group**, not **ip access group**. In addition, the command should specify whether the access group is being applied to inbound or outbound packets with the "in" or "out" identifier. Answer d is incorrect because it identifies an IP standard access list (access list number 95), not an IP extended access list. Answer e is incorrect because it identifies an IPX standard access list, not an IP extended access list.

Question 5

Which of the following can be used to permit or deny traffic with IP extended access lists? [Choose the three best answers]

❑ a. Source IP addresses

❑ b. Destination IP addresses

❑ c. IP sequence number

❑ d. TCP or UDP port numbers

The correct answers are a, b, and d. Answers a and b are correct because IP extended access lists allow traffic to be filtered based on both source and destination IP addresses. Answer d is correct because IP extended access lists allow traffic to be filtered based on TCP or UDP port numbers. Refer to Table 9.6 to see a list of the different items the IP extended access lists can use to filter traffic. Answer c is incorrect because IP extended access lists do not filter traffic based on IP sequence number.

Question 6

What is the valid range for an IP extended access list?

○ a. 1 through 99

○ b. 100 through 199

○ c. 800 through 899

○ d. 900 through 999

The correct answer is b. IP extended access lists are identified by the numeric range of 100 through 199. Answer a is incorrect because the numeric range of 0 through 99 identifies IP standard access lists. Answer c is incorrect because the numeric range of 800 through 899 identifies IPX standard access lists. Answer d is incorrect because the numeric range of 900 through 999 identifies IPX extended access lists.

Question 7

Which of the following commands identifies an IPX extended access list?

- ○ a. **ipx access-group 899 in**
- ○ b. **ipx access-group 905 in**
- ○ c. **ipx access-list 910 out**
- ○ d. **ipx access-group 105 out**

The correct answer is b. The numeric range for an IPX extended access list is 900 through 999. Answer a is incorrect because an access group number of 899 refers to an IPX standard access list, not an IPX extended access list. Answer c is incorrect because the command format **ip access-list 910 out** is incorrect; the correct format is **ipx access-group**, not **access-list**. Answer d is incorrect because the number 105 is not in the correct range for an IPX extended access list. The number 105 identifies an extended access list.

Question 8

Which of the following IP standard access lists would deny host 172.16.23.2? [Choose the two best answers]

- ☐ a. **access-list 5 deny 172.16.23.0 0.0.0.255**
- ☐ b. **access-list 105 deny host 172.16.23.2**
- ☐ c. **access-list 25 deny host 172.16.23.2**
- ☐ d. **access-list 5 deny 172.16.24.2 0.0.0.255**

The correct answers are a and c. Answer a denies traffic with the source address between 172.16.23.0 and 172.16.23.255. The source-wildcard mask of 0.0.0.255 for answer a indicates that all bit combinations in the fourth octet are identified. Answer c denies only traffic with the source IP address of 172.16.23.2. Answer b is incorrect because the access list number is 105, which identifies an IP extended access list, not an IP standard access list (although this command would function correctly). Answer d is incorrect because it indicates that source IP addresses 172.16.24.0 through 172.16.24.255 are denied access, which does not include source IP address 172.16.23.2.

Question 9

Which of the following IP extended access list entries would permit Telnet (TCP port 23) from IP source addresses 172.16.29.0 through 172.16.29.255 to access any destination address?

○ a. **access-list 105 permit tcp 172.16.29.0 0.0.0.255 any eq 23**

○ b. **access-list 105 permit tcp 172.16.29.0 0.0.0.255 172.16.0.0 0.0.255.255 eq 23**

○ c. **access-list 105 permit tcp host 172.16.29.10 any eq 23**

○ d. **access-list 105 permit udp 172.16.29.0 0.0.0.255 any eq 23**

The correct answer is a. Answer a specifies that TCP traffic with IP port number 23 should be permitted from IP source addresses 172.16.29.0 through 172.16.29.255 to any destination IP address. Answer b is incorrect because this access list permits TCP traffic with IP port number 23 from source IP addresses 172.16.29.0 through 172.16.29.255 only to the destination IP addresses 172.16.0.0 through 172.16.255.255. Answer c is incorrect because it only permits host 172.16.29.10. Answer d is incorrect because it permits UDP traffic, not TCP traffic.

Question 10

Which of the following commands can be used to show access lists? [Choose the three best answers]

❏ a. **show ip interfaces**

❏ b. **show ipx interfaces**

❏ c. **show access-lists**

❏ d. **show access lists**

The correct answers are a, b, and c. These three commands show configured access lists. Answer d is incorrect because the command format is wrong; it should be **show access-lists**, not **show access lists**.

Need to Know More?

 Chappell, Laura. *Introduction to Cisco Router Configuration*. Cisco Systems Inc., Macmillan Computer Publishing. Indianapolis, IN, 1998. ISBN 0-7645-3186-7.

This book is a great reference for introductory material about Cisco router configuration.

 Lammle, Todd, Donald Porter, and James Chellis. *CCNA Cisco Certified Network Associate*. Sybex Network Press. Alameda, CA, 1999. ISBN 0-7821-2381-3.

Chapter 4 covers IP addressing.

 McNutt, Shawn, Mark Poplar, Jason Waters, and David Stabenaw. *CCNA Routing and Switching Exam Prep*. The Coriolis Group. Scottsdale, AZ, 2000. ISBN 1-57610-440-0.

This book is a great complement to the *CCNA Exam Cram* book.

 Syngress Media with Richard D. Hornbaker, CCIE. *Cisco Certified Network Associate Study Guide*. Osborne/McGraw-Hill. Berkeley, CA, 1998. ISBN 0-07-882487-7.

Chapter 2 covers IP addressing.

 www.cisco.com/univercd/home/home.htm, Cisco's documentation home page, contains examples and syntax for all access list–related commands.

LAN Switching

Terms you'll need to understand:

✓ Switch

✓ Spanning Tree Protocol

✓ Cut-through switching

✓ Store-and-forward switching

✓ Frame tagging

Techniques you'll need to master:

✓ Describing the advantages of local area network (LAN) segmentation

✓ Describing the operation of Spanning Tree Protocol and its benefits

✓ Describing LAN segmentation using switches

✓ Distinguishing between cut-through and store-and-forward switching

✓ Describing the benefits of network segmentation with switches

Switching is a technology that has grown out of the demand for increased performance from existing network infrastructures. As applications such as email, Internet connectivity, client/server, and voice and video continue to demand more bandwidth, the need for switches is growing stronger. This increase in demand is also making switching technology more affordable. Switches are rapidly taking the place of hubs as the preferred method of connecting desktops in the wiring closet.

Layer 2 Switching Technology

Remember from earlier chapters that switches operate at layer 2 of the Open Systems Interconnection (OSI) model. The technology upon which layer 2 switches operate is the same as that provided by Ethernet bridges. The basic operation of a switch involves the following:

➤ Discovering Media Access Control (MAC) addresses

➤ Filtering or forwarding frames

➤ Preventing loops

Discovering MAC Addresses

Like a bridge, a switch monitors all frames that pass through it to learn the MAC addresses of each device connected to its ports. This information is stored in a database. The switch consults the database each time it receives a frame to determine whether to forward the frame to a different port or to drop it.

When the switch is initially booted up, the MAC address database is empty. Forwarding or filtering decisions cannot be made with an empty database, so initially each incoming packet is forwarded through all the switch's ports. This is called *flooding the frame*. As flooding occurs, the switch begins to learn the MAC addresses and associate them with one of its ports.

This address-learning process is a continual operation of the switch. Each MAC database entry is stored in memory and is valid only for a preset interval. If the entry is not refreshed by a new frame transmitting within the switch, it is discarded. So, as long as all stations have network activity within the MAC database entry lifetime, the switch builds a complete view of network devices.

Filtering and Forwarding

Each time the switch receives a frame, it examines the destination MAC address. If this address exists in the MAC database, the frame is forwarded only through the switch port associated with the address. This process frees all the segments connected to different ports of the excess bandwidth taken by the frame. This is known as *frame filtering*.

Whenever the destination MAC address is unknown, the frame is flooded to all switch ports. This is undesirable because it wastes bandwidth.

Preventing Loops

Bridges introduce the possibility of creating a bridged network with multiple paths to a single destination. Typically, this type of redundancy is considered favorable, but for bridges it can cause problems in the form of *bridging loops*, which occur when circular connections exist in a bridged network. Figure 10.1 illustrates a bridged network with bridging loops.

Figure 10.1 shows that a loop can exist in a network. For example, if someone sends a broadcast message from segment 2, the message would be forwarded to physical segment 3 by bridges B and C. Bridge A would then receive two broadcasts and forward both broadcasts to physical segment 1. Bridge D would have forwarded this broadcast to physical segment 1 as well. Subsequently, bridge D will receive the two broadcasts forwarded by bridge A and forward these packets to physical segment 2. This continuous forwarding of broadcast packets wastes bandwidth. With more complex bridged networks, the broadcast packets can be forwarded exponentially, leading to what is termed a *broadcast storm*. This occurs when so many broadcasts are being continuously forwarded that they consume all the available bandwidth. The Spanning Tree Protocol, which implements an

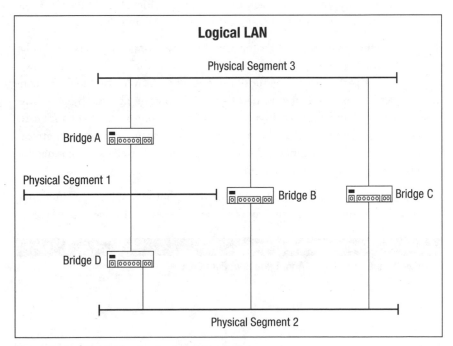

Figure 10.1   A bridged network with bridging loops.

algorithm that removes all circular connections in a bridged network, eliminates bridging loops.

Spanning Tree Protocol

The Spanning Tree Protocol creates a loop-free network topology by placing connections that create loops in a blocking state. It is important to note that this protocol does not eliminate loops but rather only blocks the connections that create the loops. Loops in a network often provide needed redundancy in the case of a physical connection being disconnected. The Spanning Tree Protocol maintains the benefits of redundancy while eliminating the disadvantages of looping. To illustrate how the Spanning Tree Protocol functions, we will use the bridged network shown earlier in Figure 10.1.

The Spanning Tree Protocol selects a root bridge in the network (in this case, bridge A). Next, every other bridge selects one of its ports with the least path cost to the root bridge. The *least path cost* is the sum of the cost to traverse every network between the indicated bridge and the root bridge. The root path cost can be determined in multiple ways; in this case, we have arbitrarily assigned costs to each path. Next, designated bridges are determined. A *designated bridge* is the bridge on each LAN with the lowest aggregate root path cost. It's the only bridge on a LAN allowed to forward frames. Table 10.1 details the bridge identifier and its root path cost to reach the root bridge. Figure 10.2 illustrates our network with the root path cost assigned to each bridge interface.

By applying the Spanning Tree Protocol, we block the connection between bridge C and physical segments 2 and 3, because bridge D and bridge B both have lower aggregate root path costs to the root bridge (bridge A). We also block the connection between bridge D and physical segment 2, because bridge B has a lower root path cost than bridge D. Figure 10.3 illustrates our bridged network after the Spanning Tree Protocol has been applied. Note that the connections between bridge C and physical segments 2 and 3 are blocked, as well as the connection between bridge D and physical segment 2.

We now have no circular routes in our network, but we maintain redundancy, because the Spanning Tree Protocol is applied whenever a bridge is powered up

Table 10.1 Spanning Tree Protocol.	
Bridge Number	**Aggregate Root Path Cost**
Bridge A	0
Bridge B	10
Bridge C	30
Bridge D	20

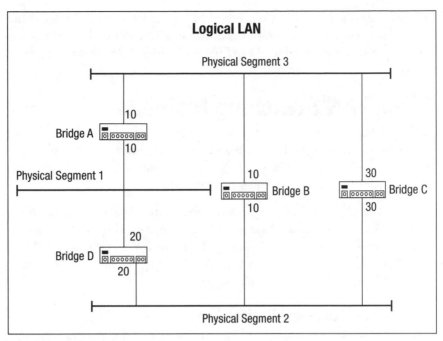

Figure 10.2   Spanning Tree Protocol root path cost.

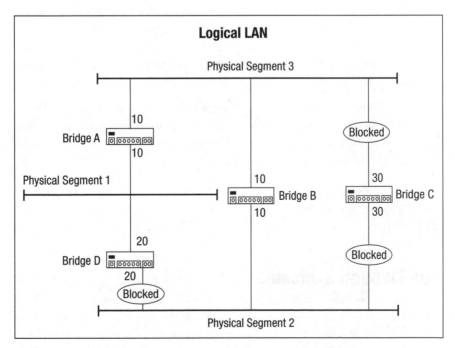

Figure 10.3   The bridged network after Spanning Tree Protocol calculation.

or a topology change occurs. Therefore, if the connection between bridge B and physical segment 2 becomes broken, the Spanning Tree Protocol would run and the connection between bridge D and physical segment 2 would no longer be blocked.

Cisco LAN Switching Methods

All the switching methods used by Cisco switches provide increased throughput in comparison to bridges. The hardware-based architectures of switches allow them to make decisions at wire speeds. The primary difference between the various methods is the process each uses to switch frames.

Note: Frames have been consistently used to represent layer 2 data messages in this chapter. The term cells *can also be used to identify layer 2 data messages. This term is used when referring to data traffic using the Asynchronous Transfer Mode (ATM) technology. The CCNA exam does not cover this technology, so only frames have been presented in this chapter to simplify the concepts.*

Store-and-Forward Switching

In store-and-forward switching mode, the switch reads the entire incoming frame and copies the frame into its buffers. After the frame has been completely read, the switch performs the layer 2 cyclical redundancy check (CRC) to determine whether an error occurred during transmission. If the frame has an error, meaning less than 64 bytes, the switch drops the frame. If no error is identified, the switch checks its forwarding table to determine the proper port (in the case of a unicast) or ports (in the case of a multicast) to which the frame must be forwarded.

Store-and-forward switches have the highest latency of any switching mode, because the switch must read the entire frame before making a forwarding decision. The added error checking of store-and-forward switching, however, reduces the number of erred frames that are forwarded.

 Store-and-forward switching is the default method used by Catalyst 5000 switches.

Cut-Through Switching

Cut-through switches introduce a lower level of latency during the switching process than store-and-forward switches do, mainly because the frame is forwarded as soon as the destination address and outgoing interface are determined. They achieve increased performance by eliminating the error checking and making forwarding decisions based only on the first 6 bytes of the incoming frame. (These first 6 bytes contain the destination MAC address of the frame.) Cut-through switches read the destination address of the incoming frame and immediately check the forwarding table to determine the proper destination ports. This increased performance does, however, allow erred frames to be forwarded more often than store-and-forward switches do.

Fragment-Free Switching

Fragment-free switching is a modification to the cut-through switching method. Like cut-through switches, fragment-free switches read only a portion of the frame before beginning the forwarding process. The difference is that fragment-free switches read the first 64 bytes, which is enough to check the frame for collisions. This allows for better error checking than with cut-through switches, with a minimal loss in latency.

 Fragment-free switching is the default method used by Catalyst 1900 switches.

Cisco Switches

Cisco produces a wide variety of switching products to meet almost any business need. At the high end are products such as the Catalyst 5000 through 8500 series, designed as high-performance multilayer switches for large network backbones. At the other end of the spectrum are products such as the 1900 and 2820 series, which are affordable solutions for workgroups and desktop connectivity.

As a CCNA candidate, you should be very familiar with the latter group of switches. You will need to be able to implement these switches as high-speed hub replacements or as backbones to small or midsize LANs.

In addition, you will need to be able to implement virtual local area networks (VLANs) and connect multiple switches using some type of trunk connection. These tasks are covered in Chapter 11.

In the following sections, you will examine the functionality and configuration of the Catalyst 1900 series switch. This is an extremely popular switch, because it provides low-cost switched connectivity for desktops or 10BaseT hubs and Fast Ethernet connectivity for servers or backbones. It is also an excellent starting point for learning switching technology. Figure 10.4 shows a Catalyst 1900 switch in a typical environment.

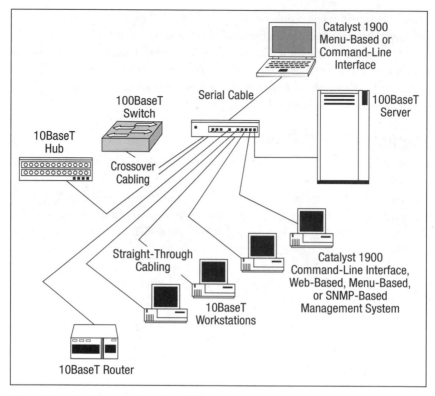

Figure 10.4   Catalyst 1900 switch environment.

Switch Startup

The startup process for a Cisco switch can be monitored in the following ways:

➤ Observing the light-emitting diodes (LEDs) on the switch chassis

➤ Examining the Cisco Internetwork Operating System (IOS) output by connecting a terminal to the switch's console port

Cisco catalyst switches have several LEDs that give a convenient visual indicator of a switch's operational status. These LEDs are green when the switch is functioning properly and amber when there's any sort of problem.

The Catalyst 1900 series switch executes a power-on self-test (POST) each time the switch is powered on and can be monitored by watching the LEDs on the switch chassis. The typical sequence is as follows:

1. Initially, all LEDs are green.

2. Each LED is associated with a specific POST. Each LED turns off after its task is complete or turns amber if there's a problem.

3. The system LED turns amber if any test fails.

4. When the POST is complete, the LEDs blink and then turn off.

In addition to monitoring LEDs, any errors encountered during startup can be checked by attaching a terminal to the console port of the switch and observing the text output. The initial output from a Catalyst 1900 switch with no errors looks similar to the following:

```
Catalyst 1900 Management Console
Copyright (c) Cisco Systems, Inc.1993-1999
All rights reserved.

Standard Edition Software
Ethernet address:    00-E0-1E-7E-B4-40

PCA Number: 73-2239-01
PCA Serial Number: SAD01200001
Model Number: WS-C1924-A
System Serial Number: FAA01200001
--------------------------------


User Interface Menu

[M] Menus
[I] IP Address
[P] Console Password

Enter Selection:
```

Configuring the Switch

There are three different options for configuring a new Catalyst 1900 switch:

➤ Menu-driven interface

➤ Command-line interface (CLI)—only available on Enterprise Edition IOS software

➤ Web-based interface

These configuration options may vary depending on which model switch you have and which version of software it is running. Using the menu-driven interface may seem like the easiest and quickest way to get your switch running. It is important, however, that you learn how to configure the switch through the CLI as well.

Note: The CLI is the standard interface used to configure any Cisco device running the IOS, Cisco's proprietary OS.

The Web-based interface is another easy visual way to monitor and configure the switch. It is important to note, however, that before you can use the Web-based interface, the switch must have a valid Internet Protocol (IP) address. For this reason, you must first configure at least an IP address using one of the other two configuration methods.

Default Configuration

Cisco switches come with a default configuration that is actually usable in many cases without any additional customization. Table 10.2 shows the default configuration settings of a Catalyst 1900 switch. For most situations, you will want to configure at least some basic options on the switch, such as an IP address, default gateway, and duplex options.

Using the Menu-Driven Interface

Using the menu-driven interface to configure a Catalyst 1900 switch is a simple and straightforward process. You must first connect to the switch through the console port using a PC with terminal emulation software or Telnet into the switch. As soon as the switch starts up, a menu that you use to select the option to configure appears. The initial management console logon screen looks like this:

```
User Interface Menu

[M] Menus
[K] Command Line
[I] IP Address
[P] Console Password

Enter Selection:
```

Table 10.2 Catalyst 1900 default configuration.	
Option	**Default Value**
IP address	0.0.0.0
CDP	Enabled
Switching mode	Fragment-free
100BaseT port	Auto-negotiate duplex mode
10BaseT port	Half duplex
Spanning tree protocol	Enabled
Console password	None

You may want to give the switch a password by pressing P and following the instructions about setting the console password. You can enter the IP Configuration menu by pressing I:

```
Catalyst 1900 - IP Configuration

Ethernet Address:00-E0-1E-7E-B4-40

----------Settings----------
[I] IP address              0.0.0.0
[S] Subnet mask             0.0.0.0
[G] Default gateway           0.0.0.0
[B] Management Bridge Group1 (fixed)
[M] IP address of DNS server 1      0.0.0.0
[N] IP address of DNS server 2      0.0.0.0
[D] Domain name
[R] Use Routing Information Protocol    Enabled

----------Actions----------
[P] Ping
[C] Clear cached DNS entries
[X] Exit to previous menu

Enter Selection:
```

You can access the management console Main Menu by pressing M:

```
Catalyst 1900 - Main Menu

[C] Console Settings
[S] System
[N] Network Management
[P] Port Configuration
[A] Port Addressing
[D] Port Statistics Detail
[M] Monitoring
[B] Bridge Group
[R] Multicast Registration
[F] Firmware
[I] RS-232 Interface
[U] Usage Summaries
[H] Help

[X] Exit Management Console

Enter Selection:
```

Almost every option that you may need to configure for a Catalyst switch has an associated menu command.

Using the CLI

The command-line interface (CLI), although slightly more difficult to learn than the menu-driven interface, is important to know because it is used for configuration across the entire Cisco product line. The CLI is available on switches that are running the Enterprise Edition of Cisco's IOS. From the initial management console logon screen, press K to enter the CLI. You will get a prompt that looks similar to the following:

```
1900>
```

Enter privileged mode by using the **enable** command. Then, enter configuration mode by using the **config terminal** command:

```
1900>enable
Enter Password: <enable password>
1900#config terminal
1900(config)#
```

Configuring TCP/IP Options

Giving the switch an IP address is one of the first things that should be done. The command used to do so is **ip address** {*ip address*} {*subnet mask*}. The default gateway should also be specified by using the **ip default-gateway** {*ip address*} command. The following is an example:

```
ip address 192.168.1.10· 255.255.255.0
ip default-gateway 192.168.1.1
```

You may also need to configure a domain name for the switch and tell it how to resolve names by giving it a name-server address.

```
ip domain-name cisco.com
ip name-server 192.168.1.20
```

Now, you can view the TCP/IP information by using the **show ip** command:

```
hostname# show ip

IP Address:192.168.1.10
Subnet Mask:255.255.255.0
Default Gateway:192.168.1.1
Management VLAN: 1
```

```
Domain name: cisco.com
Name server 1:192.168.1.20
Name server 2:198.92.30.32
HTTP server :Enabled
HTTP port : 80
RIP :Enabled
```

Using the Web Interface

Catalyst 1900 and 2820 switches come with a built-in Web server that can be used for monitoring and configuring the switch. It is very visually oriented and allows you to change configuration options in a point-and-click environment. All you have to know is the IP address of the switch, and you can point your Web browser to the switch's IP address. If the switch has been configured with a password, you will have to enter it to use the Web interface.

Practice Questions

Question 1

What is maintained in a bridge's forwarding table?

○ a. A device's IP address and the IP network on which the device resides

○ b. A device's MAC address and the physical segment on which that device resides

○ c. The MAC addresses and the best interfaces to use to forward a frame to a destination MAC address

○ d. The IP network and MAC address of devices

The correct answer is c. Forwarding tables maintain MAC addresses. In addition, forwarding tables maintain the best interfaces to use to forward a frame to a destination MAC address. Answer a is incorrect because a bridge does not maintain IP addresses in its forwarding table. IP is a layer 3 protocol and is used by routers, not bridges. Answer b is a trick answer because it is partially correct. However, bridges do not maintain the physical segment on which a device resides. Bridges only maintain the next physical segment to forward a frame en route to the device's physical segment. In some cases, the device will exist on this physical segment, but not in all cases. Answer d is incorrect because bridges do not maintain IP network information.

Question 2

What is the name of the protocol used to eliminate bridging loops?

○ a. Switching

○ b. ISL

○ c. Frame tagging

○ d. Spanning Tree Protocol

The correct answer is d. The Spanning Tree Protocol is used to remove circular routes in bridged and switched networks. Answer a is incorrect because switching is a layer 2 technology, not a protocol. Answer b is incorrect because interswitch link (ISL) is used to allow VLANs to span multiple physical switches. Answer c is incorrect because frame tagging is a process used to identify the VLAN of a frame between switches.

Question 3

Switches provide higher port densities than bridges.

○ a. True

○ b. False

The correct answer is a. Switches provide higher port densities than bridges. The increased port density is one of the main factors that allow switches to provide a higher throughput than bridges.

Question 4

Which of the following switching methods provides the greatest frame throughput?

○ a. Store-and-forward switching

○ b. Frame-tag switching

○ c. Cut-through switching

○ d. ISL switching

The correct answer is c. Cut-through switching provides high-throughput frame switching because it reads only a portion of the frame before making the forwarding decision. Cut-through switching does not provide error checking. Answer a is incorrect because store-and-forward switching has slower frame throughput rates than cut-through switching because of its error-checking capabilities and because it reads the entire frame before making a forwarding decision. Answer b is incorrect because frame-tag switching does not exist; frame tagging is a process used to identify a frame's VLAN between switches. Answer d is incorrect because it is used to allow VLANs to span multiple switches as well.

Question 5

> Which of the following are valid ways to configure a Catalyst 1900 switch?
> [Choose all that apply]
>
> ❑ a. From a configuration file
>
> ❑ b. From the switch's built-in menu interface
>
> ❑ c. From the switch's CLI
>
> ❑ d. From your Web browser

The correct answers are a, b, c, and d. Each of these answers is a valid method for configuring a Catalyst 1900 switch.

Question 6

> Which of the following commands could be used to assign an IP address to a Catalyst 1900 switch?
>
> ○ a. **ip-address 10.1.1.10 255.0.0.0**
>
> ○ b. **ip address 10.1.1.10** and **subnet-mask 255.0.0.0**
>
> ○ c. **ip 10.1.1.10/255.0.0.0**
>
> ○ d. **ip address 10.1.1.10 255.0.0.0**

The correct answer is d. The command for assigning an IP address to a switch from the command prompt is **ip address** *{address}{subnet-mask}*. Answers a and c are incorrect because these are invalid commands. Answer b is incorrect because "subnet-mask" is not a valid command.

Question 7

> What command can be used on a Catalyst 1900 switch to view its TCP/IP configuration information?
>
> ○ a. **show tcp/ip**
>
> ○ b. **show ip**
>
> ○ c. **show network**
>
> ○ d. **display network**

The correct answer is b. The **show ip** command will display information about the TCP/IP settings the switch is using. Answers a, c, and d are all invalid commands.

Question 8

What is the default switch type on Catalyst 5000 switches?

O a. Store and forward

O b. Cut through

O c. Fragment free

The correct answer is a. Store-and-forward switching is the default method used by Catalyst 5000 switches. Fragment-free switching is used on the Catalyst 1900 switches; therefore answer c is incorrect.

Need to Know More?

 Chappell, Laura. *Introduction to Cisco Router Configuration*. Cisco Systems Inc., Macmillan Computer Publishing. Indianapolis, IN, 1998. ISBN 0-7645-3186-7. This book provides a great overview of the concepts tested on the CCNA exam.

 Ford, Merilee, H. Kim Lew, Steve Spanier, and Kevin Downes. *Internetworking Technologies Handbook, 2nd Edition*. Macmillan Computer Publishing. Indianapolis, IN, 1998. ISBN 1-56205-102-3. This book is full of resourceful information on internetworking technologies.

 Lammle, Todd, Donald Porter, and James Chellis. *CCNA Cisco Certified Network Associate*. Sybex Network Press. Alameda, CA, 1999. ISBN 0-7821-2381-3. This book is a great supplement for learning the technologies tested on the CCNA exam.

 McNutt, Shawn, Mark Poplar, Jason Waters, and David Stabenaw. *CCNA Routing and Switching Exam Prep*. The Coriolis Group. Scottsdale, AZ, 2000. ISBN 1-57610-440-0. This book is a great complement to the *CCNA Exam Cram*. The switching chapters expand on the information presented here.

 Syngress Media, with Richard D. Hornbaker, CCIE. *Cisco Certified Network Associate Study Guide*. Osborne/McGraw-Hill. Berkeley, CA, 1998. ISBN 0-07882-487-7. Another great book for review before taking the CCNA exam.

 Visit **www.cisco.com/univercd/cc/td/doc/product/software/ios113ed/ 113ed_cr/switch_c/xcisl.htm** for a great article titled "Configuring Routing between VLANs with ISL Encapsulation."

Extending Switch Functionality

Terms you'll need to understand:

✓ Virtual local area network (VLAN)

✓ Trunking

✓ Interswitch link (ISL)

✓ VLAN Trunking Protocol (VTP)

Techniques you'll need to master:

✓ Describing VLAN operation

✓ Creating VLANs

✓ Establishing a trunk connection between switches

✓ Understanding VTP

In this chapter, I will introduce you to some of the advanced features available on Cisco switches. You will learn to interconnect switches through trunk connections. You will also learn how to configure and manage VLANs.

Virtual Local Area Networks (VLANs)

A VLAN is a group of switched ports that acts as a separate, isolated LAN. There can be several VLANs defined on a single switch. A VLAN can also span multiple switches. Workstations in separate VLANs will never encounter traffic from or share bandwidth with other VLANs unless the data is routed. In other words, a router or switch with routing capabilities is required if devices on different VLANs need to communicate. It should be noted that VLAN configuration is done through the switch and its software.

Remember from earlier chapters that one of the main benefits to switches is that they segment a network into many collision domains. Each port represents a single collision domain, and devices share bandwidth only with other devices on the same switch port. Unless a switch is segmented into VLANs, however, all the devices on the switch are still in the same broadcast domain; that is, all broadcasts are sent to each port throughout the switching fabric.

VLANs introduce a way to limit the broadcast traffic in a switched network (a job normally associated with routers). When you create a VLAN by defining which ports belong to it, you are really just creating a boundary for broadcast traffic. This has the effect of creating multiple, isolated LANs on a single switch.

Figure 11.1 shows a 12-port switch that has been divided into two VLANs. Ports 1 through 6 are VLAN 1, and ports 7 through 12 are VLAN 2.

It is important to understand the need for routers in a switched network. If devices on different VLANs need to communicate, routing is required to facilitate this exchange of data. Many of today's network systems are collections of routers *and* switches.

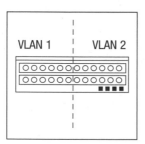

Figure 11.1   A simple VLAN configuration.

What happens when a device on one VLAN needs to communicate with a device on another VLAN? Because a VLAN is a closed layer 2 network, traffic must cross a layer 3 device to communicate with other VLANs. This means that a router is required to facilitate the exchange of packets between VLANs.

Note: The behavior described here is that of layer 2 switching. There are layer 3 switches on the market that perform routing, but these are beyond the scope of this book.

It is possible for a device to participate in more than one VLAN by using a special type of network card that performs ISL, which is discussed later in this chapter.

The real benefit to using VLANs is that they can span multiple switches. Figure 11.2 shows two switches that are configured to share VLAN information.

A large campus network may have hundreds of switches spread throughout several buildings. Users can be put on the appropriate VLANs easily, no matter where they are physically located. Users on the same VLAN do not have to be connected to the same device. Therefore, LANs are no longer tied to the physical location of users but rather can be assigned based on department, functional area, or security level. By isolating users according to department or functional area, network administrators can keep the majority of data traffic within one VLAN, thereby maximizing the amount of traffic switched at hardware speeds versus what is routed at slower software speeds.

The ability to assign a user to a VLAN on a port-by-port basis makes adding, moving, or deleting users simple. For example, let's say a user changes from the accounting department to the marketing department. If the network administrator designed the network and VLANs by functional department, this user would have changed VLANs. To accommodate this change, the administrator only has

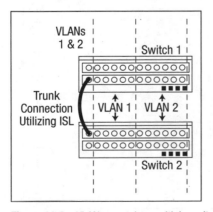

Figure 11.2 VLANs spanning multiple switches.

to make a software configuration change in the switch by assigning that user's port to the new VLAN.

In addition, VLANs provide the flexibility necessary to group users by security level. This can greatly simplify applying a security policy to a network. In summary, here are the benefits of VLANs:

➤ They simplify security administration.

➤ They allow users to be grouped by functional area versus physical location.

➤ They simplify moving and adding users.

Frame Tagging

Frame tagging is the method used by Cisco Catalyst switches to identify to which VLAN a frame belongs. As a frame enters the switch, the switch encapsulates the frame with a header that "tags" the frame with a VLAN ID. Any time a frame needs to leave one switch for another, the tagged frame is sent throughout the switching fabric. When the frame arrives at the destination switch, the tag tells the switch to which VLAN the frame belongs. This process is illustrated in Figure 11.3 using the VLAN IDs 10, 20, and 30. The tag is stripped off of the frame before the frame is sent out to the destination device. This process gives the illusion that all ports are physically connected to the same switch.

Be sure to understand the function of frame tagging, which "tags" a frame with a user-defined VLAN ID.

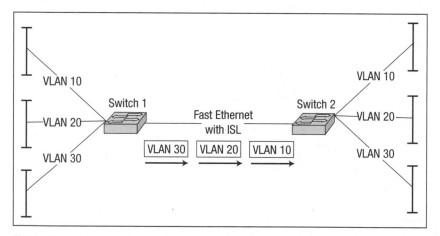

Figure 11.3   ISL and frame tagging.

Trunk Connections

Under normal circumstances, a switch port can carry traffic for a single VLAN only. For VLANs to span multiple switches, a trunk connection must be created. This trunk connection transports data from multiple VLANs. Trunk connections allow VLANs to be used throughout the switching fabric of large networks.

Any Fast Ethernet or Asynchronous Transfer Mode (ATM) port on a Catalyst switch can be designated as a trunk port. This port typically connects to another switch via a crossover 100BaseT cable in the case of a Fast Ethernet trunk.

For the trunked port to transport multiple VLANs, it must understand frame tags.

Interswitch Link (ISL)

ISL is a technology developed by Cisco that allows a single Ethernet interface to participate in multiple VLANs. When a trunk connection is made on a Catalyst switch's Ethernet port, ISL is used. ISL is also available on Ethernet cards that can be used in servers or routers.

A device utilizing an ISL Ethernet card will appear to have many physical cards, each connected to a different segment. ISL allows this single Ethernet card to have many logical (virtual) addresses. The user must configure each logical interface with an address that reflects the VLAN to which it belongs.

ISL works by allowing the frame-tagging information to be passed along to the Ethernet card. The Ethernet card then reads the frame tag, which identifies the VLAN to which the frame belongs. Conversely, the ISL Ethernet card creates the frame tags when transmitting frames.

Note: ISL is a technology proprietary to Cisco and, therefore, is not supported on equipment made by other vendors. However, in mid-1998, the Institute of Electrical and Electronics Engineers (IEEE) standardized a frame-tagging process similar to Cisco's ISL. The new standard is a protocol called 802.1Q. With 802.1Q, switches from multiple vendors can coexist in the same switching fabric.

VLAN Trunking Protocol (VTP)

VTP is a protocol used between switches to simplify the management of VLANs. Configuration changes that are made to a VTP server are propagated across trunks to all connected switches.

All switches that are to be managed in this way must be members of the same *management domain*. A VTP management domain is the entire group of switches that share configuration information.

For example, when you add a new VLAN to a member switch, the VLAN is available in all the network switches automatically. VTP allows switched networks to scale to larger environments; otherwise, VLAN configuration would have to be maintained manually on individual switches.

By default, Catalyst switches are set to a no-management-domain state. The switches remain in a no-management state until a user configures the management domain or the switches receive an advertisement for a domain over a trunk link. The default VTP configuration parameters are shown in Table 11.1.

VTP Modes

When it has a management domain, a switch operates in one of three VTP modes: server, client, or transparent. The default mode is server.

In VTP server mode, a switch can create, modify, or delete VLAN and other configuration parameters for the entire VTP domain. VTP messages are sent over all trunk links, and configuration changes are propagated to all switches in the management domain.

In VTP client mode, the switch receives VTP messages and applies configuration changes made from any VTP server. However, a client cannot create, change, or delete VLAN information.

In VTP transparent mode, the switch forwards all VTP messages to other switches in the domain but does not use the configuration from VTP advertisements. A VTP transparent switch can create, modify, or delete VLANs, but the changes apply only locally and are not transmitted to other switches.

VTP Pruning

VTP can detect whether a trunk connection is carrying unnecessary traffic. By default, all trunk connections carry traffic from all VLANs in the management domain. In many cases, however, a switch does not need a local port configured for each VLAN. In this event, it is not necessary to flood traffic from VLANs other than the ones supported by that switch. VTP pruning enables the switching

Table 11.1 Default VTP configuration parameters.	
Option	Default Value
VTP Domain Name	None
VTP Mode	Server
VTP Password	None
VTP Pruning	Disabled
VTP Trap	Enabled

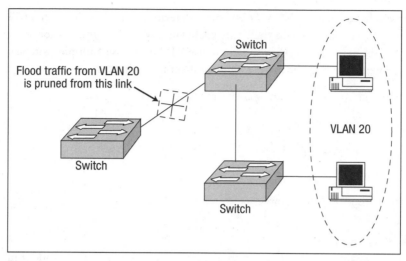

Figure 11.4   VTP pruning.

fabric to prevent flooding traffic on trunk ports that do not need it. This is illustrated in Figure 11.4.

Configuring VLANs

Three methods can be used to assign a switch port to a particular VLAN: port-centric, static, and dynamic. In a port-centric configuration, all nodes that are connected to ports within the same VLAN are given the same VLAN ID. In this type of configuration, the network administrator's job is much easier because of the ease of administering the VLAN. In a static VLAN configuration, the ports on a switch are hard-coded and remain in effect until the administrator changes them. This type of configuration is typical of a network that is very well monitored and where changes are unlikely. The third type of port configuration is dynamic. This type of configuration involves more overhead on setup for the administrator because of the database configuration. The ports on these switches automatically determine their assigned VLAN. The VLAN assignment is determined by the type of protocol (within a packet), MAC address, and logical addressing. A major benefit of this type of configuration is that the administrator will notice when any unauthorized or new user is on the network. If a workstation happens to be connected to a port that is unassigned, the switch will record the MAC address of the computer and check its database to determine which VLAN to assign the workstation to.

In the rest of this chapter, we will look at the Cisco commands used to configure, monitor, and maintain VLANs and trunk connections.

Before you begin creating VLANs, you must determine whether the switch will participate in a VTP domain that will synchronize VLAN configuration with the rest of the network. Also, if you want to use VLANs across multiple switches, a trunk connection must be made to interconnect the switches.

The steps required to configure VLANs are as follows:

1. Enable VTP (optional).

2. Enable trunking (optional).

3. Create the VLANs.

4. Assign the VLANs to ports.

Enabling VTP

When adding a new switch to an existing domain, it is good practice to add it in VTP client mode initially. This way, you can prevent the switch from propagating incorrect VLAN information to other switches. In the following example, however, we are setting up a new VTP domain and will place the switch into server mode. The commands to do so are as follows:

```
1900#conf terminal
Enter configuration commands, one per line. End with CNTL/Z
1900(config)#vtp server
1900(config)#vtp domain ccnalab
```

To verify VTP information, use the **show vtp** command from EXEC privileged mode:

```
hostname# show vtp

VTP version: 1
    Configuration revision: 3
    Maximum VLANs supported locally: 1005
    Number of existing VLANs: 5
    VTP domain name      : ccnalab
    VTP password        : vtp_server
    VTP operating mode   : Server
    VTP pruning mode    : Enabled
    VTP traps generation : Enabled
    Configuration last modified by: 0.0.0.0 at 00-00-0000 00:00:00
```

Enabling Trunking

The next step is to create a trunk connection to other switches that will be sharing VLAN information. In the following example, we'll assume that we are connecting two Catalyst 1900 switches via their 100BaseT ports using a crossover Category 5 Ethernet cable. We are using the Fast Ethernet ports known in the IOS as f0/26.

The **trunk** command has five options: on, off, desirable, auto, and negotiate. Table 11.2 shows the function of each trunk mode.

To enable trunking on a port, enter interface configuration mode for the desired port first and then use the **trunk** command with the appropriate option, as shown here:

```
1900#conf terminal
Enter configuration commands, one per line. End with CNTL/Z
1900(config)#interface f0/26
1900(config-if)#trunk on
```

The same configuration must be executed for the appropriate port on the connected device. Because we set the trunk to "on" mode in the previous example, the corresponding port must be set to on, auto, or desirable for the trunk connection to be established.

To verify the trunk operation, use the **show trunk** command. Its syntax is as follows:

```
show trunk [a | b]
```

A Catalyst 1900 switch has two Fast Ethernet ports that can act as trunk connections. They are known as interfaces f0/26 and f0/27. When you're using the **show trunk** command, option A refers to the first trunk port (in this case, f0/26), and option B is for port f0/27. Therefore, to see the trunking status for Fast Ethernet port A (f0/26), use the following command:

```
1900#show trunk a
DISL state: On, Trunking: On, Encapsulation type: ISL
```

Table 11.2	Trunk command options.
Option	**Function**
On	The port goes into permanent ISL trunk mode and negotiates with the connected device to convert the link to a trunk.
Off	This option disables trunking on the port and negotiates with the connected device to convert the link to non-trunk.
Desirable	The port will enter trunk mode if the connected device is set to on, desirable, or auto; otherwise, the port is a non-trunk.
Auto	The port will enter trunk mode if the connected device is set to on or desirable; otherwise, the port is a non-trunk.
Negotiate	The port goes into permanent ISL trunk mode, but no negotiation takes place with the connected device.

Creating the VLAN

To create a new VLAN, use the **vlan** command from global configuration mode. This command has several options that can be specified, but for our purposes, all we need to have is a four-digit number to identify the VLAN and a name for it. Each VLAN must have a unique numeric ID, which can be any number from 1 to 1005.

We will create a VLAN called Engineering and make it VLAN 2:

```
hostname(config)# vlan 2 name Engineering
```

To verify the configuration of the VLAN, use the **show vlan** *vlan#* command:

```
1900#show vlan 2

VLAN Name       Status      Ports
--------        ------      ----
2 Engineering   Enabled
------------    ------


VLAN Type   SAID   MTU   Parent RingNo BridgeNo Stp  Trans1 Trans2
--------    ----   ---   ------ ------ -------- ---  ------ ------
2 Ethernet  100009 1500  0      1      1        Unkn 0      0
```

Assigning the VLAN to Ports

Now that the VLAN has been created, you can statically assign which ports will be members of the VLAN. A port can belong to only one VLAN at a time. By default, all ports are members of VLAN 1.

To assign a VLAN to a port, enter interface configuration mode for the appropriate port and then use the **vlan-membership** command:

```
1900#conf terminal
Enter configuration commands, one per line. End with CNTL/Z
1900(config)#interface ethernet 0/8
1900(config-if)#vlan-membership static 2
```

To verify VLAN membership and to see which ports belong to what VLAN, use the **show vlan-membership** command:

```
hostname# show vlan-membership
Port  VLAN Membership Type   Port VLAN Membership Type
----  ---- ---------------   ---- ---- ---------------
 1    1    Static             14   2    Static
 2    1    Static             15   2    Static
```

3	1	Static	16	2	Static
4	1	Static	17	2	Static
5	1	Static	18	2	Static
6	1	Static	19	2	Static
7	1	Dynamic	20	2	Static
8	1	Dynamic	21	2	Static
9	1	Dynamic	22	2	Static
10	1	Dynamic	23	2	Static
11	1	Dynamic	24	2	Static
12	1	Dynamic	AUI	2	Static
13	1	Dynamic			
A	1	Static			
B	2	Static			

Practice Questions

Question 1

> Which of the following are advantages of VLANs? [Choose the two best answers]
>
> ❏ a. They reduce switching overhead.
>
> ❏ b. They increase switching throughput.
>
> ❏ c. They simplify the adding, moving, and changing of users.
>
> ❏ d. They allow users to be grouped by functional area, not physical location.

The correct answers are c and d. VLANs increase the flexibility of assigning users to LANs. This increased simplicity allows users to be grouped by functional area rather than physical location, because VLANs can span multiple switches. Answer a is incorrect because VLANs do not reduce the amount of overhead required to switch a frame. Answer b is incorrect because VLANs do not provide any increased switching throughput.

Question 2

> What must you do to allow a VLAN to span two or more switches?
>
> ○ a. Set up a VTP domain.
>
> ○ b. Set up a trunk connection.
>
> ○ c. Configure the duplex setting on the ports.
>
> ○ d. Configure port security on the switch.

The correct answer is b. A trunk connection must be established in order for a VLAN to span multiple switches. Trunk ports recognize frame tags and are therefore able to carry information on multiple VLANs. Answer a is incorrect because a VTP domain is not necessary for switches to share VLAN information. Answer c is incorrect because the duplex setting does not have to be configured manually to connect two switches. Answer d is incorrect because port security is not necessary for a VLAN to span switches.

Question 3

Which of the following are advantages of using VTP in a switching environment? [Choose the two best answers]

❏ a. It enables VLANs to span multiple switches.

❏ b. It simplifies the management of VLANs.

❏ c. It simplifies the scalability of the switched network.

❏ d. It allows switches to read frame tags.

The correct answers are b and c. VTP simplifies the management of VLANs because configuration information is propagated automatically throughout the switching fabric when changes are made. Without VTP, each switch would have to be configured manually; therefore, VTP makes it easier to scale to a larger switched environment. Answer a is incorrect because VTP is not necessary for VLANs to span multiple switches. Answer d is incorrect because VTP does not allow the switch to read frame tags.

Question 4

What is ISL used for?

○ a. To allow an Ethernet interface to understand frame tags

○ b. To make two Ethernet interfaces appear as one

○ c. To connect an Ethernet switch with a high-speed core switch such as ATM

○ d. To allow simultaneous routing and switching

The correct answer is a. ISL allows an Ethernet interface to understand frame tags, which identify the VLAN to which a packet belongs. For this reason, an ISL interface can participate in multiple VLANs, which is necessary for a trunk connection. Answer b is incorrect because ISL can actually have the opposite effect of this—a single Ethernet interface may appear to be several by having multiple layer 3 addresses. Answers c and d are incorrect because these are not functions of ISL.

Question 5

> What is the purpose of VTP pruning?
>
> ○ a. To detect loops in the switching fabric
>
> ○ b. To disable a trunk connection that creates a bridging loop
>
> ○ c. To simplify the management of VLANs
>
> ○ d. To prevent flooding unnecessary traffic across trunk connections

The correct answer is d. VTP pruning is used to prevent flooding of unnecessary traffic across trunk connections. Answer a is incorrect because this is a function of the Spanning Tree Protocol. Answer b is incorrect because this is not the purpose of VTP pruning. Answer c is incorrect because this is the purpose of the VTP, not VTP pruning.

Question 6

> Which of the following is a valid command to create a VLAN on a Catalyst 1900 switch and name it Accounting?
>
> ○ a. **switch(config)#create vlan 10 name Accounting**
>
> ○ b. **switch#create vlan 10 name Accounting**
>
> ○ c. **switch(config)#vlan 10 name Accounting**
>
> ○ d. **switch#vlan 10 name Accounting**

The correct answer is c. The correct syntax to create a VLAN in command mode is **vlan** *{number}* **name** *{name}* from global configuration mode. Answers a and b are incorrect because the word "create" is not a part of this command. Answer d has the correct syntax for the command; however, the switch is not in configuration mode. Therefore, answer d is incorrect.

Question 7

Which of the following commands will assign Ethernet port 9 on a Catalyst 1900 to VLAN 20?

○ a. **interface Ethernet 0/9** and **vlan-membership static 20**

○ b. **vlan-membership interface Ethernet 0/9 static 20**

○ c. **interface Ethernet 0/9** and **vlan 20**

○ d. **vlan 20 interface Ethernet 0/9**

The correct answer is a. To assign an interface to a VLAN, you must first enter port configuration mode by using the **interface Ethernet 0/9** command from global configuration mode. Then, you use the **vlan-membership** command to assign a VLAN to the port. Answers b, c, and d all use invalid syntax.

Question 8

Which VLAN port configuration option requires more upfront administration because of database configuration?

○ a. Static

○ b. Port-centric

○ c. Dynamic

The correct answer is c. The dynamic configuration requires more initial overhead because the administrator has to configure the switches database. Static is also labor intensive upfront but not as much as dynamic. Therefore, answer a is incorrect. Port-centric is the easiest of the three to administer. Therefore, answer b is incorrect.

Question 9

Which VLAN port configuration is the most secure?

○ a. Static

○ b. Dynamic

The correct answer is a. Static is the choice that is most often implemented and most secure of the two because the port on the switch which has been assigned by the administrator is always assigned to that port until the administrator changes it manually. Dynamic, on the other hand, is configured automatically. The assignment of the ports is done so through a database of MAC addresses and protocols. Therefore, answer b is incorrect.

Need to Know More?

 Chappell, Laura. *Introduction to Cisco Router Configuration.* Cisco Systems Inc., Macmillan Computer Publishing. Indianapolis, IN, 1998. ISBN 0-7645-3186-7. This book provides a great overview of the concepts tested on the CCNA exam.

 Ford, Merilee, H. Kim Lew, Steve Spanier, and Kevin Downes. *Internetworking Technologies Handbook 2nd Edition.* Macmillan Computer Publishing. Indianapolis, IN, 1998. ISBN 1-56205-102-3. This book is full of resourceful information on internetworking technologies.

 Lammle, Todd, Donald Porter, and James Chellis. *CCNA Cisco Certified Network Associate.* Sybex Network Press. Alameda, CA, 1999. ISBN 0-7821-2381-3. This book is a great supplement for learning the technologies tested on the CCNA exam.

 McNutt, Shawn, Mark Poplar, Jason Waters, and David Stabenaw. *CCNA Routing and Switching Exam Prep.* The Coriolis Group. Scottsdale, AZ, 2000. ISBN 1-57610-440-0. This book is a great complement to the *CCNA Exam Cram* book. The switching chapters expand on the information presented here.

 Syngress Media, with Richard D. Hornbaker, CCIE. *Cisco Certified Network Associate Study Guide.* Osborne/McGraw-Hill. Berkeley, CA, 1998. ISBN 0-07882-487-7. Another great book for review before taking the CCNA exam.

 Visit **www.cisco.com/univercd/cc/td/doc/product/software/ios113ed/ 113ed_cr/switch_c/xcisl.htm** for a great article titled "Configuring Routing between VLANs with ISL Encapsulation."

Wide Area Networking

Terms you'll need to understand:

✓ Point-to-Point Protocol (PPP)

✓ High-Level Data Link Control (HDLC)

✓ Link Control Protocol (LCP)

✓ Integrated Services Digital Network (ISDN)

✓ Reference points

✓ Dial-on-demand routing (DDR)

✓ Data terminal equipment (DTE)

✓ Data communication equipment (DCE)

✓ Frame Relay

✓ Frame check sequence (FCS)

✓ Permanent virtual circuit (PVC)

✓ Data link connection identifier (DLCI)

✓ Local Management Interface (LMI)

Techniques you'll need to master:

✓ Identifying PPP operations to encapsulate wide area network (WAN) data on Cisco routers

✓ Differentiating between the following WAN services: Frame Relay, ISDN, HDLC, and PPP

✓ Stating a relevant use and context for ISDN networking

✓ Identifying ISDN protocols, function groups, reference points, and channels

✓ Describing Cisco's implementation of ISDN BRI

✓ Recognizing key Frame Relay terms and features

✓ Listing commands to configure Frame Relay LMIs, maps, and subinterfaces

✓ Listing commands to monitor Frame Relay activity in a router

This chapter provides an overview of WAN protocols and services. More specifically, this chapter deals with PPP components and operations, and the configuration and monitoring commands are presented. This chapter continues the overview of WAN protocols and services while discussing the use and context for ISDN networking and ISDN components as well as configuration and monitoring commands. Lastly, the chapter continues the overview of WAN protocols and services by addressing the use of Frame Relay networking and addresses, Frame Relay configuration, and monitoring commands.

WAN Services

Because WANs cover long distances, organizations typically subscribe to an outside provider for WAN services. These services (usually telephone and data) are routed from an interface at one end of the customer's network through the provider's network to the other end of the customer's network. Figure 12.1 illustrates a WAN service provider's network cloud.

Table 12.1 defines the commonly used terms presented in Figure 12.1.

It is the provider's responsibility to provide the customer with the parameters necessary to connect to its network. The WAN provider's network appears as a cloud to the customer, who simply makes a point-to-point connection to the remote site.

The main interface between the customer and provider networks occurs between the data terminal equipment (DTE) and the data communication equipment

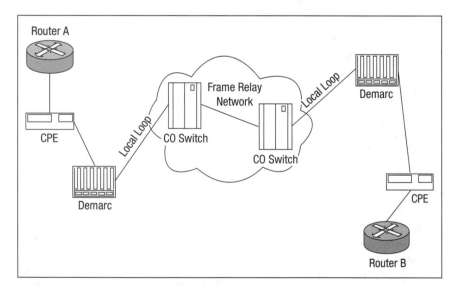

Figure 12.1   WAN service provider's network cloud.

Table 12.1 Common WAN service provider terms.	
Term	**Description**
Customer premise equipment (CPE)	Devices that are physically located on the subscriber's premises. These devices are either owned by the customer or leased from the WAN service provider.
Demarcation (Demarc)	The point where the CPE ends and the local loop begins, usually in the customer's main data closet.
Local loop (last mile)	Cabling that extends from the demarc into the service provider's central office.
Central office (CO)	The WAN service provider's switching facility, which provides the nearest point of presence (POP) for the service. The CO is also referred to as the *service provider's POP*.

(DCE). The customer's router usually serves as the DTE device and performs the packet-switching function. Sometimes, DTE devices are bridges or terminals. The DCE attaches to the DTE and provides clocking, converts the data into a suitable format, and switches the data across the provider's network. DCE devices include modems, a channel service unit/data service unit (CSU/DSU), and a terminal adapter/network termination 1 (TA/NT1). Figure 12.2 depicts DTE devices (routers) and DCE devices within a WAN.

The DTE/DCE interface serves as the boundary where responsibility for the network traffic shifts from the customer's network to the WAN provider's network. It can support several common types of WAN service connections when the DTE is a Cisco router. The first type involves switched services. Switches

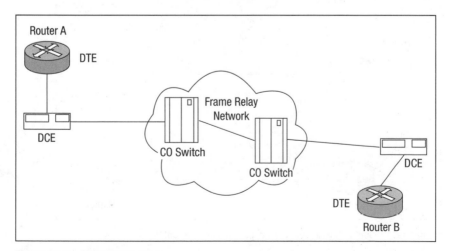

Figure 12.2   DTE/DCE interface.

within the provider's network transmit data from one customer DTE to that customer's other DTEs. Frame Relay and ISDN are examples of packet-switched and circuit-switched services, respectively.

The second type involves connecting remote devices to a central mainframe. Synchronous Data Link Control (SDLC) is the protocol used in these types of point-to-point or point-to-multipoint connections. SDLC is a bit-synchronous data link protocol that supports legacy IBM networks.

A third type involves connecting peer devices. HDLC and PPP can be used to encapsulate the data for transmission to peer DTE devices. Table 12.2 lists the types of connectivity of common WAN services, and Figure 12.3 highlights common types of connections and services supported by Cisco routers.

Table 12.2 Connectivity of common WAN services.	
Type	**Connects To**
Frame Relay, ISDN	A device in a WAN service provider's network
SDLC	An IBM enterprise data center computer (mainframe hosts)
HDLC, PPP	A peer device on the WAN

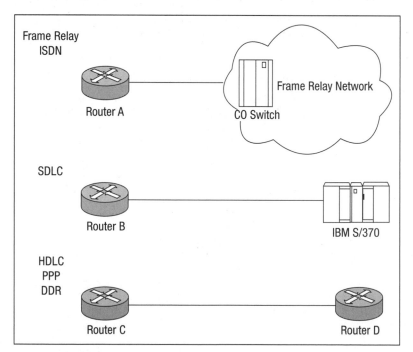

Figure 12.3 Common WAN services supported by Cisco routers.

In the remainder of this section, I will be discussing how to employ the HDLC and PPP protocols on a leased line.

HDLC Overview

High-Level Data Link Control (HDLC) is the default encapsulation used by Cisco routers over synchronous serial links. HDLC is an ISO standard data link protocol. It specifies a method to encapsulate data over synchronous serial links using frame characters and checksums.

Cisco routers use a proprietary version of HDLC. Typically, HDLC is used on leased lines between two Cisco devices. If you need to establish a link between a Cisco router and a non-Cisco device, you must use PPP encapsulation instead of HDLC.

 The ISO standard HDLC does not support multiple protocols on a single link. However, Cisco's proprietary HDLC adds a field that allows it to support multiprotocol environments.

The command to enable HDLC on an interface is relatively simple—use **encapsulation hdlc** from interface configuration mode. Because HDLC is the default encapsulation type used by Cisco routers, the only time you may need to use this command is when an interface has been configured with another encapsulation type, such as PPP, and then you need to change it back to HDLC.

PPP Overview

Point-to-Point Protocol (PPP) encapsulates Network layer information for transmission over point-to-point links. It was designed by developers on the Internet and is described by a series of documents called *Request for Comments (RFCs)*— namely, 1661, 1331, and 2153. Figure 12.4 shows how PPP's layered architecture relates to the Open Systems Interconnection (OSI) model.

 PPP consists of two main components:

➤ *Link Control Protocol (LCP)*—Establishes, configures, and tests the connection

➤ *Network Control Program (NCP)*—Configures many different Network layer protocols

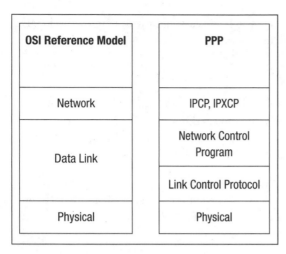

Figure 12.4 The OSI reference model and PPP.

PPP Physical Layer

PPP can operate on a variety of DTE/DCE physical interfaces, including:

➤ Asynchronous serial

➤ Synchronous serial

➤ High–Speed Serial Interface (HSSI)

➤ ISDN

Other than what is required by a particular physical interface, PPP makes no special transmission rate requirements.

PPP Connections

It is the responsibility of the LCP within PPP to establish, configure, test, maintain, and terminate the point-to-point connection. Four phases occur during the LCP process:

➤ Link establishment

➤ Link quality determination

➤ Network layer protocol negotiation

➤ Link termination

During link establishment, LCP opens the connection and negotiates configuration parameters. Acknowledgment frames must be sent and received before this phase can be considered completed successfully.

The link quality determination phase involves testing the connection to determine whether the line quality is sufficient to support the Network layer protocols. Although this phase seems very important, it is optional.

In the third phase, the appropriate Network layer protocols are configured. *Network control programs (NCPs)* configure PPP to support different Network layer protocols, including Internet Protocol (IP), Internetwork Packet Exchange (IPX), and AppleTalk. The PPP devices transmit NCP packets to select and configure one or more Network layer protocols. After each selected Network layer protocol has been configured, data can begin to be transmitted across the link. If the LCP terminates a link, it notifies the NCP, which takes appropriate action.

The link termination phase can be initiated by the LCP at any time. Link termination can occur from events such as a user request, a loss of carrier, or the expiration of a timeout parameter.

PPP Authentication

PPP authentication occurs during the link quality determination phase; therefore, authentication is optional. The calling side of the link must transmit information to ensure that the sender is authorized to establish the connection. This is accomplished by a series of authentication messages being sent between the routers. PPP supports two types of authentication: Password Authentication Protocol (PAP) and Challenge Handshake Authentication protocol (CHAP).

PAP

PAP uses a two-way handshake to allow remote hosts to identify themselves. After the link has been established and the link establishment phase is complete, PAP performs the following steps:

1. The remote host initiates the call, sends a username and password to the local host, and continues to send the information until it is accepted or rejected.

2. The local host receives the call and accepts or rejects the username and password information. If the local host rejects the information, the connection is terminated.

CHAP

CHAP uses a three-way handshake to force remote hosts to identify themselves after the link establishment phase. CHAP performs the following steps after the link establishment phase is complete:

1. The local router that received the call sends a challenge packet to the remote host that initiated the call. The challenge packet consists of an ID, a random

number, and either the name of the local host performing the authentication or a username on the remote host.

2. The remote host must respond with its encrypted unique ID, a one-way encrypted password, the remote hostname or a username, and a random number.

3. The local router performs its own calculation on the response values. It accepts or rejects the authentication request based on whether the value it received from the remote host matches the value it calculated.

Like PAP, CHAP terminates the connection immediately if the local host rejects the authentication request.

 During the PAP process, the username and password information is sent from the remote host in clear text, so PAP is not a recommended protocol. It offers no protection from a network analyzer capturing the information and using it. Because CHAP uses secret, encrypted passwords and unique IDs, it is a much stronger protocol than PAP. You can choose only one type of authentication, so CHAP is definitely recommended; however, PAP is better than no authentication at all.

LCP Configuration Options

Cisco routers support several configuration options for LCP:

➤ Authentication options include PAP and CHAP.

➤ By reducing the amount of data that must be transmitted, data compressions increase the throughput on a network link. The data is compressed as it is sent and decompressed as it is received. LCP compression options include Stacker or Predictor.

➤ The error-detection options within LCP activate processes to detect errors. The Quality and Magic Number protocols help to ensure reliable connections.

➤ The multilink PPP configuration option supports load balancing over PPP links. This option is supported in Cisco Internetwork Operating System (IOS) 11.1 and later.

Table 12.3 summarizes the different configuration options within LCP.

Note: RFC 1548 describes the different PPP LCP configuration options in detail.

Table 12.3	LCP configuration options.		
Option	**Function**	**Protocol**	**Command**
Authentication	Requires a password	PAP	**ppp authentication pap**
	Performs a challenge handshake	CHAP	**ppp authentication chap**
Compression	Compresses data at the source	Stacker	**ppp compress stacker**
	Reproduces data at the destination	Predictor	**ppp compress predictor**
Error detection	Monitors the data dropped on the link and avoids frame looping	Quality and Magic Number	**ppp quality <*number 1 - 100*>**
Multilink	Performs load balancing across multiple links	MP	**ppp multilink**

Configuring PPP

Configuring PPP on a Cisco router requires that both global and interface configuration commands be executed on both the local and remote routers. Figure 12.5 presents an example of two routers that need to establish a PPP link.

A username and password must be set, so the following global configuration command must be executed:

```
Username name password secret-password
```

In this command, *name* and *secret-password* indicate the name of the remote host and the password to use for authentication. The password must be the same on both the local and remote routers. Table 12.4 lists the interface commands that must be executed to configure PPP. Figure 12.6 presents the global and interface configuration commands for router A and router B.

Figure 12.5 PPP scenario.

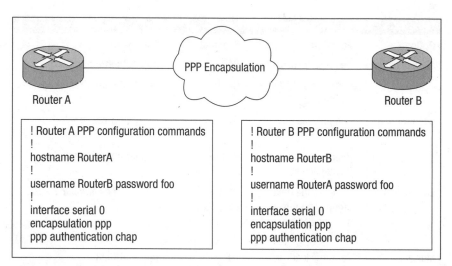

Figure 12.6 PPP configuration.

Table 12.4 PPP interface commands.	
Command	**Description**
encapsulation ppp	Encapsulates data on this interface as PPP
ppp authentication pap	Enables password checking for incoming calls
ppp authentication chap	Forces incoming calls to answer password challenges

Monitoring PPP

You can monitor PPP activity with the **show interface** and **debug ppp chap** commands. The **show interface** command enables you to view PPP LCP and NCP information. Listing 12.1 shows an example of PPP activity on an interface.

Listing 12.1 PPP activity with the **show interface** command.

```
RouterA#sh int s0
Serial0 is up, line protocol is up
  Hardware is HD64570
  Internet address is 172.16.1.1/16
  MTU 1500 bytes, BW 1544 Kbit, DLY 20000 usec,
    rely 255/255, load 1/255
  Encapsulation PPP, loopback not set, keepalive set (10 sec)
  LCP Open
  Open: IPCP, CDPCP
  Last input 00:00:06, output 00:00:06, output hang never
  Last clearing of "show interface" counters never
  Input queue: 0/75/0 (size/max/drops); Total output drops: 0
  Queueing strategy: weighted fair
```

```
Output queue: 0/1000/64/0 (size/max total/threshold/drops)
    Conversations  0/2/256 (active/max active/max total)
    Reserved Conversations 0/0 (allocated/max allocated)
 5 minute input rate 0 bits/sec, 0 packets/sec
 5 minute output rate 0 bits/sec, 0 packets/sec
    34 packets input, 1303 bytes, 0 no buffer
    Received 34 broadcasts, 0 runts, 0 giants, 0 throttles
  0 input errors, 0 CRC, 0 frame, 0 overrun, 0 ignored, 0 abort
    72 packets output, 2819 bytes, 0 underruns
    0 output errors, 0 collisions, 14 interface resets
    0 output buffer failures, 0 output buffers swapped out
    41 carrier transitions
    DCD=up  DSR=up  DTR=up  RTS=up  CTS=up
RouterA#
```

The **debug ppp chap** command displays the CHAP packet exchanges and PAP exchanges. Listing 12.2 displays an example of the authentication handshake sequence.

**Listing 12.2   PPP authentication sequence with the debug ppp chap
command.**

```
RouterA# debug ppp chap
Serial0: Unable to authenticate. No name received from peer
Serial0: Unable to validate CHAP response.
        USERNAME pioneer not found.
Serial0: Unable to validate CHAP response.
        No password defined for USERNAME pioneer
Serial0: Failed CHAP authentication with remote.
Remote message is Unknown name
Serial0: remote passed CHAP authentication.
Serial0: Passed CHAP authentication with remote.
Serial0: CHAP input code = 4 id = 3 len = 48
```

*Note: The **debug ppp chap** command displays the reason why the CHAP request failed.*

Once you have finished examining the debug output, use the **no debug all** command to turn off the debugging feature.

ISDN Overview

ISDN refers to the call-processing system that enables voice, data, and video to be transmitted over our existing telephone system. ISDN offers several advantages over existing analog modem lines. For example, ISDN connection speeds begin at 64Kbps, whereas typical modem speeds hover between 28.8Kbps and 56Kbps. The call setup time for an ISDN call is also much quicker. ISDN can transmit data packets, voice, or video. ISDN is a viable solution for remote connectivity (telecommuting) and access to the Internet. ISDN also supports any of the Network layer protocols supported by the Cisco Internetwork Operating System (IOS) and encapsulates other WAN services, such as PPP.

ISDN can be used to:

➤ Add bandwidth for telecommuting

➤ Improve Internet response times

➤ Carry multiple Network layer protocols

➤ Encapsulate other WAN services

Basic Rate Interface and Primary Rate Interface

ISDN can be ordered as either BRI or PRI. An ISDN BRI service contains two bearer channels (or B channels) of 64Kbps and one data channel (or D channel) of 16Kbps. The B channel carries user data, and the D channel carries signaling and control information. The maximum throughput for BRI is 128Kbps (two B channels at 64Kbps). In North America and Japan, an ISDN PRI service uses a T1 line that contains 23 B channels and one D channel that enables a maximum throughput of 1.544Mbps. In Europe, PRI service uses an E1 line that contains 30 B channels, enabling a throughput of 2.048Mbps.

ISDN Protocols

The International Telecommunication Union Telecommunication (ITU-T) standardization sector is an international body that develops worldwide standards for telecommunications technologies. In 1984, ITU-T published a comprehensive list of standard ISDN protocols, organized into groups that address certain topics. Table 12.5 presents some of the ISDN protocols.

Functions and Reference Points

ISDN functions and reference points are the items that describe ISDN service provider standards. Functions and reference points enable you to articulate your needs clearly as you work with service providers to engineer, implement, and

Table 12.5 ITU-T standard ISDN protocols.		
Topic	Protocol	Example
Telephone network and ISDN	E-series	E.164 (international ISDN addressing)
ISDN concepts, aspects, and interfaces	I-series	I.100 (concepts, structures, and terminology)
Switching and signaling	Q-series	Q.931 (ISDN network layer between terminal and switch)

Table 12.6 ISDN devices and functions.		
Device Name	**Abbreviation**	**Function**
Terminal adapter	TA	Converts RS-232, V.35, and so forth into BRI signals
Terminal endpoint 1	TE1	Indicates a router or other device that has a native ISDN interface
Terminal endpoint 2	TE2	Indicates a router or other device that requires a TA for its BRI signals
Network termination 1	NT1	Converts BRI signals for use by the ISDN line
Network termination 2	NT2	Indicates a device that supports on-premises ISDN concentration, such as a PBX (a more complex NT1 that also performs layer 2 and 3 functions)
Local termination	LT	The part of the local exchange that terminates the local loop
Exchange termination	ET	The part of the exchange that communicates with other ISDN components

maintain ISDN services. *Functions* represent devices or hardware functions within ISDN. Table 12.6 presents basic ISDN devices and their functions.

Reference points describe the logical interfaces between ISDN functions such as TAs or NT1s. Normally, you can connect up to eight ISDN-capable devices on a single ISDN line, enabling them to share the ISDN bandwidth. These devices may be things such as ISDN-capable phones, faxes, routers, and/or terminal adapters. Figure 12.7 shows an example of two routers connected to ISDN services.

In Figure 12.7, router A is a TE1 device that already has a built-in BRI connection. Conversely, router B does not have a built-in BRI connection; it has a serial connection and is considered a TE2 device. It requires a TA to convert the serial signals into BRI signals. Both router A and router B (with a TA device) can connect to the NT1 device.

If your router has a BRI interface, you only need to attach an NT1 device to connect to ISDN services. If your router does not have a BRI interface, you need to attach a TA and an NT1 to connect to ISDN services. In North America, ISDN BRIs can be provisioned without an NT1. In this case, the customer is responsible for providing the NT1 and power for the NT1. Unlike analog telephone lines, if you want a BRI to stay up during a power outage, you must supply uninterrupted power to the NT1. In Europe, ISDN BRIs are provisioned with the NT1 included.

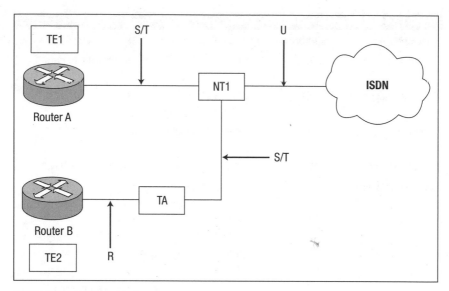

Figure 12.7 ISDN example.

Note: An ISDN BRI usually interfaces with an NT1 device, and an ISDN PRI usually interfaces with a channel service unit/data service unit (CSU/DSU).

DDR

Dial-on-demand routing (DDR) works with ISDN to establish and terminate network connections, as traffic dictates. DDR configuration commands define host and ISDN connection information. An access list and DDR dialer group define what type of traffic should initiate an ISDN call. You can configure multiple access lists to look for different types of "interesting" traffic—network traffic that, when it arrives at the router, triggers the router to initiate the ISDN connection. Figure 12.8 illustrates the DDR process when router A calls router B.

When the router notices interesting traffic, it refers to its ISDN information and initiates the setup of the ISDN call through its BRI or PRI and NT1 device. It should also be noted here that 56Kbps dial-up interfaces can also be used with DDR. When the connection is established, normal routing occurs between the two end devices. After interesting traffic stops being transmitted over the ISDN connection, the connection idle timer begins. When the idle timer expires, the connection is terminated.

Configuring ISDN

You must perform both global and interface configuration tasks when configuring a router for ISDN. Global configuration tasks include specifying the type of ISDN switch your router connects to at the provider's central office (CO) and

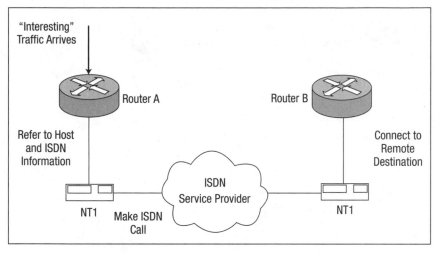

Figure 12.8 DDR with ISDN.

defining what type of traffic is interesting. Table 12.7 lists the ISDN global configuration commands.

Table 12.8 shows the ISDN commands that must be configured on an interface.

Figure 12.9 presents a simple ISDN DDR configuration for router A and router B.

Table 12.7 ISDN global configuration commands.	
Command	**Description**
ISDN switch-type *switch-type*	Defines an ISDN switch type
dialer-list dialer-group protocol	Defines or restricts callers
protocol permit	Defines any specific protocol traffic as interesting for a particular dialer group

Table 12.8 ISDN interface configuration commands.	
Command	**Description**
interface bri *interface number*	Chooses the router interface acting as a TE1 device
encapsulation ppp	Chooses PPP framing
dialer-group *number*	Assigns an interface to a specific dialer group
dialer map *protocol next hop*	Maps a layer 3 protocol to a next-hop address with a specific name
address *name hostname speed*	Defines the connection speed
number **dial-string**	Defines the telephone number to dial
dialer idle-timeout *number*	Defines the number of seconds of idle time before the ISDN connection is terminated

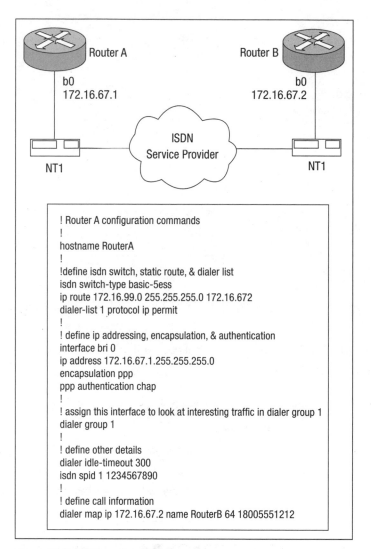

Figure 12.9 DDR configuration example.

Monitoring ISDN

The commands listed in this section enable you to monitor the activity and operation of ISDN and DDR configurations.

You can monitor ISDN and DDR configurations with the following commands:

➤ **show controller bri**

➤ **show interface bri**

➤ **show dialer**

Use the **show controller bri** command to display detailed information about the B and D channels. Listing 12.3 displays an example of the **show controller** command.

Listing 12.3   The **show controller bri** command output.

```
RouterA# show controller bri 0
BRI unit 0
D Chan Info:
Layer 1 is ACTIVATED
idb 0x32089C, ds 0x3267D8, reset_mask 0x2
buffer size 1524
RX ring with 2 entries at 0x2101600 : Rxhead 0
00 pak=0x4122E8 ds=0x412444 status=D000 pak_size=0
01 pak=0x410C20 ds=0x410D7C status=F000 pak_size=0
TX ring with 1 entries at 0x2101640: tx_count = 0,
  tx_head = 0, tx_tail = 0
00 pak=0x000000 ds=0x000000 status=7C00 pak_size=0
0 missed datagrams, 0 overruns, 0 bad frame addresses
0 bad datagram encapsulations, 0 memory errors
0 transmitter underruns
B1 Chan Info:
Layer 1 is ACTIVATED
idb 0x3224E8, ds 0x3268C8, reset_mask 0x0
buffer size 1524
RX ring with 8 entries at 0x2101400 : Rxhead 0
00 pak=0x421FC0 ds=0x42211C status=D000 pak_size=0
01 pak=0x4085E8 ds=0x408744 status=D000 pak_size=0
02 pak=0x422EF0 ds=0x42304C status=D000 pak_size=0
03 pak=0x4148E0 ds=0x414A3C status=D000 pak_size=0
04 pak=0x424D50 ds=0x424EAC status=D000 pak_size=0
05 pak=0x423688 ds=0x4237E4 status=D000 pak_size=0
06 pak=0x41AB98 ds=0x41ACF4 status=D000 pak_size=0
07 pak=0x41A400 ds=0x41A55C status=F000 pak_size=0
TX ring with 4 entries at 0x2101440: tx_count = 0,
  tx_head = 0, tx_tail = 0
00 pak=0x000000 ds=0x000000 status=5C00 pak_size=0
01 pak=0x000000 ds=0x000000 status=5C00 pak_size=0
02 pak=0x000000 ds=0x000000 status=5C00 pak_size=0
03 pak=0x000000 ds=0x000000 status=7C00 pak_size=0
0 missed datagrams, 0 overruns, 0 bad frame addresses
0 bad datagram encapsulations, 0 memory errors
0 transmitter underruns
B2 Chan Info:
Layer 1 is ACTIVATED
idb 0x324520, ds 0x3269B8, reset_mask 0x2
buffer size 1524
```

```
RX ring with 8 entries at 0x2101500 : Rxhead 0
00 pak=0x40FCF0 ds=0x40FE4C status=D000 pak_size=0
01 pak=0x40E628 ds=0x40E784 status=D000 pak_size=0
02 pak=0x40F558 ds=0x40F6B4 status=D000 pak_size=0
03 pak=0x413218 ds=0x413374 status=D000 pak_size=0
04 pak=0x40EDC0 ds=0x40EF1C status=D000 pak_size=0
05 pak=0x4113B8 ds=0x411514 status=D000 pak_size=0
06 pak=0x416ED8 ds=0x417034 status=D000 pak_size=0
07 pak=0x416740 ds=0x41689C status=F000 pak_size=0
TX ring with 4 entries at 0x2101540: tx_count = 0,
   tx_head = 0, tx_tail = 0
00 pak=0x000000 ds=0x000000 status=5C00 pak_size=0
01 pak=0x000000 ds=0x000000 status=5C00 pak_size=0
02 pak=0x000000 ds=0x000000 status=5C00 pak_size=0
03 pak=0x000000 ds=0x000000 status=7C00 pak_size=0
0 missed datagrams, 0 overruns, 0 bad frame addresses
0 bad datagram encapsulations, 0 memory errors
0 transmitter underruns
```

Note: Both B channels and the D channel are active.

Use the **show interface bri** command to display BRI status, encapsulation, and counter information. Listing 12.4 displays an example of the **show interface** command.

Listing 12.4   The **show interface bri** command output.

```
RouterA# show interface bri 0
BRI0 is up, line protocol is up (spoofing)
Hardware is BRI
Internet address is 172.16.67.1, subnet mask is 255.255.255.0
MTU 1500 bytes, BW 64 Kbit, DLY 20000 usec,
rely 255/255, load 1/255
Encapsulation PPP, loopback not set, keepalive set (10 sec)
Last input 0:00:07, output 0:00:00, output hang never
Output queue 0/40, 0 drops; input queue 0/75, 0 drops
Five minute input rate 0 bits/sec, 0 packets/sec
Five minute output rate 0 bits/sec, 0 packets/sec
16263 packets input, 1347238 bytes, 0 no buffer
Received 13983 broadcasts, 0 runts, 0 giants
2 input errors, 0 CRC, 0 frame, 0 overrun, 0 ignored, 2 abort
22146 packets output, 2383680 bytes, 0 underruns
0 output errors, 0 collisions, 2 interface resets, 0 restarts
1 carrier transitions
```

Note: The encapsulation type is PPP, and two errors were received on the BRI.

Use the **show dialer bri** command to display general diagnostic information for serial interfaces configured to support DDR. Listing 12.5 displays an example of the **show dialer** command.

Listing 12.5   The show dialer bri command output.

```
RouterA# show dialer interface bri 0
BRIO - dialer type = IN-BAND NO-PARITY
Idle timer (900 secs), Fast idle timer (20 secs)
Wait for carrier (30 secs), Re-enable (15 secs)
Time until disconnect 838 secs
Current call connected 0:02:16
Connected to 8986
```

Dial String	Successes	Failures	Last called	Last status	
8986	0	0	never		Default
8986	8	3	0:02:16	Success	Default

Note: "IN-BAND" indicates that DDR is enabled and the router is currently connected. The Dial String table provides a history of logged calls.

Frame Relay

Frame Relay is a high-speed, packet-switching WAN protocol. Packet-switching protocols enable devices to share the available network bandwidth. As its name implies, Frame Relay operates at layer 2 of the Open Systems Interconnection (OSI) model and runs on nearly any type of serial interface. Frame Relay encapsulates packets from the upper layers of the OSI model and switches them through the provider's network. Figure 12.10 provides a quick comparison of Frame Relay and the OSI model.

Frame Relay services have been streamlined to gain more throughput. Services such as flow control, robust congestion management, and error checking are left to upper-layer protocols such as Transmission Control Protocol (TCP); however, Frame Relay does include some error checking and congestion management.

Frame Relay uses cyclic redundancy checking (CRC) to perform error checking quickly. CRC produces a frame check sequence (FCS), which is appended to each frame that is transmitted. When a node receives the frame, it calculates a new FCS (based on the data portion of the frame) and compares it with the one contained in the frame. If the values are different, the frame is dropped.

Frame Relay manages congestion through the use of a discard eligibility bit. This bit is set to a value of 1 if the frame has lower importance than other frames; the DTE device is responsible for setting the bit and sets the bit to 1 for frames that have lower importance than other frames. Switches within the WAN provider's

OSI Reference Model	Frame Relay
Application	o
Presentation	o
Session	o
Transport	o
Network	o
Data Link	Frame Relay
Physical	Physical

Figure 12.10 The OSI reference model and Frame Relay.

network may discard frames to manage congestion. However, the switches only discard frames with the discard eligibility bit set to 1; frames with bits set to 0 are still transmitted. This feature protects against critical data being dropped during periods of network congestion.

Virtual Circuits

Communication in a Frame Relay network is connection oriented, and a defined communication path must exist between each pair of DTE devices. Virtual circuits provide the bidirectional communication within Frame Relay networks. In essence, a virtual circuit is a logical connection established between two DTE devices. Many virtual circuits can be multiplexed into one physical circuit, and a single virtual circuit can cross multiple DCE devices within the Frame Relay network.

Virtual circuits can be grouped into two categories: switched virtual circuits (SVCs) and permanent virtual circuits (PVCs). SVCs are temporary connections and can be used when only sporadic data communication is necessary between DTE devices. SVCs require the connection to be set up and terminated for each session. Conversely, PVCs are permanent connections. They support frequent and consistent data communications across a Frame Relay network. When the PVC is established, DTE devices can begin transmitting data when they are ready. PVCs are used more widely in Frame Relay networks than SVCs.

DLCI

A data link connection identifier (DLCI) serves as the addressing scheme within a Frame Relay network. The service provider assigns a DLCI for each PVC, and the DLCI is locally significant within the network. In other words, the DLCI must be unique within the network like an Internet Protocol (IP) address. Two DTE devices that have a PVC established between them may or may not use the same DLCI value. Figure 12.11 illustrates how PVCs and DLCIs appear within a Frame Relay network. Table 12.9 clarifies how each router maps its ports to DLCI numbers.

Two methods can be used to map a DLCI to a Network layer address (such as an IP address)—dynamically via inverse ARP or manually using the **map** command. Both methods are discussed in the "Configuring Frame Relay" section.

LMI

Local Management Interface (LMI) is a set of enhancements to the Frame Relay protocol specifications. Developed in 1990 by four companies (nicknamed the

Table 12.9 DLCI mapping.		
From Router	**To Router**	**Use DLCI**
A	B	111
A	C	222
B	A	333
C	A	444

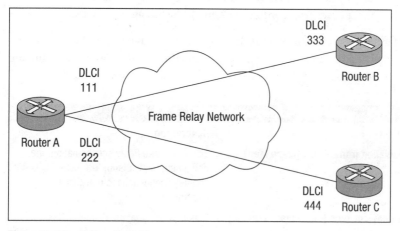

Figure 12.11 PVCs with DLCIs.

"Gang of Four"), LMI extensions offer several features for better management of complex Frame Relay networks. These extensions include global addressing, virtual circuit status messaging, and multicasting.

Note: The "Gang of Four" includes Cisco Systems, StrataCom, Northern Telecom, and Digital Equipment Corporation.

The LMI global addressing extension enables a DLCI to have global instead of local significance. With LMI, DLCI values are unique within a Frame Relay network, and standard address resolution protocols, such as Address Resolution Protocol (ARP) and reverse ARP (or inverse ARP), and discovery protocols can be used to identify nodes within the network. Virtual circuit status messaging improves the communication and synchronization between DTE and DCE devices. The status messages, which are similar to hello packets, report on the status of PVCs. LMI multicasting enables multicast groups to be assigned. Multicasting reduces overhead by allowing route updates and address resolution messages to be sent to specific groups of DTE devices.

Cisco supports the following Frame Relay LMI protocol variations:

➤ *ANSI*—American National Standards Institute

➤ *q933a*—International Telecommunication Union–Telecommunication standardization sector

➤ *cisco*—Gang of Four

Configuring Frame Relay

Configuring a Cisco router to serve as a DTE device within a Frame Relay network involves configuring interfaces on the router. Table 12.10 lists the commands you must execute to configure Frame Relay on an interface.

In configurations where inverse ARP is not used to dynamically discover network protocol addresses on the virtual circuit, the **frame-relay map** command must be used to map the layer 3 protocol address to the layer 2 DLCI.

Table 12.10 Frame Relay basic configuration.	
Command	**Description**
encapsulation frame-relay [cisco I ietf]	Enables Frame Relay encapsulation; the default setting is **cisco**; **ietf** (see RFC 1490) enables connections to non-Cisco equipment.
frame-relay lmi-type [ansi I cisco I q933a]	Sets the LMI type; the default setting is **cisco**.

Configure the **frame-relay map** command as follows:

```
Frame-relay map protocol protocol-address dlci [broadcast]
[cisco | ietf]
```

In this example, *protocol* is a supported protocol, such as IP or IPX, *protocol-address* is the destination protocol address, and *dlci* is the DLCI number used to connect to the specified protocol address on the interface. Also, **broadcast** (optional) forwards broadcasts to this address (although this is optional, it's usually a good idea to include it), and **ietf** (optional) uses the Internet Engineering Task Force (IETF) form of Frame Relay encapsulation (use this parameter when the router or access server is connected to another vendor's equipment across a Frame Relay network). Finally, **cisco** (optional) is the Cisco encapsulation method.

Nonbroadcast Multiaccess

Because Frame Relay connections are established by direct PVCs, Frame Relay cannot support broadcast transmissions. If broadcast services are required, a router must copy the broadcast and then transmit it on each of its PVCs. The term that describes this behavior is *nonbroadcast multiaccess (NBMA)*. NBMA simply describes any multiaccess layer 2 protocol that does not provide a mechanism for broadcasting messages (such as route updates between routers). For broadcast messages to be communicated in an NBMA network, each router within the network serves as a peer and is part of the same subnet. In a Frame Relay network, broadcast messages must be duplicated and then sent out each PVC to each peer.

Subinterfaces

A single, physical serial interface can be configured with several virtual interfaces called *subinterfaces*. These subinterfaces can be configured on a serial line; different information is sent and received on each serial subinterface. Using subinterfaces, a single router can support PVCs to several other routers. Figure 12.12 depicts a simple Frame Relay network with subinterfaces.

Before configuring a subinterface for a Frame Relay network, the Frame Relay configuration on the physical interface must be complete. Execute the following command to create a subinterface and assign it a DLCI value:

```
Interface type .subinterface point-to-point
Frame-relay interface-dlci dlci [broadcast]
```

In this command, *type* is the physical serial interface number, *subinterface* is the subinterface number, *dlci* is the DLCI number used to connect to the specified protocol address on the interface, and *broadcast* (optional) forwards broadcasts to this address.

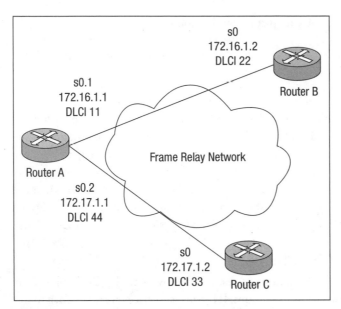

Figure 12.12   Frame Relay network with subinterfaces.

 The proper syntax for creating and accessing a subinterface is the interface number followed by a period (.) followed by the subinterface number. For example, **serial 0.11** indicates subinterface 11 on serial interface 0.

 A common practice in choosing subinterface numbers is to use the same number as the DLCI value.

Monitoring Frame Relay

After the Frame Relay configuration is complete, you can use the **show interface** and **debug frame-relay** commands to monitor and troubleshoot the configuration. Listing 12.6 shows the output from the **show interface** command.

Listing 12.6   The **show interface** command output.

```
Router# show interface serial 0
  Serial0 is up, line protocol is up
  Hardware is MCI Serial
```

```
Internet address is 172.59.1.1,
  subnet mask is 255.255.255.252
MTU 1500 bytes, BW 1544 Kbit, DLY 20000 usec, rely 249/255,
  load 1/255
Encapsulation FRAME-RELAY, loopback not set,
  keepalive set (10 sec)
LMI enq sent   4, LMI stat recvd 0, LMI upd recvd 0,
  DTE LMI UP
LMI enq recvd 268, LMI stat sent   264, LMI upd sent   0
LMI DLCI 1023  LMI type is CISCO  frame relay DTE
Last input 0:00:09, output 0:00:07, output hang never
Last clearing of "show interface" counters 0:44:57
Output queue 0/40, 0 drops; input queue 0/75, 0 drops
Five minute input rate 0 bits/sec, 0 packets/sec
Five minute output rate 0 bits/sec, 0 packets/sec
    309 packets input, 6641 bytes, 0 no buffer
    Received 0 broadcasts, 0 runts, 0 giants
    0 input errors, 0 CRC, 0 frame, 0 overrun,
    0 ignored, 0 abort
    0 input packets with dribble condition detected
    268 packets output, 3836 bytes, 0 underruns
    0 output errors, 0 collisions, 2 interface resets,
    0 restarts
    180 carrier transitions
```

Note: The encapsulation type, DLCI, LMI type, and router status as DTE are displayed.

Use the **show frame-relay pvc** command to display the status of the virtual circuit:

```
RouterA#show frame-relay pvc

PVC Statistics for interface Serial0 (Frame Relay DTE)

DLCI = 222, DLCI USAGE = LOCAL, PVC STATUS = ACTIVE,INTERFACE =
Serial0

  input pkts 50          output pkts 20         in bytes 11431
  out bytes 1474         dropped pkts 2         in FECN pkts 0
  in BECN pkts 0         out FECN pkts 0        out BECN pkts 0
  in DE pkts 0           out DE pkts 0
  pvc create time 04:14:12, last time pvc status changed 00:39:06
RouterA#
```

Note: No packets have had their discard eligibility bits set.

Use the **show frame-relay lmi** command to determine whether LMI is being transmitted successfully:

```
RouterA#show frame-relay lmi

LMI Statistics for interface Serial0
(Frame Relay DTE) LMI TYPE = CISCO
  Invalid Unnumbered info 0          Invalid Prot Disc 0
  Invalid dummy Call Ref 0           Invalid Msg Type 0
  Invalid Status Message 0           Invalid Lock Shift 0
  Invalid Information ID 0            Invalid Report IE Len 0
  Invalid Report Request 0           Invalid Keep IE Len 0
  Num Status Enq. Sent 292           Num Status msgs Rcvd 292
  Num Update Status Rcvd 0           Num Status Timeouts 0
RouterA#
```

Note: No LMI status messages have been lost.

Use the **show frame-relay map** command to display mappings among protocol, protocol address, and DLCI:

```
RouterA#show frame-relay map
Serial0 (up): ip 172.59.1.1 dlci 222(0xDE,0x34E0), dynamic,
              broadcast, status defined, active
RouterA#
```

Note: IP address 172.59.1.1 is mapped to DLCI 222, and the PVC is active.

The **debug frame-relay** command enables you to monitor the Frame Relay activity closely. The **debug frame-relay lmi** command enables you to monitor LMI activity on a router closely. Listing 12.7 shows sample output from the **debug frame-relay lmi** command.

Listing 12.7   The **debug frame-relay lmi** command.

```
RouterA#debug frame-relay lmi
Frame Relay LMI debugging is on

RouterA#
Serial0(out): StEnq, myseq 20, yourseen 67, DTE up
 datagramstart = 0x23A3820, datagramsize = 13

 FR encap = 0xFCF10309
00 75 01 01 01 03 02 14 43

Serial0(in): Status, myseq 20
RT IE 1, length 1, type 1
```

```
KA IE 3, length 2, yourseq 68, myseq 20
RouterA#
Serial0(out): StEnq, myseq 21, yourseen 68, DTE up
 datagramstart = 0x23A3820, datagramsize = 13
```

*Note: The sequence counters for the LMI transmission are being increased properly. Enabling a single **debug** command on a router does not use much of the router's system resources; however, enabling several **debug** commands may severely affect the router's ability to perform its functions. The **no debug all** command quickly disables all debug commands on a router.*

Practice Questions

Question 1

Which of the following commands allows you to monitor a PPP authentication sequence on interface serial 0?

○ a. **sh ppp**

○ b. **sh ppp s0**

○ c. **debug ppp authentication s0**

○ d. **debug ppp authentication**

The correct answer is d. The command **debug ppp authentication** displays the authentication handshake sequence as it is occurring. Answers a, b, and c are incorrect because they are all invalid commands.

Question 2

Which protocol is responsible for establishing, configuring, testing, maintaining, and terminating PPP connections?

○ a. BRI

○ b. PRI

○ c. LCP

○ d. NCP

The correct answer is c. LCP has the primary responsibility for a PPP connection. Answers a and b are incorrect because BRI and PRI are not components within PPP. Answer d is incorrect because NCP is responsible for the configuration supporting Network layer protocols.

Question 3

Which of the following is an authentication type that would be appropriate for an environment that requires strong encrypted passwords?

○ a. PAP

○ b. CHAP

○ c. LCP

○ d. NCP

The correct answer is b. CHAP uses encrypted passwords, making it a much stronger protocol than PAP. Answer a is incorrect because PAP uses clear text to send passwords. Answers c and d are incorrect because neither is an authentication type.

Question 4

Which of the following physical interfaces will PPP operate on?

○ a. Asynchronous serial

○ b. Synchronous serial

○ c. HSSI

○ d. ISDN

○ e. All of the above

The correct answer is e. PPP can operate on a variety of DTE/DCE physical interfaces, including asynchronous serial, synchronous serial, HSSI, and ISDN.

Question 5

Which PPP authentication protocol uses a three-way handshake?

○ a. PAP

○ b. CHAP

○ c. LCP

○ d. NCP1

The correct answer is b. The CHAP three-way handshake includes the local host requesting authentication, the remote host sending an encrypted response, and the local host comparing the received information and then accepting or rejecting the connection. PAP only uses a two-way handshake. Therefore, answer a is incorrect. LCP and NCP1 are not authentication protocols. Therefore, answers c and d are incorrect.

Question 6

If your router does not have a built-in BRI, which devices will you need to connect to ISDN services? [Choose the two best answers]

❑ a. NT1

❑ b. TA

❑ c. TE1

❑ d. TE2

The correct answers are a and b. You need a TA to convert the serial signal from your router into a BRI signal, and you need an NT1 to convert the BRI signal for use by the ISDN digital line. A TE1 is a device that *has* a built-in BRI and already transmits BRI signals. Therefore, answer c is incorrect. Answer d is incorrect because a device that does *not* have a built-in BRI is considered a TE2.

Question 7

How can you use ISDN? [Choose all that apply]

❑ a. To improve Internet response times

❑ b. To encapsulate other WAN services

❑ c. To add bandwidth for telecommuting

❑ d. To carry multiple Network-layer protocols

The correct answers are a, b, c, and d.

Question 8

What commands should you use to monitor ISDN or DDR activity? [Choose the three best answers]

- ❏ a. **show interfaces**
- ❏ b. **show controllers**
- ❏ c. **show dialer**
- ❏ d. **show bri**

The correct answers are a, b, and c. The **show interfaces** command displays status and statistics for each interface on the router, including BRI. The **show controllers** command displays detailed information about BRI channels. The **show dialer** command presents information about current dialer activity and simple call history. Answer d is incorrect because the **show bri** command is invalid.

Question 9

According to ITU-T standards for ISDN protocols, which series of standards deals with switching and signaling?

- ◯ a. A-series
- ◯ b. E-series
- ◯ c. R-series
- ◯ d. Q-series

The correct answer is d. The Q-series standards address switching and signaling topics. Answers a and c are incorrect because A-series and R-series do not exist for ISDN. Although E-series is a valid grouping of standards, it addresses telephone network and ISDN topics. Therefore, answer b is incorrect.

Question 10

What is the correct command to define all IPX traffic as "uninteresting" for dialer group 7?

- ○ a. **dialer-group 7 no ipx**
- ○ b. **dialer-group 7 no ipx all**
- ○ c. **dialer-group 7 protocol no ipx**
- ○ d. **dialer-group 7 protocol ipx deny**

The correct answer is d. The syntax for the **dialer-group** command requires a dialer group, the keyword "protocol", the protocol you want to define (IP, IPX, AppleTalk, and so on), and the keyword "permit" or "deny" to indicate whether the protocol should be permitted or denied. Answers a, b, and c are incorrect because they each generate syntax error messages.

Question 11

Which of the following commands will display Frame Relay information about serial interface 0?

- ○ a. **sh frame-relay s0**
- ○ b. **sh frame-relay interface s0**
- ○ c. **sh interface s0**
- ○ d. **sh ip interface brief**

The correct answer is c. The **sh interface s0** command displays the configuration and statistics for the serial 0 interface on the router. The **sh frame-relay s0** and **sh frame-relay interface s0** commands are invalid, so answers a and b are incorrect. The **sh ip interface brief** command displays IP addressing and status information for all interfaces, so answer d is incorrect.

Question 12

Frame Relay operates at which layer of the OSI model?

○ a. Transport

○ b. Network

○ c. Data Link

○ d. Physical

The correct answer is c. Frame Relay operates at the Data Link layer. Answers a and b are incorrect because Frame Relay does not include any specifications for layer 4 (Transport) or layer 3 (Network). Although Frame Relay can operate on several different physical media, it does not include specifications for layer 1 (Physical). Therefore, answer d is incorrect.

Question 13

Which of the following devices can serve as a DTE device? [Choose the two best answers]

❏ a. Router

❏ b. Terminal

❏ c. Modem

❏ d. CSU

The correct answers are a and b. Routers and terminals can be configured to act as DTE devices. Modems and CSUs cannot be configured as DTE devices, but they can be configured as DCE devices. Therefore, answers c and d are incorrect.

Question 14

> Which of the following are common WAN services supported by Cisco? [Choose the five best answers]
>
> ❑ a. ISDN
>
> ❑ b. Frame Relay
>
> ❑ c. PPP
>
> ❑ d. BGP
>
> ❑ e. HDLC
>
> ❑ f. SDLC

The correct answers are a, b, c, e, and f. ISDN, Frame Relay, PPP, HDLC, and SDLC are all WAN services supported by Cisco equipment. Although BGP is supported by Cisco equipment, it is an exterior routing protocol. Therefore, answer d is incorrect.

Question 15

> Which of the following can be used to establish bidirectional communication between two DTE devices? [Choose the two best answers]
>
> ❑ a. CVC
>
> ❑ b. DVC
>
> ❑ c. PVC
>
> ❑ d. SVC

The correct answers are c and d. A permanent virtual circuit (PVC) remains established between two DTE devices, even when data is not being transmitted. A switched virtual circuit (SVC) is established only when two DTE devices need to transmit data; it is disconnected when the transmission is over. CVC and DVC are not related to virtual circuits between DTE devices. Therefore, answers a and b are incorrect.

Question 16

Which of the following serves as the addressing scheme within a Frame Relay network?

○ a. DLCI

○ b. LMI

○ c. NBMA

○ d. SVC

The correct answer is a. A DLCI number serves as the addressing scheme and is assigned to each PVC. LMI provides several enhancements to Frame Relay specifications. Therefore, answer b is incorrect. Answer c is incorrect because NBMA describes how a router must send broadcasts within a Frame Relay network. An SVC is established to enable DTE to communicate. Therefore, answer d is incorrect.

Question 17

Cisco supports which of the following Frame Relay LMI protocol variations? [Choose the three best answers]

❑ a. IETF

❑ b. ANSI

❑ c. Q933A

❑ d. Cisco

The correct answers are b, c, and d. Cisco supports LMI extensions from American National Standards Institute (ANSI), International Telecommunication Union–Telecommunication standardization sector (Q933A), and Cisco's "Gang of Four." Answer a is incorrect because IETF is a type of frame encapsulation supported by Cisco that enables Cisco devices to communicate with non-Cisco devices across a Frame Relay network.

Question 18

Frame Relay uses what mechanism to perform error checking?

- ○ a. CRC
- ○ b. LMI
- ○ c. TA/NT1
- ○ d. Inverse ARP

The correct answer is a. Frame Relay uses CRC to derive the FCS, which is a calculated value based on the data portion of each frame. If a device calculates an FCS value that is different from the FCS value it receives, the frame is dropped. LMI is communicated between DTE and DCE devices and contains the status of the virtual circuit. Therefore, answer b is incorrect. Answer c is incorrect because a TA/NT1 is a DCE device and has nothing to do with error checking. Answer d is incorrect because inverse ARP is the method by which DTE devices discover layer 3 protocol address information about each other.

Question 19

DCE devices provide which of the following functions?

- ○ a. Provides a clock to the DTE
- ○ b. Converts data into a suitable format
- ○ c. Switches data across the provider's network
- ○ d. All of the above

The correct answer is d. Answers a, b, and c are all functions of DCE devices.

Question 20

Which of the following commands allow you to closely monitor Frame Relay activity? [Choose the two best answers]

- ❑ a. **debug frame-relay lmi**
- ❑ b. **debug frame-relay activity**
- ❑ c. **debug frame-relay all**
- ❑ d. **debug frame-relay verbose**

The correct answers are a and d. The **debug frame-relay lmi** command monitors link information between the DCE and DTE devices. The **debug frame-relay verbose** command displays detailed information. Answers b and c are incorrect because the commands are not valid.

Need to Know More?

 Downes, Kevin, Merilee Ford, H. Kim Lew, Steve Spanier, and Tim Stevenson. *Internetworking Technologies Handbook, 2nd Edition*. Macmillan Computer Publishing. Indianapolis, IN, 1998. ISBN 1-57870-102-3. Chapters 12 and 13 present more information about PPP.

 McNutt, Shawn, Mark Poplar, Jason Waters, and David Stabenaw. *CCNA Routing and Switching Exam Prep*. The Coriolis Group. Scottsdale, AZ, 2000. ISBN 1-57610-440-0. This book is a great complement to the *CCNA Exam Cram* book. Chapters 12 and 13 contain information on PPP.

 Reed, Kenneth. *Data Network Handbook*. Van Nostrand Reinhold Publishing. New York, 1996. ISBN 0-442-02299-9. Chapter 11 provides more information about voice and data telecommunications.

 Syngress Media, with Richard D. Hornbaker, CCIE. *Cisco Certified Network Associate Study Guide*. Osborne/McGraw-Hill. Berkeley, CA, 1998. ISBN 0-07-882487-7. Chapter 10 addresses wide area networking.

 Using Cisco's documentation CD-ROM, you can immediately access Cisco's entire library of end-user documentation, selected product news, bug databases, and related information. The documentation CD-ROM is produced monthly.

 www.cisco.com, the official Cisco Web site, contains several Cisco white papers on topics such as PPP configuration and troubleshooting.

 www.cis.ohio-state.edu/hypertext/information/rfc.html, the Computer and Information Science Web site at Ohio State University, provides information about Internet RFC documents. You can review detailed information on PPP in RFCs 1661, 1331, and 2153.

Sample Test

Question 1

What are the primary purposes of the OSI model's Network layer? [Choose the two best answers]

- ❏ a. Path determination
- ❏ b. Code formatting
- ❏ c. Flow control
- ❏ d. Packet switching
- ❏ e. Error notification

Question 2

Which router commands, if executed from the global configuration prompt, will enable RIP routing for network 172.23.0.0?

- ○ a. **router rip 13** and **network 172.23.0.0**
- ○ b. **router rip all**
- ○ c. **router rip** and **network 172.23.0.0**
- ○ d. **network 172.23.0.0**

Question 3

Which of the following are performed at the Data Link layer of the OSI model? [Choose the three best answers]

- ❑ a. Error notification
- ❑ b. Packet switching
- ❑ c. Physical addressing
- ❑ d. Establishing, maintaining, and terminating sessions
- ❑ e. Frame sequencing

Question 4

Which of the following are examples of LAN protocols? [Choose the three best answers]

- ❑ a. Frame Relay
- ❑ b. Token ring
- ❑ c. Ethernet
- ❑ d. FDDI
- ❑ e. ISDN

Question 5

What is the vendor code of the following address?

```
BBD1.4822.53AA
```

- ○ a. BBD148
- ○ b. 2253AA
- ○ c. BBD1
- ○ d. 53AA
- ○ e. 4822

Question 6

Which two answers are characteristics of connection-oriented communication? [Choose the two best answers]

❑ a. Setup and maintenance procedures are performed to ensure delivery of messages.

❑ b. A physical circuit exists between the two communicating devices.

❑ c. It is a best-effort type of communication.

❑ d. A virtual connection exists between the two devices.

Question 7

Which of the following are examples of layer 3 addressing? [Choose the two best answers]

❑ a. 172.29.5.12

❑ b. CB255467.3000.B433.A232

❑ c. 0000.B333.A232

❑ d. A4XX

Question 8

If you want to view the currently executing configuration file, which of the following commands should you use?

○ a. **show startup-config**

○ b. **show running-config**

○ c. **configure terminal**

○ d. **configure memory**

Question 9

What command would be used to back up a running configuration file?

○ a. **router#copy tftp running-config**

○ b. **router>copy tftp running-config**

○ c. **router#copy running-config tftp**

○ d. **router>copy tftp running**

Question 10

Which of the following commands would set an "enable secret" password on a Cisco router?

- ○ a. **router#enable secret** *password*
- ○ b. **router(config-line)#password phoenix**
- ○ c. **router(config)#enable secret** *password*
- ○ d. **router(config)#enable password**

Question 11

Which of the following commands would create a text description on an interface of a router?

- ○ a. **router#description** I am going to pass the CCNA exam
- ○ b. **router(config)#description** I am going to pass the CCNA exam
- ○ c. **router(config-line)description** I am going to pass the CCNA exam
- ○ d. **router(config-if)#description** I am going to pass the CCNA exam

Question 12

What are methods used to map a Frame Relay virtual circuit's DLCI to a destination Network layer address such as an IP address? [Choose the two best answers]

- ❏ a. CIR
- ❏ b. Inverse ARP
- ❏ c. Manually
- ❏ d. LMI
- ❏ e. PVC

Question 13

Which of the following are advantages of using the ISDN BRI service? [Choose the three best answers]

❑ a. The ability to simultaneously carry voice and data.

❑ b. It offers faster call setup as opposed to modem connections.

❑ c. It creates a permanent virtual circuit between two networks.

❑ d. It provides a dedicated, full-time connection to the Internet.

❑ e. It provides end-to-end digital service.

Question 14

Which of the following services is used to copy files between Cisco routers?

○ a. SMTP

○ b. SNMP

○ c. TFTP

○ d. RARP

○ e. HTTP

Question 15

Which of the following are characteristics of TCP? [Choose the three best answers]

❑ a. Performs error and duplication checking

❑ b. Performs acknowledgment windowing to increase efficiency of bandwidth use

❑ c. Initiates a three-way handshake

❑ d. Provides logical addressing

Question 16

What is the function performed by Address Resolution Protocol (ARP)?

- ○ a. Maps a known physical address to a logical address
- ○ b. Maps a known logical address to a physical address
- ○ c. Communicates error messages and control messages between devices
- ○ d. Obtains physical and logical addresses from a TFTP server

Question 17

Which best describes the process of connection-oriented services?

- ○ a. Repackaging data for transmission on a different physical network.
- ○ b. Flow control/sequencing/data transfer.
- ○ c. A data link is permanently established.
- ○ d. Connection establishment/data transfer/connection termination.

Question 18

Which of the following functions do both UDP and TCP perform? [Choose the two best answers]

- ❏ a. They provide destination and source port numbers.
- ❏ b. They initiate a three-way handshake.
- ❏ c. They allocate dynamic datagram size.
- ❏ d. They perform checksums.
- ❏ e. They acknowledge datagram receipt.

Question 19

The following IP address is listed in decimal format:

```
172.16.8.8
```

What is the corresponding binary value of this IP address?

- ○ a. 10101100.00010000.00001000.00001000
- ○ b. 10101100.00100000.11100000.00000100
- ○ c. 10101100.00010000.00000010.00000111
- ○ d. 11001100.00001111.00011001.00001000

Question 20

Given the Ethernet specification 100BaseFL, what do each of the following parts mean: 100, Base, and FL?

- ○ a. LAN speed, signaling method, and media type
- ○ b. LAN speed, media type, and signaling method
- ○ c. LAN speed, topology, and media type
- ○ d. LAN speed, signaling method, and topology

Question 21

Which of the following addresses are Class C addresses? [Choose the two best answers]

- ❑ a. 221.15.130.254
- ❑ b. 10100000.11000000.11111111.11110000
- ❑ c. 11010001.11001100.10101010.00001111
- ❑ d. 127.0.0.0

Question 22

Encapsulation, or *tunneling*, can be described as which of the following?

- ○ a. Taking frames from one network system and placing them inside frames from another network system
- ○ b. Stripping data off of a packet as it moves up the protocol stack
- ○ c. Creating a stream of ones and zeros for transmission across a physical wire
- ○ d. The exchange of route summary messages between routers

Question 23

With an IP address and subnet mask of 172.10.10.4 255.255.255.128, what is the full range of IP addresses in this subnet?

- ○ a. 172.10.10.1 through 172.10.10.254
- ○ b. 172.10.10.129 through 172.10.10.254
- ○ c. 172.10.10.0 through 172.10.10.127
- ○ d. 172.10.10.1 through 172.10.10.12

Question 24

With an IP address and subnet mask of 172.10.10.4 255.255.255.128, what is the number of possible subnets?

- ○ a. 510
- ○ b. 254
- ○ c. 1,024
- ○ d. 14
- ○ e. 4,094

Question 25

Which of the following commands identifies an IP standard access list?

○ a. **ip access-group 400 out**

○ b. **ip access-group 11 out**

○ c. **ip access-group 145 out**

○ d. **ip access-group 105 out**

○ e. **ipx access-group 805 in**

Question 26

If you are extremely security conscious, which PPP authentication protocol should you implement?

○ a. CHAP

○ b. DDR

○ c. PAP

Question 27

Which of the following cannot be used to permit or deny traffic with IP extended access lists?

○ a. TCP port number

○ b. Destination IP address

○ c. IP sequence number

○ d. Source IP address

Question 28

What is the valid range for an IPX extended access list?

○ a. 0 through 99

○ b. 100 through 199

○ c. 800 through 899

○ d. 900 through 999

Question 29

Which of the following commands can be used to show access lists? [Choose the three best answers]

- ❑ a. **show ip interfaces**
- ❑ b. **show ipx interfaces**
- ❑ c. **show access-lists**
- ❑ d. **show access lists**

Question 30

Which of the following are disadvantages of using a bridge to segment a LAN? [Choose the two best answers]

- ❑ a. It increases the latency period to forward frames by 20 percent.
- ❑ b. A bridge logically segments a LAN and, therefore, isolates nonlocal devices from local traffic.
- ❑ c. A bridge can extend the physical distance of a LAN by amplifying the electrical signal of the physical media.
- ❑ d. It introduces the possibility of bridging loops.

Question 31

What is maintained in a bridge's forwarding table?

- ○ a. A device's IP address and the IP network on which the device resides
- ○ b. A device's MAC address and the physical segment on which the device resides
- ○ c. A device's MAC address and the next physical segment to forward a frame to while in route to the physical segment on which the device resides
- ○ d. The IP network and the MAC address of devices

Question 32

What is the name of the protocol used to pass VLAN information between switches?

○ a. Switching

○ b. ISL

○ c. Frame tagging

○ d. Spanning tree

Question 33

Which of the following are disadvantages of routing in comparison with bridging and switching? [Choose the two best answers]

❑ a. Routing provides the functionality to allow complex networks with dissimilar technologies to be connected.

❑ b. Increased latency.

❑ c. Reduced security.

❑ d. Increased complexity.

Question 34

Frame tagging is used to tag a frame with a unique VLAN ID between switches.

○ a. True

○ b. False

Question 35

Which of the following switching methods provides error-checking capabilities?

○ a. Store-and-forward switching

○ b. Frame-tag switching

○ c. Cut-through switching

○ d. ISL switching

Question 36

You have connected six PCs to a Fast Ethernet switch. Each PC is plugged into a single switch port. All PCs are equipped with 10/100 NICs. How much bandwidth is available to each PC?

○ a. 16.6Mbps

○ b. 0.6Mbps

○ c. 100Mbps

○ d. 10Mbps

Question 37

Which of the following are not services provided by the Transport layer? [Choose the three best answers]

❑ a. Establishing a session

❑ b. Ensuring that the segment sent is error-free

❑ c. Ending a session

❑ d. Keeping the sending and receiving station from sending segments at the same time

Question 38

Which of the following addresses represents a Class D IP address that is used for multicast applications?

○ a. 255.255.0.0

○ b. 10.1.1.0

○ c. 224.0.1.1

○ d. 192.0.0.255

Question 39

Which PPP authentication protocol uses a two-way handshake?

○ a. PAP

○ b. CHAP

○ c. LCP

○ d. NCP

Question 40

How do devices on different VLANs communicate?

○ a. Through a layer 2 switch

○ b. Through a bridge

○ c. Through a router

○ d. Through a layer 2 switch with properly configured access lists

○ e. Through a switch that supports ISL

Question 41

Which of the following commands will display Frame Relay information about serial interface 1?

○ a. **sh frame-relay s1**

○ b. **sh frame-relay interface s1**

○ c. **sh interface s1**

○ d. **sh ip interface brief**

Question 42

Given the following output from the **show interface** command, what can you assume about this interface?

```
Ethernet0 is administratively down, line protocol
        is down
```

○ a. Ethernet0 is operational.

○ b. Ethernet0 is not plugged into the network.

○ c. There is a hardware problem with the Ethernet0 interface.

○ d. Ethernet0 has been disabled or shut down.

Question 43

Frame Relay operates primarily at which layers of the OSI model?

○ a. Transport and Network

○ b. Network and Data Link

○ c. Data Link and Physical

Question 44

What key or keys would you press to complete a partially entered command?

○ a. Ctrl+E

○ b. Tab

○ c. Shift+right arrow

○ d. Ctrl+A

○ e. Up arrow

Question 45

Which of the following is an interior routing protocol? [Choose the three best answers]

❑ a. RIP

❑ b. IGRP

❑ c. OSPF

❑ d. BGP

Question 46

Which of the following is a valid IPX address for network 4d?

○ a. 4d80.c747.b122

○ b. 4d.0080.c747.b122

○ c. 4d.172.16.101.123

○ d. 4d

Question 47

Which command, when executed successfully, verifies that two routers are routing packets between each other successfully? [Choose the three best answers]

❑ a. **ping**

❑ b. **show interface**

❑ c. **trace**

❑ d. **telnet**

Question 48

To enable IPX, what is the first IPX configuration command that must be executed on a router?

○ a. **ipx routing**

○ b. **ipx protocol**

○ c. **ipx interface**

○ d. **ipx network**

Question 49

What was the primary purpose for the creation of the OSI model?

- ○ a. So that mainframe networks could interoperate with newer cllent/server networks
- ○ b. To help computer vendors create interoperable network equipment
- ○ c. As a learning tool for people who were new to network engineering
- ○ d. To reduce the burden on software programmers

Question 50

How are collisions handled by Fast Ethernet when running in full-duplex mode?

- ○ a. When a collision is detected, data is retransmitted after a random waiting period.
- ○ b. The NIC checks to make sure that the line is free before transmitting, so no collisions are created.
- ○ c. There are no collisions.
- ○ d. When a collision is detected, data is retransmitted at predetermined intervals.

Question 51

Which router commands, if executed from the global configuration prompt, will enable IGRP routing for autonomous system 77 and network 172.25.0.0?

- ○ a. **router igrp 77** then **network 172.25.0.0**
- ○ b. **router igrp 172.25.0.0**
- ○ c. **router igrp** then **network 172.25.0.0**
- ○ d. **network 172.25.0.0**

Question 52

Which of the following is not a solution to problems experienced by distance vector routing protocols?

○ a. Split horizon

○ b. Route poisoning

○ c. Counting to infinity (loops)

○ d. Maximum hop count

○ e. Hold-down timers

Question 53

The Presentation layer provides which of the following services? [Choose the three best answers]

❑ a. Data representation

❑ b. Data compression

❑ c. Dialog management

❑ d. Data transmission

❑ e. Data encryption

Question 54

Which of the following prompts indicates that the router is in user mode?

○ a. **Router>**

○ b. **Router#**

○ c. **Router(config)#**

○ d. **Router:**

Question 55

What is the purpose of ICMP?

○ a. To report errors and provide other information relevant to IP packet processing

○ b. To map a known IP address to a physical address

○ c. To pass mail messages between devices

○ d. To obtain data on remote devices

Question 56

Which of the following router commands displays a list of keywords needed for the **show** command?

○ a. **sh?**

○ b. **sh ?**

○ c. **show?**

Question 57

When you first log in to a Cisco router under normal circumstances, what router mode are you in?

○ a. RXBOOT

○ b. Privileged

○ c. Global configuration

○ d. User

Question 58

Examine the following output from the initial configuration dialog on a Cisco 2500 router:

```
Configuring interface Serial 0:
Is this interface in use? [yes] <Return>
Configure IP on this interface? [yes] <Return>
Configure IP unnumbered on this interface? [no] :
    <Return>
IP Address for this interface: 172.29.3.4
Number of bits in subnet field [8]: <Return>
Class B network is 172.29.0.0, 8 subnet bits; mask is
255.255.255.0
```

What does the information contained in brackets represent?

○ a. Allowable answers

○ b. An answer that was previously entered

○ c. The default answer

○ d. The answer that was entered manually by the person configuring this router

Question 59

To display a brief description of the help system in privileged mode, which of the following keys or commands must be typed at the prompt?

○ a. **help**

○ b. F1

○ c. Ctrl+H

○ d. **?**

Question 60

Which of the following layers is most concerned with the representation of data?

○ a. Application

○ b. Presentation

○ c. Session

○ d. Transport

Question 61

Which of the following devices will segment a LAN into separate collision domains? [Choose the three best answers]

❑ a. Hub

❑ b. Bridge

❑ c. Switch

❑ d. Router

❑ e. Repeater

Question 62

With what is the Application layer primarily concerned?

○ a. Providing services for user applications

○ b. Data representation

○ c. Dialog management

○ d. Data transport

Question 63

A packet, frame, and bits conversion process includes which layers (in order)?

○ a. Session, Transport, and Network

○ b. Network, Data Link, and Physical

○ c. Presentation, Session, and Transport

○ d. Network, Transport, and Data Link

Question 64

Which of the following represent the reason the industry uses a layered model? [Choose the best answers that apply]

❑ a. Network operations and troubleshooting can be simplified.

❑ b. Standard interfaces can be defined for vendor compatibility.

❑ c. Enhancements for one layer can be isolated from the other layers.

❑ d. Designs and development efforts can be made in a modular fashion.

❑ e. Complex internetworking components can be divided into discrete subsets.

Question 65

Which of the following layers is most concerned with end-to-end communication?

○ a. Application

○ b. Presentation

○ c. Session

○ d. Transport

Question 66

A BDPU is sent to a device every _____ seconds.

○ a. 2

○ b. 4

○ c. 6

○ d. 8

Question 67

Which router component stores the router's backup/startup configuration file?

- ○ a. RAM
- ○ b. ROM
- ○ c. NVRAM
- ○ d. Flash

Question 68

Which Cisco router component is reprogrammable ROM that holds the IOS image?

- ○ a. RAM
- ○ b. ROM
- ○ c. NVRAM
- ○ d. Flash

Question 69

How is a VLAN membership configured? [Choose the two best answers]

- ❑ a. Via a TFTP server
- ❑ b. Statically
- ❑ c. Via DHCP
- ❑ d. Dynamically

Question 70

The IP routing table of a Cisco router can be viewed with which command?

- ○ a. **show ip**
- ○ b. **show route**
- ○ c. **show ip config**
- ○ d. **show ip route**

Question 71

What is the broadcast address of the subnet address 20.254.255.20
255.255.255.248?

○ a. 20.254.255.23

○ b. 20.255.255.23

○ c. 20.255.254.23

○ d. 255.0.0.0

Question 72

What is the broadcast address of the subnet address 134.153.178.80
255.255.255.0?

○ a. 134.153.255.0

○ b. 134.153.178.255

○ c. 134.153.255.255

○ d. 134.153.0.0

Question 73

What is the broadcast address of the subnet address 178.55.20.88
255.255.0.0?

○ a. 178.55.255.255

○ b. 178.255.255.0

○ c. 178.255.0.0

○ d. 178.55.255.0

Question 74

What is the broadcast address of the subnet address 201.244.18.2 255.255.255.0?

○ a. 201.244.255.255

○ b. 201.244.18.0

○ c. 201.244.18.254

○ d. 201.244.18.255

Question 75

What is the network address of the subnet address 156.192.200.15 255.255.192.0?

○ a. 156.192.192.0

○ b. 156.192.0.0

○ c. 156.192.200.0

○ d. 156.192.192.255

Answer Key

1. a, d	20. a	39. a	58. c
2. c	21. a, c	40. c	59. a
3. a, c, e	22. a	41. c	60. b
4. b, c, d	23. c	42. d	61. b, c, d
5. a	24. a	43. c	62. a
6. a, d	25. b	44. b	63. b
7. a, b	26. a	45. a, b, c	64. a, b, c, d, e
8. b	27. c	46. b	65. d
9. c	28. d	47. a, c, d	66. a
10. c	29. a, b, c	48. a	67. c
11. d	30. a, d	49. b	68. d
12. b, c	31. c	50. c	69. b, d
13. a, b, e	32. b	51. a	70. d
14. c	33. b, d	52. c	71. a
15. a, b, c	34. a	53. a, b, e	72. b
16. b	35. a	54. a	73. a
17. d	36. c	55. a	74. d
18. a, d	37. a, c, d	56. b	75. a
19. a	38. c	57. d	

Question 1

The correct answers are a and d. The Network layer of the OSI model performs both path determination and packet switching. Path determination is the process of identifying the best path to a destination across an internetwork. Packet switching is the process of moving a packet from one network interface to another. Answer b is incorrect because code formatting occurs at the Presentation layer of the OSI model, not the Network layer. Answer c is incorrect because flow control occurs at the Data Link or Transport layer. Answer e is incorrect because the Network layer does not perform any error notification.

Question 2

The correct answer is c. The **router rip** command enables RIP routing, and the **network 172.23.0.0** command enables the router to advertise that network to other routers. Answers a and b are incorrect because the **router rip** command does not require an autonomous system or additional parameters. Answer d is incorrect because you must first enter routing protocol configuration mode before configuring a network to be advertised.

Question 3

The correct answers are a, c, and e. The Data Link layer performs error notification, physical addressing, and frame sequencing, among other things. Answer b is incorrect because packet switching is performed at the Network layer. Answer d is incorrect because establishing, maintaining, and terminating sessions occurs at the Session layer.

Question 4

The correct answers are b, c, and d. Token ring, Ethernet, and FDDI are all layer 2 LAN protocols. Answers a and e are incorrect because Frame Relay and ISDN are WAN protocols; however, they both do function at layer 2 of the OSI model.

Question 5

The correct answer is a. The first six digits of the physical address represent the vendor code. Answer b is incorrect because the last six numbers of the physical address represent the serial number, not the vendor code. Answers c, d, and e have no meaning on their own and are therefore incorrect.

Question 6

The correct answers are a and d. Both a virtual connection and setup and maintenance functions are performed during connection-oriented communication. Answer b is incorrect because a physical circuit is not necessary for connection-oriented communication. Answer c is a characteristic of connectionless communication, not of connection-oriented communication, and is therefore incorrect.

Question 7

The correct answers are a and b. Answer a is an example of an IP logical address or a Network layer address. Answer b is an example of an IPX logical address or a Network layer address. Answer c is incorrect because it is an example of a Physical or layer 2 address, not a Network or layer 3 address. Answer d has no meaning and is therefore incorrect.

Question 8

The correct answer is b. The command to display the executing configuration/running configuration file to a console terminal is **show running-config**. Answer a is incorrect because this command displays the backup configuration/startup configuration file. Answers c and d are incorrect because these commands are used to modify configuration files, not to show configuration files.

Question 9

The correct answer is c. When you're backing up a running configuration file, the file needs to be copied from the router to a TFTP server. Answer a is incorrect because it would copy a file from a TFTP server to the router, whereas the goal is the opposite. Answer b is incorrect because the command is being executed from user EXEC mode. Answer d is incorrect because the command is executed from user EXEC mode, and it is in the wrong format.

Question 10

The correct answer is c. The **enable secret** command is the correct command. Answer b is incorrect because the word "password" is not used for setting an enable secret password. Answer a is incorrect because the enable secret password is set while in configuration mode, not privileged EXEC mode. Answer d is incorrect because this command is used to set the enable password, not the enable secret password.

Question 11

The correct answer is d. The command description is executed from the interface configuration mode and is the correct command to create a text description on an interface of a router. Answer a is incorrect because the command is executed from privileged EXEC mode. Answer b is incorrect because the command is executed from global configuration mode. Answer c is incorrect because the syntax of "**router(config-line)**" is incorrect.

Question 12

The correct answers are b and c. A local DLCI is mapped to a Network layer address dynamically using inverse ARP or manually by configuring a static map in the map table. Answer a is incorrect because CIR is the rate at which Frame Relay transfers data. Answer d is incorrect because LMI is a signaling standard. Answer e is incorrect because a PVC is a permanently established virtual circuit.

Question 13

The correct answers are a, b, and e. ISDN BRI service includes the ability to carry voice and data simultaneously, offers faster call setup than modem connections, and provides end-to-end digital service. Answer c is incorrect because PVCs are used by Frame Relay. Answer d is incorrect because an ISDN BRI connection is not a dedicated, full-time connection.

Question 14

The correct answer is c. TFTP is a scaled-down version of FTP used to copy files between Cisco routers or to TFTP servers. Answer a is incorrect because SMTP is a mail protocol, not a file-transfer protocol. SNMP is a network-management protocol, not a file-transfer protocol. Therefore, b is incorrect. RARP is a protocol used to map an unknown logical address to a known physical address. Therefore, d is incorrect. HTTP is used for Web browsing. Therefore, e is incorrect.

Question 15

The correct answers are a, b, and c. Error and duplication checking, acknowledgment windowing, and the three-way handshake are some of the characteristics of TCP. IP performs logical addressing in the TCP/IP suite. Therefore, answer d is incorrect.

Question 16

The correct answer is b. ARP maps a known logical address to an unknown physical address. Answer a is incorrect because it describes RARP, not ARP. Answer c is incorrect because it has nothing to do with ARP. Answer d is incorrect because ARP does not retrieve logical addresses, nor does a TFTP server have to be in the picture.

Question 17

The correct answer is d. Connection-oriented services have no permanently established connection; therefore, for two devices to communicate via a connection-oriented network environment, they must establish a connection, transfer data, and then terminate the connection. Answer b is incorrect because it describes specific methods used by some protocols to ensure reliable data transport. Answer c is incorrect because this describes connectionless communication. Answer a is incorrect because this is not a function of connection-oriented services. Answer a describes the process of encapsulation.

Question 18

The correct answers are a and d. Destination and source port numbers are provided in both the UDP and TCP headers, and both TCP and UDP provide for a checksum in the header to verify accurate delivery. Answer b is incorrect because only TCP performs the three-way handshake. Answer c is incorrect because UDP does not set datagram sizes dynamically but rather assigns each datagram the same size. Only TCP provides reliability in its data transport. Therefore, answer e is incorrect because UDP does not generate acknowledgments for the receipt of datagrams.

Question 19

The correct answer is a. The dotted decimal value 172.16.8.8 is equivalent to the binary value 10101100.00010000.00001000.00001000. Answers b, c, and d are incorrect because these binary values are not equivalent to 172.16.8.8.

Question 20

The correct answer is a. The Ethernet naming convention breaks down into three components that summarize its characteristics: LAN speed, signaling method, and media type. 100BaseFL means 100Mbps LAN speed, baseband signaling, and fiber-optic media.

Question 21

The correct answers are a and c. Answer a can be identified as correct because it has a decimal value between 192 and 223. Answer c can be identified as correct because the first three binary digits are 110. Answer b can be eliminated because the first three binary digits are 101, not 110. Answer d can be eliminated because the dotted decimal value is not between 192 and 223.

Question 22

The correct answer is a. Tunneling refers to the process of taking frames from one network system and placing them inside frames from another network system. Answer b is incorrect because stripping data from a packet is a function of de-encapsulation. Answer c is incorrect because this is a function of the Data Link layer of the OSI model. Answer d is incorrect because it does not accurately describe the process of encapsulation or tunneling.

Question 23

The correct answer is c. An IP address of 172.10.10.4 255.255.255.128 indicates a class B address with a nine-bit subnet mask. The valid range in dotted decimal notation for this IP address is 172.10.10.0 through 172.10.10.127. Answers a, b, and d can be eliminated because they do not fall within this range of IP addresses.

Question 24

The correct answer is a. The number of subnets can be derived by using the formula $2^n - 2$. A class B address of 172.10.10.4 with a nine-bit subnet mask indicates that nine bits are used for identifying networks. Therefore, take 2 to the power of 9 and subtract 2 to yield the number of networks. Answers b, c, d, and e do not show the correct result of the formula and can therefore be eliminated.

Question 25

The correct answer is b. The command in answer b identifies an IP standard access list by the access list number 11, which is the proper numeric range for identifying an IP standard access list. Answer a is incorrect because it uses the access list number 400. The access list number 400 is not reserved for IP standard access lists. Answer c is incorrect because the access list number 145 is reserved for IP extended access lists, not IP standard access lists. Answer d is incorrect because the number 105 is reserved for IP extended access lists, not IP standard access lists. Answer e is incorrect because it is an IPX access list, not an IP access list.

Question 26

The correct answer is a. CHAP uses a three-way handshake and transmits encrypted data between remote and local hosts. Answer b is incorrect because DDR is not a PPP authentication protocol. Answer c is incorrect because PAP transmits authentication data in clear text from the remote host to the local host.

Question 27

The correct answer is c. The IP sequence number cannot be used to permit or deny traffic with IP extended access lists. IP extended access lists can permit or deny traffic using a TCP port number, destination IP address, and source IP address. Therefore, answers a, b, and d are incorrect.

Question 28

The correct answer is d. IPX extended access lists are identified by a numeric range between 900 and 999. Answers a, b, and c are incorrect because they do not fall within the correct numeric range for IPX extended access lists.

Question 29

The correct answers are a, b, and c. The **show ip interfaces, show ipx interfaces,** and **show access-lists** commands can all be used to show access lists. Answer d is incorrect because the **show access lists** command is not in the correct format.

Question 30

The correct answers are a and d. Bridges increase frame-forwarding rates at approximately 20 percent in comparison with repeaters or physical media. In addition, implementing bridges to segment a layer 2 network introduces the possibility of bridging loops in a network. Answers b and c are incorrect because these are actually advantages of bridges.

Question 31

The correct answer is c. A bridge only maintains a device's physical MAC address and the next physical segment to forward a frame to while in route to the destination device. Answer a is incorrect because bridges do not maintain IP addresses. Answer b is incorrect because bridges don't maintain the physical segment on which a device resides but rather only maintain the next physical segment to forward a frame to while in route to the destination device. Answer d is incorrect because bridges do not maintain IP networks.

Question 32

The correct answer is b. ISL is a communication protocol used between switches to communicate common VLANs between devices. Answer a is incorrect because a switch is a physical device, not a protocol. Answer c is incorrect because frame tagging is a process employed by switches, not a protocol. Answer d is incorrect because the spanning tree protocol is used to eliminate loops in bridged networks.

Question 33

The correct answers are b and d. Routers increase the latency of forwarding packets/frames between networks. In addition, the increased functionality provided by routers often increases the complexity of networks. Answers a and c are incorrect because these are actually advantages of routing in comparison with bridging and switching.

Question 34

The correct answer is a. Frame tagging is used to tag a frame with a unique VLAN ID between switches.

Question 35

The correct answer is a. Store-and-forward switching is a method of forwarding frames by copying an entire frame into the buffer of the switch and making a forwarding decision. Answer a is correct because store-and-forward switching provides error checking that is not provided by cut-through switching. Answers b and d are not switching methods and are therefore incorrect. Answer c is incorrect because cut-through switching does not provide error-checking capabilities.

Question 36

The correct answer is c. A Fast Ethernet switch provides dedicated bandwidth to each port. This is unlike hubs, which share bandwidth among all ports. By definition, Fast Ethernet runs at 100Mbps. Note that if these PCs were connected through a single switch port, they would share the 100Mbps available to that port; however, the question states that each PC is given its own switch port.

Question 37

The correct answers are a, c, and d. The Session layer provides services to establish sessions, end sessions, and manage the dialog between the sending and receiving stations. Ensuring that the segment sent is error free *is* handled within the Transport layer. Therefore, answer b is incorrect.

Question 38

The correct answer is c. The Internet Assigned Numbers Authority (IANA) has assigned various class D addresses as well-known addresses for use by multicast applications. 224.0.1.1 is one such address, and it should be recognizable from the other choices as the only IP address that is a class D address. Answer a is incorrect because this is a subnet mask, not an IP address. Answer b is incorrect because this is a class A IP address. Answer d is incorrect because this is a class C IP address.

Question 39

The correct answer is a. PAP only uses a two-way handshake to allow the remote host to identify itself to the local host. Answer b is incorrect because CHAP uses a three-way handshake in its procedure. LCP and NCP are not authentication protocols. Therefore, answers c and d are incorrect.

Question 40

The correct answer is c. Devices on separate VLANs require a router to communicate, just as devices on separate LANs would. Answers a and b are incorrect because neither a layer 2 switch nor bridge provides inter-VLAN communication. Answer d is incorrect because access lists will not allow inter-VLAN communication. Answer e is incorrect because ISL is required for trunk connections, not inter-VLAN communication.

Question 41

The correct answer is c. The **sh interface s1** command displays the configuration and statistics for serial interface 1 on the router. Answers a and b are incorrect because the **sh frame-relay s1** and **sh frame-relay interface s1** commands are invalid. Answer d is also incorrect because the **sh ip interface brief** command displays IP addressing and status information for all interfaces, not Frame Relay information.

Question 42

The correct answer is d. The most common reason to see this message is because the interface was manually shut down through an IOS command. Answer a is incorrect because an operational interface would not give this message. Answer b is incorrect because the network connection may or may not be present given the output from the **show interface** command. Answer c is incorrect because this message does not mean there is a hardware problem.

Question 43

The correct answer is c. Frame Relay operates within the Data Link layer and over the Physical layer. Answers a and b are incorrect because Frame Relay does not contain any layer 3 (Network) or layer 4 (Transport) information.

Question 44

The correct answer is b. Pressing the Tab key will complete a partially entered command. Answer a is incorrect because it will place the cursor at the end of a line. Answer c is incorrect because it is not an IOS command. Answer d is incorrect because it will place the cursor at the beginning of a line. Answer e is incorrect because it will recall the most recent command from the command history buffer.

Question 45

The correct answers are a, b, and c. RIP, IGRP, and OSPF are interior routing protocols used to communicate route information within an autonomous system. Answer d is incorrect because BGP is designed to communicate route information between autonomous systems. Therefore, it is an exterior routing protocol.

Question 46

The correct answer is b. It is a complete IPX logical address for network 4d and node 0080.c747.b122. Answer a is incorrect because it is a node address and does not contain network information. Answer c is incorrect because it contains an IPX network number (4d) but also includes an IP address. Answer d is incorrect because it is only the IPX network number and is not a valid IPX logical address.

Question 47

The correct answers are a, c, and d. The **ping** and **trace** commands verify routing by sending and receiving packets across the network. For the **telnet** command to be successful, packets must be sent and received properly, so it also verifies that packets are being routed. Although the **show interface** command displays the status of the interfaces on a router, it does not indicate whether packets are reaching their destination. Therefore, answer b is incorrect.

Question 48

The correct answer is c. The **ipx routing** command enables IPX routing within the router; the other commands can be executed after IPX has been enabled. Answer d is incorrect because the **ipx network** command assigns a network number to a router interface. Answers b and c are also incorrect because the **ipx protocol** and **ipx interface** commands are not valid commands.

Question 49

The correct answer is b. Although many additional benefits have been realized by the networking industry, including the use of the OSI model as an educational tool, the International Organization for Standardization (ISO) released the OSI reference model with the primary purpose of helping computer vendors create interoperable network equipment. Therefore, answers a, c, and d are incorrect.

Question 50

The correct answer is c. When Fast Ethernet is in full-duplex mode, dedicated wires are used for sending and receiving. Therefore, collisions are not possible. Answer a is incorrect because this is the behavior of standard or half-duplex Ethernet operation. Answers b and d are incorrect because neither is valid in any instance of Ethernet.

Question 51

The correct answer is a. The **router igrp 77** command enables IGRP routing for autonomous system 1, and the **network 172.25.0.0** command enables the router to advertise that network to other routers. Answers b and c are incorrect because the **router igrp** command requires an autonomous system to be specified. Answer d is incorrect because you must first specify a routing protocol and then enter routing protocol configuration mode before configuring a network to be advertised.

Question 52

The correct answer is c. Counting to infinity can result from the slow convergence inherent with distance vector protocols. Answers a, b, d, and e are incorrect. Split horizon, route poisoning, maximum hop count, and hold-down timers are techniques used to reduce the occurrence and impact of the counting-to-infinity situation.

Question 53

The correct answers are a, b, and e. The Presentation layer concerns itself with data representation, data compression, and data encryption. Because the Session layer handles dialog management, answer c is incorrect. The Transport layer handles data transmission, so answer d is incorrect.

Question 54

The correct answer is a. A greater than sign (>) after the hostname (in this case, Router) indicates that the router is in user mode. Answer b is incorrect because a pound sign (#) immediately following the hostname indicates that the router is in privileged mode. The text "(config)#" after the hostname indicates that the router is in global configuration mode. Therefore, answer c is incorrect. A colon (:) after the hostname is not a valid router mode indicator. Therefore, answer d is incorrect.

Question 55

The correct answer is a. ICMP reports errors and provides other information relevant to IP packet processing. Answer b is incorrect because this is the function of ARP. Answer c is incorrect because this is the function of SMTP. Answer d is incorrect because this is the function of SNMP.

Question 56

The correct answer is b. The **sh ?** command displays the keyword needed to complete the **show** command. The **sh?** and **show?** commands display the commands beginning with the text "sh" and "show," respectively. Therefore, answers a and c are incorrect.

Question 57

The correct answer is d. Upon login, the router is placed in user mode. Answer a is incorrect because RXBOOT mode is for router recovery. Answer b is incorrect because you must first enter user mode before entering privileged mode. Answer c is incorrect because global configuration mode is enabled after you have entered privileged mode.

Question 58

The correct answer is c. Bracketed items represent the default answer in dialog sessions within the Cisco IOS. You can press Enter to accept the default answer or some other key to change it. Answer b is incorrect because even though this might be the case in some scenarios, answer c is better. Answer a is incorrect because the information in brackets is certainly allowable, but listing allowable answers is not why the information is there. Answer d is incorrect because this will never be the case in a configuration dialog.

Question 59

The correct answer is a. The **help** command displays a brief description of the help system for any command mode. Answer b is incorrect because pressing F1 will not provide help on a Cisco router. Answer d is incorrect because the question mark (?) displays the list of possible commands when it is typed at the prompt, regardless of the router's current mode. The Ctrl+H keystrokes display nothing. Therefore, answer c is incorrect.

Question 60

The correct answer is b. The Presentation layer's chief concern is data representation. The Application layer provides services for user applications. Therefore, answer a is incorrect. The Session layer mainly performs session management. Therefore, answer c is incorrect. Answer d is incorrect because the Transport layer handles different aspects of data transport that include end-to-end communication, sending segments from one host to another, and reliable transport.

Question 61

The correct answers are b, c, and d. Bridges, switches, and routers all segment a LAN into separate collision domains. Only routers, however, segment broadcast domains. Answer a is incorrect because all devices on a hub are in the same collision domain. Answer e is incorrect because a repeater provides no network segmentation.

Question 62

The correct answer is a. The Application layer provides services for user applications. Answer b is incorrect because the Presentation layer's chief concern is data representation. The Session layer mainly performs session management. Therefore, answer c is incorrect. The Transport layer focuses primarily on aspects of data transport. Therefore, answer d is incorrect.

Question 63

The correct answer is b. The Network layer converts segments into packets. The Data Link layer converts packets into frames. The Physical layer converts frames into bits. Answer a is incorrect because the Session layer sends *data* to the Transport layer. Answer c is incorrect because the Transport layer converts data into segments. Answer d is incorrect because the layers are out of order: The Transport layer communicates with the Network layer, and the Network layer communicates with the Data Link layer.

Question 64

The correct answers are a, b, c, and d.

Question 65

The correct answer is d. The Transport layer handles different aspects of data transport, including end-to-end communication, sending segments from one host to another, and reliable transport. Answer a is incorrect because the Application layer provides services for user applications. Because the Presentation layer's chief concern is data representation, answer b is incorrect. The Session layer mainly performs session management. Therefore, answer c is incorrect.

Question 66

The correct answer is a. BDPUs are sent out every two seconds by default, thus making answers b, c, and d incorrect.

Question 67

The correct answer is c. Nonvolatile RAM stores the router's backup/startup configuration file. Answer a is incorrect because RAM provides temporary running memory for a router's config file, while the router is powered on. Answer b is incorrect because ROM contains power-on diagnostics. Answer d is incorrect because Flash contains erasable, reprogrammable ROM that contains the Cisco IOS and microcode.

Question 68

The correct answer is d. Flash contains erasable, reprogrammable ROM that contains the Cisco IOS and microcode. Answer a is incorrect because RAM provides temporary running memory for a router's config file, while the router is powered on. Answer b is incorrect because ROM contains power-on diagnostics. Answer c is incorrect because nonvolatile RAM (NVRAM) stores the router's backup/startup configuration file.

Question 69

The correct answers are b and d. The administrator can configure a VLAN membership either statically or dynamically. A TFTP server is generally used to upgrade the router's IOS while DCHP is used to assign dynamic IP addressing.

Question 70

The correct answer is d. The IP routing table of a Cisco router can be viewed with the **show ip route** command. Answer a is incorrect because the **show ip** command will show the default IP configuration of a switch. Answer b is incorrect because the **show route** command will generate an error, and answer c is incorrect because the **show ip config** command will show the configurations of all interfaces on the router.

Question 71

The correct answer is a. Question 71 involves the ability to subnet ip addressing. If you are unsure of how to arrive at the answers provided, please reread the chapter on IP addressing and subnetting as this is essential to your success on the CCNA examination.

Question 72

The correct answer is b. Question 72 involves the ability to subnet ip addressing. If you are unsure of how to arrive at the answers provided, please reread the chapter on IP addressing and subnetting as this is essential to your success on the CCNA examination.

Question 73

The correct answer is a. Question 73 involves the ability to subnet ip addressing. If you are unsure of how to arrive at the answers provided, please reread the chapter on IP addressing and subnetting as this is essential to your success on the CCNA examination.

Question 74

The correct answer is d. Question 74 involves the ability to subnet ip addressing. If you are unsure of how to arrive at the answers provided, please reread the chapter on IP addressing and subnetting as this is essential to your success on the CCNA examination.

Question 75

The correct answer is a. Question 75 involves the ability to subnet ip addressing. If you are unsure of how to arrive at the answers provided, please reread the chapter on IP addressing and subnetting as this is essential to your success on the CCNA examination.

Glossary

Access layer
A layer of the hierarchical model that provides users access to the network.

access list
Rules applied to a router that will determine traffic patterns for data.

administrative distance
A value that ranges from 0 through 255 that determines the validity of a source's routing information.

advanced distance vector protocol
A routing protocol that combines the strengths of the distance vector and link state routing protocols. Cisco's Enhanced Interior Gateway Routing Protocol (EIGRP) is considered an advanced distance vector protocol.

Application layer
The highest layer of the OSI model (layer 7). It is closest to the end user and selects appropriate network services to support end-user applications such as email and FTP.

area
See *autonomous system*.

ARP (Address Resolution Protocol)
Used to map a known logical address to an unknown physical address. A device performs an ARP broadcast to identify the physical address of a destination device. This physical address is then stored in cache memory for later transmissions.

autonomous system
A group of networks under common administration that share a routing strategy. An autonomous system is sometimes referred to as a *domain* or *area*.

bandwidth
The available capacity of a network link over a physical medium.

BGP (Border Gateway Protocol)
An exterior routing protocol that exchanges route information between autonomous systems.

boot field

The lowest four binary digits of a configuration register. The value of the boot field determines the order in which a router searches for Cisco IOS software.

BRI (Basic Rate Interface)

An ISDN interface that contains two B channels and one D channel for circuit-switched communication for data, voice, and video.

bridge

A device used to segment a LAN into multiple physical segments. A bridge uses a forwarding table to determine which frames need to be forwarded to specific segments. Bridges isolate local traffic to the originating physical segment but forward all nonlocal and broadcast traffic.

broadcast

A data frame that every node on a local segment will be sent.

buffering

A method of flow control used by the Transport layer that involves the memory buffers on the receiving hosts. The Transport layer of the receiving system ensures that sufficient buffers are available and that data is not transmitted at a rate that exceeds the rate at which the receiving system can process it.

carrier detect signal

A signal received on a router interface that indicates whether the Physical layer connectivity is operating properly.

CDP (Cisco Discovery Protocol)

A Cisco proprietary protocol that operates at the Data Link layer. CDP enables network administrators to view a summary protocol and address information about other directly connected Cisco routers (and some Cisco switches).

channel

A single communications path on a system. In some situations, channels can be multiplexed over a single connection.

CHAP (Challenge Handshake Authentication Protocol)

An authentication protocol for the Point-to-Point Protocol (PPP) that uses a three-way, encrypted handshake to force a remote host to identify itself to a local host.

checksum

A field that performs calculations to ensure the integrity of data.

CIDR (Classless Interdomain Routing)

Implemented to resolve the rapid depletion of IP address space on the Internet and to minimize the number of routes on the Internet. CIDR provides a more efficient method of allocating IP address space by removing the concept of classes in IP addressing. CIDR enables routes to be summarized on powers-of-two boundaries, thus reducing multiple routes into a single prefix.

CIR (Committed Information Rate)

The rate at which a Frame Relay link transmits data, averaged over time. CIR is measured in bits per second.

classful addressing
Categorizes IP addresses into ranges that are used to create a hierarchy in the IP addressing scheme. The most common classes are A, B, and C, which can be identified by looking at the first three binary digits of an IP address.

CO (central office)
The local telephone company office where all local loops in an area connect.

configuration register
A numeric value (typically displayed in hexadecimal form) used to specify certain actions on a router.

congestion
A situation that can occur during data transfer if one or more computers generate network traffic faster than it can be transmitted through the network.

connectionless network services
Connectionless network services involve using a permanently established link. Path selection and bandwidth allocation are done dynamically.

connection-oriented network services
Connection-oriented network services involve using a nonpermanent path for data transfer. In order for two systems to communicate, they must establish a path that will be used for the duration of their connection.

console
A terminal attached directly to the router for configuring and monitoring the router.

convergence
The process by which all routers within an internetwork route information and eventually agree on optimal routes through the internetwork.

counting to infinity
A routing problem in which the distance metric for a destination network is continually increased because the internetwork has not fully converged.

CPE (customer premise equipment)
Terminating equipment such as telephones and modems supplied by the service provider, installed at the customer site, and connected to the network.

CRC (cyclic redundancy check)
An error-checking mechanism by which the receiving node calculates a value based on the data it receives and compares it with the value stored within the frame from the sending node.

CSMA/CD (Carrier Sense Multiple Access/Collision Detection)
A physical specification used by Ethernet to provide contention-based frame transmission. CSMA/CD specifies that a sending device must share physical transmission media and listen to determine whether a collision occurs after transmitting.

cut-through switching
A method of forwarding frames based on the first 6 bytes contained in the frame. Cut-through switching provides higher throughput than

store-and-forward switching because it requires only 6 bytes of data to make the forwarding decision. Cut-through switching does not provide error checking like its counterpart store-and-forward switching.

DARPA (Defense Advanced Research Projects Agency)

A government agency that develops advanced defense capabilities. It is now known as *ARPA*.

DCE (data communication equipment)

The device at the network end of a user-to-network connection that provides a physical connection to the network, forwards traffic, and provides a clocking signal used to synchronize data transmission between the DCE and DTE devices.

DDR (dial-on-demand routing)

The technique by which a router can initiate and terminate a circuit-switched connection over ISDN or telephone lines to meet network traffic demands.

deencapsulation

The process by which a destination peer layer removes and reads the control information sent by the source peer layer in another network host.

default mask

A binary or decimal representation of the number of bits used to identify an IP network. The class of the IP address defines the default mask. A default mask is represented by four octets of binary digits. The mask can also be presented in dotted decimal notation.

default route

A network route (that usually points to another router) established to receive and attempt to process all packets for which no route appears in the route table.

delay

The amount of time necessary to move a packet through the internetwork from source to destination.

demarc

A point of demarcation between the carrier's equipment and the customer premise equipment (CPE).

discard eligibility bit

A bit that can be set to indicate that a frame may be dropped if congestion occurs within the Frame Relay network.

distance vector protocol

An interior routing protocol that relies on distance and vector or direction to choose optimal paths. A distance vector protocol requires each router to send all or a large part of its route table to its neighboring routers periodically.

DLCI (data link connection identifier)

A value that specifies a permanent virtual circuit (PVC) or switched virtual circuit (SVC) in a Frame Relay network.

DNS (Domain Name System)

A system used to translate fully qualified hostnames or computer names into IP addresses, and vice versa.

domain

See *autonomous system*.

dotted decimal notation
A method of representing binary IP addresses in a decimal format. Dotted decimal notation represents the four octets of an IP address in four decimal values separated by decimal points.

DTE (data terminal equipment)
The device at the user end of the user-to-network connection that connects to a data network through a data communication equipment (DCE) device.

dynamic route
A network route that adjusts automatically to changes within the internetwork.

EGP (Exterior Gateway Protocol)
An exterior routing protocol that exchanges route information between autonomous systems. EGP has become obsolete and is being replaced by the Border Gateway Protocol (BGP).

EIGRP (Enhanced Interior Gateway Routing Protocol)
A Cisco proprietary routing protocol that includes features of both distance vector and link state routing protocols. EIGRP is considered an advanced distance vector protocol.

encapsulation
Generally speaking, encapsulation is the process of wrapping data in a particular protocol header. In the context of the OSI model, encapsulation is the process by which a source peer layer includes header and/or trailer control information with a Protocol Data Unit (PDU) destined for its peer layer in another network host. The information encapsulated instructs the destination peer layer how to process the information.

EXEC
The user interface for executing Cisco router commands.

exterior routing protocol
A routing protocol that conveys information between autonomous systems; it is widely used within the Internet. The Border Gateway Protocol (BGP) is an example of an exterior routing protocol.

FCS (frame check sequence)
Extra characters added to a frame for error control purposes. FCS is the result of a cyclic redundancy check (CRC).

Flash
Router memory that stores the Cisco IOS image and associated microcode. Flash is erasable, reprogrammable ROM that retains its content when the router is powered down or restarted.

flat routing protocol
A routing environment in which all routers are considered peers and can communicate with any other router in the network as directly as possible. A flat routing protocol functions well in simple and predictable network environments.

flow control
A mechanism that throttles back data transmission to ensure that a sending system does not overwhelm the receiving system with data.

Frame Relay
A switched, Data Link layer protocol that supports multiple virtual circuits using High-level Data Link Control (HDLC) encapsulation between connected devices.

frame tagging
A method of tagging a frame with a unique user-defined virtual local area network (VLAN). The process of tagging frames allows VLANs to span multiple switches.

FTP (File Transfer Protocol)
A protocol used to copy a file from one host to another host, regardless of the physical hardware or operating system of each device. FTP identifies a client and server during the file-transfer process. In addition, it provides a guaranteed transfer by using the services of the Transmission Control Protocol (TCP).

full-duplex
The physical transmission process on a network device by which one pair of wires transmits data while another pair of wires receives data. Full-duplex transmission is achieved by eliminating the possibility of collisions on an Ethernet segment, thereby eliminating the need for a device to sense collisions.

function
A term that refers to the different devices and the hardware tasks these devices perform within ISDN.

global configuration mode
A router mode that enables simple router configuration commands, such as router names, banners, and passwords, to be executed. Global configuration commands affect the whole router rather than a single interface or component.

GNS (Get Nearest Server)
A request sent by an Internetwork Packet Exchange (IPX) client to locate the closest active server of a particular service. Depending on where the service can be located, either a server or a router can respond to the request.

half-duplex
The physical transmission process whereby one pair of wires is used to transmit information and the other pair of wires is used to receive information or to sense collisions on the physical media. Half-duplex transmission is required on Ethernet segments with multiple devices.

handshake
The process of one system making a request to another system prior to a connection being established. Handshakes occur during the establishment of a connection between two systems, and they address matters such as synchronization and connection parameters.

HDLC (High-level Data Link Control)
A bit-oriented, synchronous Data Link layer protocol that specifies data encapsulation methods on serial links.

header
Control information placed before the data during the encapsulation process.

hierarchical routing protocol

A routing environment that relies on several routers to compose a backbone. Most traffic from nonbackbone routers traverses the backbone routers (or at least travels to the backbone) to reach another nonbackbone router. This is accomplished by breaking a network into a hierarchy of networks, where each level is responsible for its own routing.

hold-down

The state into which a route is placed so that routers will not advertise or accept updates for that route until a timer expires.

hop count

The number of routers a packet passes through on its way to the destination network.

hostname

A logical name given to a router.

HSSI (High-Speed Serial Interface)

A physical standard designed for serial connections that require high data transmission rates. The HSSI standard allows for high-speed communication that runs at speeds up to 52Mbps.

ICMP (Internet Control Message Protocol)

A protocol that communicates error messages and controls messages between devices. Thirteen different types of ICMP messages are defined. ICMP allows devices to check the status of other devices, to query the current time, and to perform other functions such as ping and traceroute.

IEEE (Institute of Electrical and Electronics Engineers)

An organization that defines standards for network LANs, among other things. The IEEE is the industry standard used in today's computing world.

IGRP (Interior Gateway Routing Protocol)

A Cisco proprietary distance vector routing protocol that uses hop count as its metric.

initial configuration dialog

The dialog used to configure a router the first time it is booted or when no configuration file exists. The initial configuration dialog is an optional tool used to simplify the configuration process.

integrated routing

A technique in which a router that is routing multiple routed protocols shares resources. Rather than using several routing protocols to support multiple routed protocols, a network administrator can use a single routing protocol to support multiple routed protocols. The Enhanced Interior Gateway Routing Protocol (EIGRP) is an example of a routing protocol that supports integrated routing.

interdomain router

A router that uses an exterior routing protocol, such as the Border Gateway Protocol (BGP), to exchange route information between autonomous systems.

interfaces

Router components that provide the network connections where data packets move in and out of the router. Depending on the model of router, interfaces exist either on the motherboard or on separate, modular interface cards.

interior routing protocol

A routing protocol that exchanges information within an autonomous system. Routing Information Protocol (RIP), Interior Gateway Routing Protocol (IGRP), and Open Shortest Path First (OSPF) are examples of interior routing protocols.

intradomain router

A router that uses an interior routing protocol, such as the Interior Gateway Routing Protocol (IGRP), to convey route information within an autonomous system.

IP (Internet Protocol)

One of the many protocols maintained in the TCP/IP suite of protocols. IP is the transport mechanism for Transmission Control Protocol (TCP), User Datagram Protocol (UDP), and Internet Control Message Protocol (ICMP) data. It also provides the logical addressing necessary for complex routing activity.

IP extended access list

An access list that provides a way of filtering IP traffic on a router interface based on the source and destination IP address or port, IP precedence field, TOS field, ICMP-type, ICMP-code, ICMP-message, IGMP-type, and TCP established connections.

IP standard access list

An access list that provides a way of filtering IP traffic on a router interface based on the source IP address or address range.

IPX (Internetwork Packet Exchange)

The layer 3 protocol used within NetWare to transmit data between servers and workstations.

IPX extended access list

An access list that provides a way of filtering IPX traffic on a router interface based on the source and destination IPX address or address range, IPX protocol, and source and destination sockets.

IPX SAP filter

A method of filtering SAP traffic on a router interface. SAP filters are used to filter SAP traffic origination or traffic destined for specific IPX addresses or address ranges.

IPX standard access list

An access list that provides a way of filtering IPX traffic on a router interface based on the source IPX address or address range.

ISDN (Integrated Services Digital Network)

A communication protocol offered by telephone companies that permits telephone networks to carry data, voice, and other traffic.

ISL (interswitch link)

A protocol used to allow virtual local area networks (VLANs) to span multiple switches. ISL is used between switches to communicate common VLANs between devices.

keepalive frames
Protocol Data Units (PDUs) transmitted at the Data Link layer that indicate whether the proper frame type is configured.

LAN protocols
Protocols that identify layer 2 protocols used for the transmission of data within a local area network (LAN). The three most popular LAN protocols used today are Ethernet, token ring, and Fiber Distributed Data Interface (FDDI).

LCP (Link Control Protocol)
A protocol that configures, tests, maintains, and terminates Point-to-Point Protocol (PPP) connections.

link state packet
A broadcast packet that contains the status of a router's links or network interfaces.

link state protocol
An interior routing protocol in which each router sends only the state of its own network links across the network but sends this information to every router within its autonomous system or area. This process enables routers to learn and maintain full knowledge of the network's exact topology and how it is interconnected. Link state protocols use a "shortest path first" algorithm.

LLC (Logical Link Control) sublayer
A sublayer of the Data Link layer. The LLC sublayer provides the software functions of the Data Link layer.

LMI (Local Management Interface)
A set of enhancements to the Frame Relay protocol specifications.

load
An indication of how busy a network resource is. CPU utilization and packets processed per second are two indicators of load.

local loop
The line from the customer's premises to the telephone company's central office (CO).

logical addressing
Network layer addressing is most commonly referred to as *logical addressing* (versus the physical addressing of the Data Link layer). A logical address consists of two parts: the network and the node. Routers use the network part of the logical address to determine the best path to the network of a remote device. The node part of the logical address is used to identify the specific node to forward the packet on the destination network.

logical ANDing
A process of comparing two sets of binary numbers to result in one value representing an IP address network. Logical ANDing is used to compare an IP address against its subnet mask to yield the IP subnet on which the IP address resides.

MAC address
A physical address used to define a device uniquely.

MAC (Media Access Control) layer
A sublayer of the Data Link layer that provides the hardware functions of the Data Link layer.

metric
The relative cost of sending packets to a destination network over a specific network route. Examples of metrics include bandwidth, delay, and reliability.

MIB (management information database)
A database that maintains statistics on certain data items. The Simple Network Management Protocol (SNMP) uses MIBs to query information about devices.

multicasting
A process of using one IP address to represent a group of IP addresses. Multicasting is used to send messages to a subset of IP addresses in a network or networks.

multipath routing protocol
A routing protocol that load-balances over multiple optimal paths to a destination network when the costs of the paths are equal.

multiplexing
A method of flow control used by the Transport layer in which application conversations are combined over a single channel by interleaving packets from different segments and transmitting them.

NBMA (nonbroadcast multiaccess)
A multiaccess network that either does not support broadcasts or for which sending broadcasts is not feasible.

NCP (NetWare Core Protocol)
A collection of upper-layer server routines that satisfy requests from other applications.

NCP (network control protocol)
A collection of protocols that establishes and configures different Network layer protocols for use over a Point-to-Point Protocol (PPP) connection.

NetBIOS (Network Basic Input/Output System)
A common Session layer interface specification from IBM and Microsoft that enables applications to request lower-level network services.

NetWare
A popular LAN operating system developed by Novell Corporation that runs on a variety of different types of LANs.

NetWare shell
An upper-layer NetWare service that determines whether application calls require additional network services.

network discovery
When a router starts up, this is the process by which it learns of its internetwork environment and begins to communicate with other routers.

NIC (network interface card)
A board that provides network communication capabilities to and from a network host.

NLSP (NetWare Link State Protocol)
A link state routing protocol used for routing Internetwork Package Exchange (IPX).

NOS (network operating system)

A term used to describe distributed file systems that support file sharing, printing, database access, and other similar applications.

NVRAM (nonvolatile random access memory)

A memory area of the router that stores permanent information, such as the router's backup configuration file. The contents of NVRAM are retained when the router is powered down or restarted.

OSI (Open Systems Interconnection) model

A layered networking framework developed by the International Organization for Standardization. The OSI model describes seven layers that correspond to specific networking functions.

OSPF (Open Shortest Path First)

A hierarchical link state routing protocol that was developed as a successor to the Routing Information Protocol (RIP).

packet switching

A process by which a router moves a packet from one interface to another.

PAP (Password Authentication Protocol)

An authentication protocol for the Point-to-Point Protocol (PPP) that uses a two-way, unencrypted handshake to enable a remote host to identify itself to a local host.

parallelization

A method of flow control used by the Transport layer in which multiple channels are combined to increase the effective bandwidth for the upper layers; synonymous with *multilink*.

path length

The sum of the costs of each link traversed up to the destination network. Some routing protocols refer to path length as *hop count*.

PDU (Protocol Data Unit)

A unit of measure that refers to data that is transmitted between two peer layers within different network devices. Segments, packets, and frames are examples of PDUs.

peer-to-peer communication

A form of communication that occurs between the same layers of two different network hosts.

physical connection

A direct connection between two devices.

ping

A tool for testing IP connectivity between two devices. Ping sends multiple IP packets between a sending and a receiving device. The destination device responds with an Internet Control Message Protocol (ICMP) packet to notify the source device of its existence.

POP (point of presence)

A physical location where a carrier has installed equipment to interconnect with a local exchange carrier.

PPP (Point-to-Point Protocol)

A standard protocol that enables router-to-router and host-to-network connectivity over synchronous and asynchronous circuits such as telephone lines.

Presentation layer
Layer 6 of the OSI model. The Presentation layer is concerned with how data is represented to the Application layer.

PRI (Primary Rate Interface)
An ISDN interface that contains 23 B channels and 1 D channel for circuit-switched communication for data, voice, and video. In North America and Japan, a PRI contains 23 B channels and 1 D channel. In Europe, it contains 30 B channels and 1 D channel.

privileged mode
An extensive administrative and management mode on a Cisco router. This router mode permits testing, debugging, and commands to modify the router's configuration.

protocol
A formal description of a set of rules and conventions that defines how devices on a network must exchange information.

PSTN (public switched telephone network)
The circuit-switching facilities maintained for voice analog communication.

PVC (permanent virtual circuit)
A virtual circuit that is permanently established and ready for use.

RAM (random access memory)
A memory area of a router that serves as a working storage area. RAM contains data such as route tables, various types of caches and buffers, as well as input and output queues and the router's active configuration file. The contents of RAM are lost when the router is powered down or restarted.

RARP (Reverse Address Resolution Protocol)
This protocol provides mapping that is exactly opposite to the Address Resolution Protocol (ARP). RARP maps a known physical address to a logical address. Diskless machines that do not have a configured IP address when started typically use RARP. RARP requires the existence of a server that maintains physical-to-logical address mappings.

reference point
An identifier of the logical interfaces between functions within ISDN.

reliability
A metric that allows the network administrator to assign arbitrarily a numeric value to indicate a reliability factor for a link. The reliability metric is a method used to capture an administrator's experience with a given network link.

RIP (Routing Information Protocol)
A widely used distance vector routing protocol that uses hop count as its metric.

ROM (read-only memory)
An area of router memory that contains a version of the Cisco IOS image—usually an older version with minimal functionality. ROM also stores the bootstrap program and power-on diagnostic programs.

ROM monitor

A mode on a Cisco router in which the executing software is maintained in ROM.

ROM monitor mode (RXBOOT)

A router-maintenance mode that enables router recovery functions when the IOS file in Flash has been erased or is corrupt.

route aggregation

The process of combining multiple IP address networks into one superset of IP address networks. Route aggregation is implemented to reduce the number of route table entries required to forward IP packets accurately in an internetwork.

route poisoning

A routing technique by which a router immediately marks a network as unreachable as soon as it detects that the network is down. The router broadcasts the update throughout the network and maintains this poisoned route in its route table for a specified period of time.

route table

An area of a router's memory that stores the network topology information used to determine optimal routes. Route tables contain information such as destination network, next hop, and associated metrics.

routed protocol

A protocol that provides the information required for the routing protocol to determine the topology of the internetwork and the best path to a destination. The routed protocol provides this information in the form of a logical address and other fields within a packet. The information contained in the packet allows the router to direct user traffic. The most common routed protocols include Internet Protocol (IP) and Internetwork Packet Exchange (IPX).

router modes

Modes that enable the execution of specific router commands and functions. User, privileged, and setup are examples of router modes that allow you to perform certain tasks.

routing algorithms

Well-defined rules that aid routers in the collection of route information and the determination of the optimal path.

routing loop

An event in which two or more routers have not yet converged and are propagating their inaccurate route tables. In addition, they are probably still switching packets based on their inaccurate route tables.

routing protocols

Routing protocols use algorithms to generate a list of paths to a particular destination and the cost associated with each path. Routers use routing protocols to communicate among each other the best route to use to reach a particular destination.

RS-232

A physical standard used to identify cabling types for serial data transmission for speeds of 19.2Kbps or less. RS-232 connects two devices communicating over a serial link with either a 25-pin (DB-25) or 9-pin (DB-9) serial interface. RS-232 is now known as *EIA/TIA-232*.

running configuration file
The executing configuration file on a router.

SAP (Service Advertisement Protocol)
An Internetwork Package Exchange (IPX) protocol that serves as a means to inform network clients of available network resources and services.

SDLC (Synchronous Data Link Control)
Primarily used for terminal-to-mainframe communication, SDLC requires that one device is labeled as the primary station and all other devices are labeled as secondary stations. Communication can only occur between the primary station and a secondary station.

session
A dialogue between the Presentation layers on two or more different systems.

Session layer
As layer 5 of the OSI model, the Session layer is concerned with establishing, managing, and terminating sessions between applications on different network devices.

setup mode
The router mode triggered on startup if no configuration file resides in nonvolatile random access memory (NVRAM).

shortest path first
See *link state protocol*.

single-path routing protocol
A routing protocol that uses only one optimal path to a destination.

sliding windows
A method by which TCP dynamically sets the window size during a connection, allowing either device involved in the communication to slow down the sending data rate based on the other device's capacity.

SMTP (Simple Mail Transfer Protocol)
Used to pass mail messages between devices, SMTP uses Transmission Control Protocol (TCP) connections to pass the email between hosts.

socket
The combination of the sending and destination Transmission Control Protocol (TCP) port numbers and the sending and destination Internet Protocol (IP) addresses defines a socket. Therefore, a socket can be used to define any User Datagram Protocol (UDP) or TCP connection uniquely.

Spanning Tree Protocol
A protocol used to eliminate all circular routes in a bridged or switched environment while maintaining redundancy. Circular routes are not desirable in layer 2 networks because of the forwarding mechanism employed at this layer.

split horizon
A routing mechanism that prevents a router from sending information that it received about a network back to its neighbor that originally sent the information. This mechanism is very useful in preventing routing loops.

SPX (Sequenced Packet Exchange)

The layer 4 protocol used within NetWare to ensure reliable, connection-oriented services.

startup configuration file

The backup configuration file on a router.

static route

A network route that is manually entered into the route table. Static routes function well in very simple and predictable network environments.

store-and-forward switching

A method of forwarding frames by copying an entire frame into the buffer of a switch and making a forwarding decision. Store-and-forward switching does not achieve the same throughput as its counterpart, cut-through switching, because it copies the entire frame into the buffer instead of copying only the first 6 bytes. Store-and-forward switching, however, provides error checking that is not provided by cut-through switching.

subinterface

One of possibly many virtual interfaces on a single physical interface.

subnetting

A process of splitting a classful range of IP addresses into multiple IP networks to allow more flexibility in IP addressing schemes. Subnetting overcomes the limitation of address classes and allows network administrators the flexibility to assign multiple networks with one class of IP addresses.

switch

A switch provides increased port density and forwarding capabilities as compared to bridges. The increased port densities of switches allow LANs to be microsegmented, thereby increasing the amount of bandwidth delivered to each device.

TCP (Transmission Control Protocol)

One of the many protocols maintained in the TCP/IP suite of protocols. TCP provides a connection-oriented and reliable service to the applications that use it.

TCP three-way handshake

A process by which TCP connections send acknowledgments between each other when setting up a TCP connection.

TCP windowing

A method of increasing or reducing the number of acknowledgments required between data transmissions. This allows devices to throttle the rate at which data is transmitted.

Telnet

A standard protocol that provides a virtual terminal. Telnet enables a network administrator to connect to a router remotely.

TFTP (Trivial File Transfer Protocol)

A protocol used to copy files from one device to another. TFTP is a stripped-down version of FTP.

tick

A measure of network delay time—about 1/18th of a second. In RIP version 2, ticks serve as the primary value used to determine the best path.

traceroute

An IP service that allows a user to utilize the services of the User Datagram Protocol (UDP) and the Internet Control Message Protocol (ICMP) to identify the number of hops between sending and receiving devices and the paths taken from the sending to the receiving device. Traceroute also provides the IP address and DNS name of each hop. Typically, traceroute is used to troubleshoot IP connectivity between two devices.

trailer

Control information placed after the data during the encapsulation process.

Transport layer

As layer 4 of the OSI model, the Transport layer is positioned between the upper and lower layers of the model. It is concerned with segmenting upper-layer applications, establishing end-to-end connectivity through the network, sending segments from one host to another, and ensuring the reliable transport of data.

trunk

A switch port that connects to another switch to allow virtual local area networks (VLANs) to span multiple switches.

tunnel

A tunnel takes packets or frames from one protocol and places them inside frames from another network system. See *encapsulation*.

UDP (User Datagram Protocol)

One of the many protocols maintained in the TCP/IP suite of protocols, UDP is a layer 4, best-effort, delivery protocol and, therefore, maintains connectionless network services.

user mode

A display-only mode on a Cisco router. Only limited information about the router can be viewed within this router mode; no configuration changes are permitted.

V.35

A physical standard used to identify cabling types for serial data transmission for speeds up to 4Mbps. The V.35 standard was created by the International Telecommunication Union-Telecommunication (ITU-T) standardization sector.

virtual connection

A logical connection between two devices created through the use of acknowledgments.

VLAN (virtual local area network)

A technique of assigning devices to specific LANs based on the port to which they attach on a switch rather than the physical location. VLANs extend the flexibility of LANs by allowing devices to be assigned to specific LANs on a port-by-port basis versus a device basis.

VLSM (variable-length subnet masking)

VLSM provides more flexibility in assigning IP address space. (A common problem with routing protocols is the necessity of all devices in a given routing protocol domain to use the same subnet mask.) Routing protocols that support VLSM allow administrators to assign IP networks with different subnet masks. This increased flexibility saves IP address space because administrators can assign IP networks based on the number of hosts on each network.

WANs (wide area networks)

WANs use data communications equipment (DCE) to connect multiple LANs. Examples of WAN protocols include but are not limited to Frame Relay, Point-to-Point Protocol (PPP), High-level Data Link Control (HDLC), and Integrated Services Digital Network (ISDN).

well-known ports

A set of ports between 1 and 1,023 that are reserved for specific TCP/IP protocols and services.

Index

Bold page numbers indicate sample exam questions.

10Base2 cable, 13
10Base5 cable, 13
10/100 BaseT, 12–13, **30–31**
100BaseFL, 13

A

access-group command, 170
Access layer, 128–129
access-list commands, 170, 177
Access lists, 166
  access list entries, 167
  access list number, 167
  adding entries to, 170
  deny all statement, 167
  deny statement, **185**
  IP, 166–176
  IPX, 176–180
  for ISDN connection initialization, 238
  monitoring, 180–181
  outbound, 171
  reordering entries in, 170
  showing, 181, **186, 272**
  statements in, 167
  types of, 166
  verifying, 180–181
ACK messages, 39
Acknowledgment numbers, 40
Acknowledgment timers, 39
Acknowledgment windowing, **267**
Acknowledgments, 20–21
  during link establishment, 230
address *name hostname speed* command, 239
Address Resolution Protocol. *See* ARP.
"administratively down, line protocol is down"
  message, 66–67, **71, 276**
Agents, 38
ANDing process, 113–115, **140–141**
ANSI LMI protocol extension, 246, **259**
Application layer, TCP/IP, services at, 37–38, **45**
Application layer (layer 7), 17
  Telnet operation at, 64
  uses of, 17, **282**

Applications
  communication between, 19
  port numbers of, 41
  services for, **282**. *See also* Application layer (layer 7).
  sharing of data, 19
Areas, 128
ARP, 43, **46, 48**
  for DLCI to Network layer address mapping,
    245, **266**
  function of, **268**
arpa encapsulation type, **160**
ARPAnet, 36
Asynchronous Transfer Mode (ATM), 15
ATM ports, as trunk ports, 211
Authentication
  PPP, 231–232, **252, 275**
  showing sequence of, 235
aux keyword, 89
auxiliary password command, 89

B

B channels, 236
  showing information about, 241–242
Backbone routers, 128–129
Bandwidth, 130
  dedicated, 54, **274**
  demand for, 56
Bandwidth utilization
  efficiency of, 40, **267**
  of link state protocols, 136, **145**
banner motd command, 90–91
Basic rate interface (BRI) service, 236, **254**
  advantages of, **267**
BDPUs, **283**
Best-effort protocol, 41
Binary numbering
  converting from decimal, 109
  converting to decimal, 109, **140, 269**
Bits, frame conversion into, 28, **30, 282**
Boot images, showing, 79–80
Booting up, with TFTP, 67
Bootstrap file, storage of, 78
Border Gateway Protocol (BGP), 129
Border routers, 137

Break key, 77
Bridges, 26, **29**, 52–54, **60**
    advantages of, **58**
    collision domains, separating with, **282**
    designated, 192
    forwarding tables for, 53, **202**, **272**
    frame-forwarding rates and, **272**
    hubs on, 52–53
    layer 2 functionality of, 52, **59**
    least path cost, 192
    for multicast frames, 53–54
    ports on, 52–53
    root path cost, 192–193
    transparency of, 52
Bridging loops, 191, **272**
    eliminating, 192, **202**
Broadcast addresses, 111, **285–286**
Broadcast domains, 208
    all segments in same, 52–54, **60–61**
    separate, 55, 57, **61**
Broadcast frames, 57
Broadcast messages
    Frame Relay and, 247
    limiting, 208
Broadcast packets, 15
    forwarding, 191
Broadcast storms, 57, 191
Buffer management, 39
Buffering, 20

C

Cabling
    coaxial cable, 13
    fiber-optic cable, 13
    twisted pair, 12–13
Career Certifications home page, 7–9
Carrier detect signal, verifying, 66
Carrier Sense Multiple Access with Collision
    Detection (CSMA/CD), 13–14
Catalyst 500 switches, store-and-forward
    switching default, 194
Catalyst 1900 switches, 195–201
    CLI for, 197, 200, **204**
    configuration, 197–200, **204**
    configuration, default, 198
    configuration, showing, **204–205**
    Fast Ethernet ports, 215, **221**
    fragment-free switching default, 195
    IP address for, 198, 200, **204**
    menu-driven interface, 198–200, **204**
    passwords for, 199
    power-on self-test, 196–197
    switch environment, 196
    switch startup, 196–197
    VLAN creation on, **220**
    Web-based interface, 198, 201, **204**
Catalyst 2820 switches, 195
    Web interface, 201
Catalyst 5000 switches, 195, **205**
Catalyst 8500 switches, 195
Catalyst switches
    frame tagging, 210
    no-management-domain state, 212
    trunk ports on, 211
Category 3 (CAT 3) twisted pair copper cable, 13
Category 5 (CAT 5) twisted pair copper cable, 13
Cells, 194
Central office (CO), 226–227

Challenge Handshake Authentication protocol.
    See CHAP.
Channel access administrator, 14
Channels, sharing, 13–14
CHAP, 231–232, **253–254**, **271**
    showing packet exchange information, 234–235
Checksums, 39–42, 47, **268**
Circuit-switched services, 228
Circular routes, removing, 192–194, **202**
Cisco certification exams
    exam software, 5
    exhibits, 4–5
    layout and design of, 3–5
    practice exam, 7
    preparing for, 6–7
    question formats, 3–5
    question-handling strategies, 6
    resources for, 7–9
    test-taking strategies, 5–6
    testing situation, 2–3
    time limit for, 3
    updates for, 2
Cisco Certified Professional site, 7–9
Cisco Discovery Protocol (CDP), at Data Link
    layer, **70**
Cisco LMI protocol extension, 246, **259**
Cisco proprietary HDLC, 229
Cisco routers
    Flash memory, **284**
    HDLC encapsulation, 229
    LCP configuration options, 232–233
    LMI protocol support, 246, **259**
    logging in to, **280**
    PPP configuration on, 233–234
    user mode, **280**
    WAN services support, 227–228, **258**
Cisco switches, 195–201. *See also* Catalyst switches.
    CLI for, 197, 200
    configuring, 197–200
    switch startup, 196–197
Cisco Systems, 246
Class A addresses, 110–111
    default mask of, **142**
    subnetting example, 116–117
Class B addresses, 111
    subnet masks for, 115
Class C addresses, 111, **269**
    host IDs, determining, 117–118
    logical ANDing, 114
    subnetting, 117–118
Class D addresses, 14, 112, **274**
Class E addresses, 112
Classful addressing, 108, 110–112
Client/server architecture, 148
Coaxial cable, 13
Code bits number, 40
Collision domains, 57
    all devices in same, 52, **60**
    separate, 53–55, **60–61**, **282**
Collisions, 14, 57, **278**
    bridges and switches and, 54
Command-line interface (CLI), switch
    configuration through, 197, 200
Command mode, help system description in, **281**
Commands, partial, completion of, **276**
Communication. *See also* Connection-oriented
    protocols; Connectionless protocols.
    connectionless versus connection-oriented, 23

Complexity
  reducing with layered network model, 31
  of routed networks, 273
Compression. *See* Data compression.
con keyword, 89
config terminal command, 200
Configuration dialog
  default values, 92, **281**
  initial, booting into, **102**
  initial output of, **281**
  syntax help, 92
Configuration files
  backing up, 87–88
  backup files, displaying, 82–83, **98**
  copying, 68, **72**
  managing, 84–88
  restoring, 68–69, 87–88, **100**
  running. *See* Running configuration file.
  showing, 79–80
  startup. *See* Startup configuration files.
  types of, 84–85
Configuration modes, 76–77
  for IP address configuration, 119
Configuration registers, 103
configure memory command, **100**
configure terminal command, 138–139
Congestion, 20
  management of, 243
Connection-oriented communication, 23, **265**
  process of, **268**
Connection-oriented protocols
  Frame Relay, 244
  SPX, 149
Connectionless communication, 23
Connectionless protocols
  IPX, 149
  TFTP, 37
  UDP, 41, **49**
console password command, 89
Contention, 13–14
Convergence, 125–126
  of distance vector protocols, 129, 135
  of link state protocols, 129
Copy run tftp command, **72**
Copy running-configuration TFTP command, **72**
Copy Startup TFTP command, **72**
Counting to infinity, 135, **143–144**, **279**
CRC, 194, 243, **260**
Ctrl+Z command, 138–139
Customer premise equipment (CPE), 226–227
Cut-through switching, 194–195, **203**
Cyclical redundancy check. *See* CRC.

D

D channels, 236
  showing information about, 241–242
Data communication equipment. *See* DCE.
Data compression, 18, **279**
  LCP, 232
Data link connection identifier. *See* DLCI.
Data Link layer (layer 2), 22–25, 27, **29**
  bridges at, 52, **59**
  CDP operation at, **70**
  error notification at, **264**
  Frame Relay at, **257**, **276**
  frame sequencing at, **264**
  LAN protocols at, **264**
  LLC sublayer, 22–24

MAC sublayer, 14, 22
  NetWare protocols at, 149
  packet conversion at, **282**
  physical addressing at, **264**
Data representation, 279, 282
Data terminal equipment. *See* DTE devices.
Data transmission methods, 14–15
Data transport, 19
  reliable, 21
Datagrams
  conversion into frames, 28, **30**
  segment conversion into, 28, **30**
DCE
  devices, 227
  functions of, 226–227, **260**
DDR, 238
  configuration example, 240
  monitoring, 240–243, **255**
De-encapsulation, 26–28
debug commands, system resource use of, 156, 251
debug frame-relay command, 250–251
debug frame-relay lmi command, 250–251, **261**
debug frame-relay verbose command, **261**
debug ipx routing activity command, 157
debug ipx sap activity command, 157
debug ppp authentication command, **252**
debug ppp chap command, 234–235
Decimal numbering
  converting from binary, 109, **140**, **269**
  converting to binary, 109
Decompression, 18
Decryption, 18
Default mask, 112–113
  of Class A addresses, **142**
  subnet masks and, 113
Default route, 128
Defense Advanced Research Projects Agency
  (DARPA), 36
Delay, 130
Demarcation (demarc), 226–227
deny all statement, 167
deny command, 170, **185**
description command, 91
Desktop connectivity, hubs for, 52
Destination addresses, filtering by, 172–176, **184**
Destination and source port numbers, 40–41, **47**, **268**
Destination networks, **143**
Destination unreachable message, 44
Devices
  bandwidth sharing by, 52
  MIBs of, 38
  physical addresses of, 24
  virtual connections between, **265**
Dial-on-demand routing. *See* DDR.
Dial-up interfaces, DDR with, 238
dialer-group *number* command, 239, **256**
dialer idle-timeout *number* command, 239
dialer-list dialer-group protocol command, 239
dialer map *protocol next hop* command, 239
Digital Equipment Corporation, 246
Discard eligibility bit, 243–244
Diskless machines, RARP use, 43, **49**
Distance vector routing protocols, 129–139
  convergence of, 135
  versus link state protocols, 137
  maximum hop counts, 135
  network discovery process, 133–134
  problems with, 135, **143–144**, **279**

stabilizing, 135–136
topology change handling, 134
Distribution layer, 128–129
DLCI, 245, **259**
global significance, 246
Network layer addresses, mappings to, 245, **266**
DNS, 38, **46**
port number of, 42
DNS server, 38
Domain name resolution, DNS service for, 37
Domain Name Service. *See* DNS.
Domains, 128
Dotted decimal notation, 108–109, **140**, **269**
DTE/DCE interface, 226–228
PPP on, 230
DTE devices, 227, **257**
clock for, **260**
discard eligibility bit setting, 243
functions of, 226–227
virtual circuits between, 244, **258**
Duplication checking, 39–40
TCP capabilities for, **267**
Dynamic routes, 128

E

Echo message, 44
Echo reply message, 44
EIGRP, 129–130, 151
Electromagnetic interference (EMI), preventing, 12
enable command, 200
enable password command, 89, **102**
enable secret *password* command, 89–90, **102**, **266**
Encapsulation, 26–28, **270**
conversion steps, 27–28
order of, 27–28, **30**
encapsulation frame-relay [cisco | ietf] command, 246
encapsulation hdlc command, 229
encapsulation ppp command, 234, 239
Encapsulation types, 150
for Ethernet interfaces, **161–162**
HDLC, 229
IPX support for, 150, **160**
multiple, 152
PPP, 242
setting, 152
Encryption, 18, **279**
for passwords, 89–90, **253**
End-to-end connections, 19–20, 38, **283**
Enhanced Interior Gateway Routing Protocol. *See*
EIGRP.
Error checking, 39–40, 243
CRC for, 243, **260**
with store-and-forward switching, **273**
TCP capabilities for, **267**
Error detection, LCP, 232
Error messages, from routers, 65
Error notification, 22, **264**
ICMP reporting of, **280**
Ethernet, 15, 44, 56, **264**
CSMA/CD use, 13–14
naming conventions, 15, **269**
Ethernet interfaces
encapsulation type for, 150, **160**, **161–162**
frame tags, understanding of, **219**. *See also* ISL.
Ethernet networks
broadcast storms on, 56
collisions on, 56
latency of, 56

Evolution, accelerating with layered network
model, **31**
Exchange termination (ET), 237
EXEC privileged mode, restoring configuration
files in, 88, **100**
Exterior Gateway Protocol (EGP), 129
Exterior routing protocols, 129

F

Fast Ethernet, 15, **278**
Fast Ethernet ports, as trunk ports, 211
Fast Ethernet switches, **274**
FCS, 243, **260**
Fiber Distributed Data Interface (FDDI), 44, **264**
Fiber-optic cable, 13
File Transfer Protocol. *See* FTP.
Files
copying from host to host, 37
transferring from host to host, 37
Flash memory, 78
information on, displaying, 84
IOS images in, **98**
router, 78, **284**
size available in, 94–95
Flat routing environments, 128–129
Flooding the frame, 190
Flow control, 20–22, 243
TCP for, 39
for upper-layer protocols, 24
Forwarding tables, 53, **202**, **272**
Fragment-free switching, 195
Frame check sequence. *See* FCS.
Frame filtering, 190
Frame Relay, 228, 243–246
Cisco support for, **258**
configuration information, showing, 248–249,
256, **275**
configuring, 246–248
at Data Link layer, **257**
DLCI addressing scheme, 245, **259**
error-checking mechanism, 243, **260**
global addressing extension, 246
LMI enhancements, 245–246
LMI protocols, Cisco support for, 246, **259**
monitoring, 248–251, **261**
multicasting extension, 246
NetWare over, 149
nonbroadcast multiaccess, 247
OSI model, relationship to, 244, **276**
subinterfaces, 247–248
virtual circuit status messaging extension, 246
virtual circuits for, 244
frame-relay lmi-type [ansi | cisco | q933a]
command, 246
frame-relay map command, 247
Frame sequencing, 22, **264**
Frame tagging, 210, **273**
IEEE standard 802.1Q, 211
passing data to Ethernet card, 211, 219
Frames, 22
conversion into bits, 28, 30, **282**
datagram conversion into, 28, 30
discard eligibility setting for, 243–244
flooding, 191
forwarding, 190
packet conversion into, 28, 30, **282**
sequencing of, 24

Framing, 24–25
FTP, 37
  at Application layer, **45**
  port number of, 42
Full-duplex media access, 54
Functions, ISDN, 236–237

G

Gang of Four, 246
Gateways, 25
Get Nearest Server (GNS) requests, 151
Gigabit Ethernet, 15
Global configuration mode, 76–77

H

Handshakes, 19–20
  three-way, 39, 231–232, **253–254, 267**
  two-way, 231, **275**
Hardware
  configuration of, showing, 79–80
  interoperable, **278**. *See also* Open Systems
    Interconnection (OSI) model.
  for networking, 52–56
Hardware addressing, 22, **46**. *See also* MAC addresses.
HDLC, 228–229
  Cisco support for, **258**
Header information, 26
Headers
  IP packet headers, 42–43
  length of, 40–42
  TCP, 40–41
  UDP, 41
help command, **281**
Hexadecimal notation, for IPX addresses, 150
Hierarchical routing environments, 128–129
High-Level Data Link Control. *See* HDLC.
Hold-down timers, 135
Hop counts, 131, 150–151, **159**
  maximum, 135
Hops
  identifying, 65–66, **73**, 120–121, **141**
  information about, **143**
Host IDs, 108, 111
  determining, 113–115, 117–118
  number of bits for, 110, 115–117
hostname command, 90
Hostnames, 90–91
  configuring, 92–93
  default, 90
  mapping to IP addresses, 119
  resolution of, 38, **46**
Hubs, 52, 56, **60**
  layer 1 functionality, 52, 56
  plugging into bridges, 52–53
Hypertext Transfer Protocol (HTTP), port
  number of, 42

I

ICMP, 43–44, **280**
  echo and echo reply packets, 120
  "TTL exceeded" message, 121
ICMP messages, 44
Idle timer, 238
IEEE standard 802.1Q, 211
IGRP, 129–130, **277**
  configuration commands for, 139, **278**
  maximum hop count, 139
  update interval, 139

Integrated Services Digital Network. *See* ISDN.
Interdomain routers, 129
Interesting traffic, 238–239, **256**
interface bri *interface number* command, 239
interface Ethernet 0/9 command, **221**
Interfaces, 78
  configuration parameters, displaying, 153–154, **256**
  descriptions of, 91, **266**
  filtering traffic on. *See* Access lists.
  Frame Relay information, showing, **275**
  HDLC, enabling on, 229
  IPX routing, configuring for, 152–153, **160**
  logical aspects on, 66
  network numbers for, 152, **160**
  physical aspects on, 66
  PPP on, **253**
  router, 78
  shutdown of, manual, **276**
  statistics on, 66, **71**, 83–84.
    See also **show interface** command.
Interior Gateway Routing Protocol. *See* IGRP.
Interior routing protocols, 129, **277**
International Organization for Standardization
  (ISO), 16
International Telecommunication Union
  Telecommunication (ITU-T) standardization
  sector, 236, **255**
Internet Control Message Protocol. *See* ICMP.
Internet layer, 42–44, **48**
Internet Protocol. *See* IP.
Internet response times, improving, 236, **254**
Internetwork Operating System. *See* IOS.
Internetwork Packet Exchange. *See* IPX.
Interswitch link. *See* ISL.
Intradomain routers, 129
Inverse ARP, 245, **266**
IOS
  backing up, 67–68, 94–96, **104**
  Enterprise Edition, 200
  extended **ping**, 44
  load balancing over PPP, support for, 232
  upgrading, 94–97
IOS file
  backing up, 67–68
  storage of, 78
  upgrading, 68
IOS images, in Flash memory, **98**
IOS names, for encapsulation types, 150
IP, 36
  monitoring, 121–124
  packet-switching capabilities, 42
  path determination capabilities, 42
  reliability of, 42
  routing table for, 42
  user traffic flow, 131
ip access-group command, 178, **182–183, 271**
IP access lists, 166–176
  access-list-number field, 167–169, 174
  "any" keyword, 175
  applying, 169–172, 174–176, **182**
  command field descriptions, 174
  command operators for extended lists, 175
  commands for, 167–168, **271**
  creating, 167, 169–172, 174–176
  deny all entry, 173, 176
  deny field, 167–168, 170
  destination field, 174

destination-wildcard field, 174
extended, 172–176, **183–184, 271**
"host" keyword, 175
operator port [port] field, 173
permit field, 167–168
protocol field, 173
source field, 167–168, **183**
source-wildcard field, 167–168, **183**
standard, 167–172, **182–183**
ip address {*address*} {*subnet-mask*} command, 200, **204**
IP addresses, 108–118, **265**
address space allocation, 110–112
binary and decimal systems,
  converting between, 109
broadcast IP addresses, 111, **285–286**
classes of, 110–112
configuring, 119
configuring routers for, 92–93
current and future requirements for, 115–117
default mask for, 112–113
dotted decimal notation, 108–109, **140, 269**
grouping, 171
host ID, 108, 110–111
logical ANDing, 113–115
mapping hostnames to, 119
mapping to physical addresses, 43, **46, 48, 268**
network ID, 108, 110
octets (bytes) in, 108
ranges of, permitting access to, 171, **182**
resolution of, 38, **46**
subnetting, 112–118, **285–286**
for switches, 198, 200
verifying, 119–121
IP Configuration menu, 199
IP connectivity
end-to-end, testing, 64–65
testing, 64–69, **70–73,** 120, **141**
ip default-gateway {*ip address*} {*subnet mask*}
  command, 200
IP headers, 42–43
bit version field, 42
checksum field, 42
destination IP address field, 42
header length field, 42
identification field, 42
options field, 42
protocol field, 42
source IP address field, 42
time-to-live field, 42
total length field, 42
type-of-service field, 42
IP traffic
filtering with access lists, 166. *See also* Access lists.
packet processing, **280**
IP Version 4 (IPv4), 108
IP Version 6 (IPv6), 108
IPX
addressing, 149–150, **158, 160, 265, 277**
chatty nature of, 156
configuring, 152–153
enabling, **277**
encapsulation, 150, **160–161**
features of, 151, **161**
monitoring, 153–156
at Network layer, 149
RIP usage, 150–151, **159, 161**
routing, 150–151, **159**
service advertisement, 151–152

troubleshooting, 156–157
user traffic flow, 131
ipx access-group command, 178, **185**
IPX access lists, 176–180
applying, 177–178
creating, 177
deny all statement in, 177
destination socket field, 179
extended, 178–180, **185–186, 271**
"input" keyword, 180
"output" keyword, 180
protocol field, 179
"router" keyword, 180
source field, 179
standard, 177–178
ipx maximum-paths [paths] command, 152
ipx network command, **160**
ipx routing [node] command, 152, **277**
IPX SAP filters, 179–180
ISDN, 228, 235–238
basic rate interface service, 236–238, **254, 267**
call setup time, 235, **267**
Cisco support for, **258**
configuring, 238–240
connection speeds, 235
data, voice, and video transmission capabilities, 235
DDR and, 238
devices, 237
functions, 236–237
global configuration commands, 239
idle timer, 238
interesting traffic, 238–239, **256**
interface configuration commands, 239
monitoring, 240–243, **255**
NetWare over, 149
Network layer protocol support, 236
primary rate interface service, 236, 238
reference points, 236–237
standard protocols, 236, **255**
uses for, 236, **254**
WAN services encapsulation, 236
ISDN switch-type *switch-type* command, 239
ISL, 210–211, **219, 273**
ISL Ethernet cards, 211

K

Keepalive frames, verifying, 66

L

LAN switching, 194–195
cut-through switching, 194–195
fragment-free switching, 195
store-and-forward switching, 194
LANs
access to, 44
cabling for, 12
Ethernet for, **264.** *See also* Ethernet.
FDDI for, 44, **264**
independence from upper-layer protocols, 23
segmentation of, 52–57, **58, 282**
segmentation of, logical, 55
speed designation, **269**
token ring for, **264.** *See also* Token ring.
virtual. *See* VLANs.
Latency, 56
of bridges, **272**
of cut-through switches, 194
routers and, 55, **273**
of store-and-forward switches, 194

Layer 2 switching, 190–194
Layer 3 addressing, **265**.
    See also Network layer addresses.
Layered network model. *See also* Open Systems
    Interconnection (OSI) model.
    advantages of, **31**
    PDU transmission through, 26
LCP, 229, **252**
    configuration options, 232–233
    data compression, 232
    error detection, 232
    link establishment, 230
    link quality determination, 231
    link termination, 231
    Network layer protocol negotiation, 231
    showing information on, 234
Learning, simplifying with layered network model, **31**
Leased lines, HDLC on, 229
Least path cost, 192
Link Control Protocol. *See* LCP.
Link state, broadcasting, 132
Link state packets, 132, 134
Link state routing protocols, 129–139
    bandwidth usage, 136
    versus distance vector protocols, 137
    network discovery process, 134
    overhead of, 136, **145**
    problems with, 136, **145**
    stabilizing, 136–137, **144**
    topology change handling, 134–135
    update coordination, 137, **144**
    update synchronization problems, 136, **145**
Links
    LCP establishment of, 230
    quality determination, 231
    reliability of, 131
    termination of, 231
LLC sublayer, 22–24
LMI, 245–246
    Cisco support for, 246, **259**
    monitoring, 250–251
    status information, showing, 249
Load, 131
Load balancing
    enabling, 152
    over PPP links, 232
Local area networks. *See* LANs.
Local loop (last mile), 226–227
Local management interface. *See* LMI.
Local termination (LT), 237
Logical addressing, 22, **265**
Logical ANDing, 113–115, **140–141**
login command, 89
Loops. *See also* Bridging loops; Routing loops.
    blocking connections creating, 192–194, **202**
    preventing, 191–192

M

MAC addresses, 14, 22, 24
    bridging based on, 53, **59**
    discovering, 190
    forwarding based on, 53, 56
    locating, **22**
    manufacturer identification, 24, **30, 264**
    manufacturer serial number, 24
    for node numbers, 149–150
MAC database, 190, **202**

MAC sublayer, 14, 22
    framing, 24–25
    SAPs for, 23
Magic Number protocol, 232
Mail transfer, SMTP for, 37
Maintenance functions, **265**
Management console Main menu, 199
Management domains, 211–212
Management information base (MIB), 38
Managers, 38
map command, 245
Maximum transmission unit (MTU), 121, **142**
Media access administrator, 14
Media access methods, 13–14
Media type, notation of, **269**
Message-of-the-day (MOTD) banners,
    displaying, 90–91
Multicast frames, bridging for, 53–54
Multicast group addresses, 14
Multicast packets, 14
Multicasting, 112, 246, **274**
Multipath protocols, 128
Multiplexing, 20
Multistation access unit (MSAU), 15

N

NetBIOS, 148, **162**
NetWare Core Protocol (NCP), 149, **162**
NetWare Link State Protocol (NLSP), 151
NetWare protocol suite, 148–149
    NCP, 149, **162**
    NetBIOS emulation, **162**
    NetWare shell, **162**
    OSI model, mapping to, 148
    RIP. *See* RIP.
    SAP. *See* SAP.
    SPX, 149
    Transport layer protocol, 149, **158**
Network Access layer, 44, **48**
Network addressing, 149–150, **158, 160, 286**
Network administrators, static route configuration
    by, 128
Network Basic Input/Output System. *See* NetBIOS.
Network Control Program (NCP), 229, 231
    showing information on, 234
Network delay, 130
Network discovery, 133–134
Network events, detection of, 134–135
Network Filing System (NFS), 18
Network ID, 108
    default mask for, 112–113
    determining, 113–115, **140–141**
    number of bits for, 110, 115–117
Network interface cards. *See* NICs.
Network layer addresses, **265**
    DLCI mappings to, 245, **266**
Network layer (layer 3), 21–22, 27, **29**
    IPX at, 148–149
    packet switching, 21–22, **263**
    path determination, 21–22, **263**
    Ping operation at, 64
    routing at, 54, 124. *See also* Routing.
    segment conversion at, **32, 282**
Network layer protocols
    multiple, carrying, 236, **254**
    PPP configuration for, 231
Network links. *See* Links.
Network maintenance, device testing, 64–69, **70–73**

Network management, SNMP for, 37
network *number* command, 138–139, **145, 263, 278**
Network numbers, 149
   assigning, 152, **160**
Network Operating System (NOS), NetWare, 148
Network paths
   hop counts, 150–151
   tick values, 150–151
Network segmentation, 52–57, **58**. *See also* Segments.
   bridges for, **272**
   logical, 55
Network standards, 15
Network termination (NT1 and NT2) devices,
   237, **254**
Network transport methods, 12
Networking, 12–15
   data transmission methods, 14–15
   hardware for, 52–56
   media access methods, 13–14
   transmission media, 12–13
Networks
   complexity of, **273**
   dissimilar, connecting, **58–59**
NICs, 24
   frame processing, 57
no debug all command, 157, 235, 251
Node numbers, MAC addresses as, 149–150
Nodes, MAC addresses of, 22
Nonbroadcast multiaccess (NBMA), 247
Nonvolatile random access memory. *See* NVRAM.
Northern Telecom, 246
NOVELL-ETHER encapsulation type, 150, **160,**
   161–162
number dial-string command, 239
NVRAM, 77–78
   configuration files, saving to, 88
   configuration files in, 91–92, **99, 284**
   running configuration files, copying to, **101**
   startup configuration files in, 85, **284**
   viewing contents of, **98**

O

Open Shortest Path First. *See* OSPF.
Open Systems Interconnection (OSI) model, 15–17
   Application layer, 17. *See also* Application layer
      (layer 7).
   Data Link layer, 22–25, **29**. *See also* Data Link
      layer (layer 2).
   encapsulation and de-encapsulation, 26–28
   Frame Relay relationship to, 244, **276**
   layers of, 17
   NetWare protocol mapping to, 148
   Network layer, 21–22, **29, 32**. *See also* Network
      layer (layer 3).
   Physical layer, 25–28. *See also* Physical layer
      (layer 1).
   PPP relationship to, 229–230
   Presentation layer, 18. *See also* Presentation
      layer (layer 6).
   protocol stack, 16–17
   purpose of, **278, 283**
   quick reference for, 25–26
   Session layer, 18–19
   TCP/IP suite mapping to, 36
   transmission media, 2
   Transport layer, 19–21. *See also* Transport layer
      (layer 4).
OSPF, 129–130, **277**
   router tables maintenance, 131

P

Packet-switched networks, 36
Packet-switched services, 228
Packet switching, 21–22, 42, **48,** 124, **142–143, 263**
   Frame Relay for, 243
Packets
   addressing and transmitting, 14–15
   conversion into frames, 28, **30, 282**
   routing of, **32–33**
   segment conversion into, 28, **30, 32, 282**
PAP, 231–232, **275**
   showing packet exchange information, 234–235
Parallelization, 21
Password Authentication Protocol. *See* PAP.
Passwords
   configuring, 92–93, **102**
   enabling, **266**
   encrypted, 231–232, **253**
   router passwords, 89–90
Path determination, 21–22, 42, **48,** 124, **142–143, 263**
Path length, 131
Permanent virtual circuits. *See* PVCs.
permit command, 170
Physical addresses. *See also* MAC addresses.
   at Data Link layer, **264**
   mapping to IP addresses, 43, **268**
   vendor code segment, **264**
Physical layer (layer 1), 25–28, **32**
   frame conversion at, **282**
   Frame Relay at, **276**
   hubs at, 52, 56
   NetWare protocols at, 149
ping command, 44, 64–65, 67, **73,** 120, **141, 277**
Point-to-Point Protocol. *See* PPP.
Polling, 14
POP3, port number of, 42
Port density, of switches, 54, 203
Port numbers, 37, 41
   for DNS, 42
   filtering traffic by, 172–173, **184, 186**
   for FTP, 42
   for HTTP, 42
   for POP3, 42
   TCP and UDP supply of, **268**
   for TCP/IP Application layer services, 37
   for Telnet, 42
Ports, 41–42
   assigning VLANs to, 216–217
   dedicated bandwidth for, **274**
   trunk ports, 211
   trunking, enabling on, 215
   well-known, 41–42
PPP, 228–230
   authentication, 231–232, **252–254**
   Cisco support for, **258**
   configuring, 233–234
   connection process, 230–231
   LCP component, 229, **252**
   monitoring, 234–235
   multilink configuration, 232
   NCP component, 229
   NetWare over, 149
   OSI model, relationship to, 229–230
   physical interfaces supported by, **253**
   Physical layer, 230
ppp authentication chap command, 233–234
ppp authentication pap command, 233–234
ppp compress predictor command, 233

ppp compress stacker command, 233
ppp multilink command, 233
ppp quality <*number 1 - 100*> command, 233
Predictor, 232
Presentation layer (layer 6), 18, **282**
    data types and standards, 18
    functions of, 18, **279**
Primary rate interface (PRI) service, 236, 238
Privileged mode, 76–77
    show command keywords, 78–79
    show commands from, 86
Protocol Data Units (PDUs), 26
    control information in, 26
protocol permit command, 239
Protocols, 15
PVCs, 244, **258**
    DLCI for, 245
    status of, 246

Q

Q933A LMI protocol extension, 246, **259**
Quality protocol, 232

R

RADIUS, 89
RAM, 78
    configuration files, copying to, 88
    configuration files, restoring to, **100**
    contents, displaying, **99**
    router, 78
    running configuration files in, 84–85, **99**, **103**
RARP, 43, **49**
Reference points, ISDN, 236–237
Reliability, 131
    TCP for, 39–40
reload command, 97
Remote devices
    configuring from central location, 38
    polling, 38
Remote procedure call (RPC), 19
Repeaters, 26, **32**
Reverse Address Resolution Protocol. *See* RARP.
RFC 1331, 229
RFC 1548, 232
RFC 1661, 229
RFC 2153, 229
Ring topology, 15
RIP, 129–130, 148, **277**
    configuration commands for, 137–138, **145**
    enabling, **145**, **263**
    hold-down timer, 138
    hop counts, 150–151, **159**
    NetWare support for, 148, **159**
    router tables maintenance, 131
    ticks, 150–151, **159**
    update interval, 132, 138
RIP version 2, 150–151, **159**
ROM, 78
    monitor mode, 77
    reprogrammable, **284**
    router, 78
    router boot from, **103**
Root path cost, 192–193
Route distribution timers, 134
Route poisoning, 135
Route summarization, 112
Route tables, **143**
    broadcasting, 131–132
    metric value, 131

Route-update process, 128
Routed protocols, 22
Router# configure memory command, 87
Router# configure terminal command, 87
router# copy running-config tftp command, 87, 265
Router# Copy startup-config running-config
    command, 88
Router# copyTFTP running-config command,
    88, **100**
#router igrp *system number* command, 139, **278**
Router passwords, 89–90
Router# prompt, 86, 97
Router> prompt, **279**
Router# reload command, 97
#router rip command, 138, **145**, 263
router(config-if)#description command, 266
Router#configure terminal command, 119
router#copy flash TFTP command, 104
Router#copy running-config startup-config
    command, 88, **101**
Router#erase startup-config command, 88
Routers, 21–22, 25, **29**, 32–33, 54–57, **61**
    advantages and disadvantages of, 55, **58–59**, 273
    booting from ROM, **103**
    booting with TFTP, 67
    broadcast forwarding, 55
    collision domains and. *See* Collision domains.
    configuration files. *See* Configuration files.
    configuration modes, 76–77
    configuration of, 131–139
    configuration of, initial, 91–94
    copying files between, 68, **72**, 267
    as DTE devices, **257**
    forwarding rate, **59**
    functions of, 55, **61**, 142–143
    global configuration mode, 76–77
    hostnames, 90–91
    interface modes, 76–77
    IP address use, 56
    latency, 55
    layer 3 functionality, 54
    memory statistics, 80–81
    network discovery process, 133–134
    network topology, knowledge of, 132
    for packet exchange between VLANs, 208–209
    powering on, **102**
    privileged mode, 76–77
    protocols on, displaying, 81
    reloading, 97
    remote, connecting to, 64
    resource usage, minimizing, 136–137, **144**
    restarting, 85
    RXBOOT mode, 76–77
    setup mode, 76–77
    status of, 78–84
    testing, 65
    upgrading software on, 94–97
    user mode, 76–77, **279**
Routing
    algorithms for, 124
    best path, identifying, 22
    displaying information about, 122–123
    flat or hierarchical environments, 128–129
    metrics for, 130–131
    at Network layer, 124
    optimal paths, 125–126
    packet switching. *See* Packet switching.
    path determination. *See* Path determination.

tracing, 65–66
verifying, **277**
between VLANs, 208–209, **275**
Routing Information Protocol. *See* RIP.
Routing loops, 125–127, 129, 135
remedying, 135
Routing protocols, 22, 124. *See also* Distance
vector routing protocols; Link state routing
protocols.
configuring, 92–93
displaying, **144**
flat or hierarchical, 128–129
flexibility of, 125
goals of, 124–127
interior or exterior, 129, **277**
optimality of, 125
rapid convergence capabilities, 125–126
robustness of, 126
simplicity of, 126–127
single path or multipath, 128
static or dynamic, 128
types of, 127–130
Routing tables, 42
displaying, 123, **284**
distributing, 129
Running configuration file, 84–85
changes in, 85
configuring, 86–87
copying to NVRAM, 88, **101**, **284**
copying to TFTP server, 68, 72, **265**
displaying, 81–82, 85–86, **101**, **265**
in RAM, **103**
RXBOOT mode, 76–77

S

SAP, 149, 151–152
hex numbers for, 152
NetWare support for, 149
SAP advertisements, filtering, 179–180
SAP broadcasts, 151
SAP encapsulation type, 150, **160**
SAP table information, 151, 154–155, **161**
Scalability, of switched networks, **219**
SDLC, 228
Cisco support for, **258**
Security. *See also* CHAP; PAP.
access lists for, 166. *See also* Access lists.
router passwords, 89–90
routing and, **58–59**
Segments, 19
collision domains. *See* Collision domains.
conversion into packets, 28, **30**, **32**, **282**
data conversion into, 27, **30**, 39
reliable transport of, 21
sending from one host to another, 20
size of, 39
Sequence numbers, 40, **271**
checking, 39
for link state updates, 137
Sequence Packet Exchange (SPX), NetWare
support for, 149, **158**
Servers, service advertisements of, 149, 151–152
Service Access Points (SAPs), 23
Service Advertisement Protocol. *See* SAP.
service password-encryption command, 90
Session layer (layer 5), 18–19
Sessions, 18

Setup functions, **265**
Setup mode, 76–77
sh ? command, **280**
Shared media, 13
Shortest Path First algorithms. *See* SPF algorithms.
show access-lists command, 181, **186**, **272**
show command, 78
keywords, 78–79, **280**
show configuration command, **98**
show controller bri command, 241–242
show controllers command, for monitoring ISDN
and DDR activity, **255**
show dialer bri command, 243
show dialer command, for monitoring ISDN and
DDR activity, **255**
show flash command, 84
show frame-relay lmi command, 250
show frame-relay map command, 250
show frame-relay pvc command, 249
show interface bri command, 242
show interface command, 66–67, **70**, 83–84
"administratively down, line protocol is down"
message, 66–67, **71**, **276**
line status and line protocol combinations, 67, **71**
for monitoring ISDN and DDR activity, **255**
for monitoring PPP activity, 234
for viewing Frame Relay configuration, 248–249,
256, **275**
show ip command, 200–201, **204–205**
show ip interface command, 121–122, **142**,
180–181, **186**
for showing access lists, **272**
show ip protocol command, 122–123, 138, **144**
show ip route command, 123–124, **284**
show ipx interface command, 153–154, **186**, **272**
show ipx route command, 154
show ipx server command, 154–155, **161**
show ipx traffic command, 155–156
show memory command, 80–81
show protocols command, 81, **99**
show running-config command, 81–82, 85–86,
99, **101**, **104**, **265**
show startup-config command, 82–83, 85–86, **98**, **104**
show trunk command, 215
show version command, 79–80, 94–95, **99**, **104**
show vlan-membership command, 216–217
show vlan *vlan#* command, 216
show vtp command, 214
Signaling method, notation of, **269**
Simple Mail Transport Protocol. *See* SMTP.
Single-path protocols, 128
Sliding windows, 40
SMTP, 38
at Application layer, **45**
SNAP encapsulation type, 150, **160**
Sockets, 42
Software version, showing, 79–80
Source IP addresses. *See also* IP addresses.
filtering by, 167–176, **182**, **184**
wildcard masks for, 168, 170–171
Source-wildcard masks, 167–168, 170–171, **183**
binary and decimal formats, 172
Spanning Tree Protocol, 191–194, **202**
SPF algorithms, 132
Split horizon, 135
Stacker, 232
Stanford University, 36

Startup configuration files, 84–85
    commands, entering, 100
    configuring, 86–87
    copying, 88
    copying to TFTP server, 72
    displaying, 85–86
    erasing, 88
    overwriting, 101
    storing in NVRAM, 284
Static routes, 128
Store-and-forward switching, 194, 205
    error-checking capabilities, 273
StrataCom, 246
Structured Query Language (SQL), 18
Subinterfaces, 247–248
Subnet masks, 113, 115, 118, **140–141**, 270
    number of bits for, 115–117
Subnetting, 47, 108, 112–118
    broadcast addresses for, **285–286**
    for Class A networks, 116–117
    current and future requirements for, 115–117
    default mask, 112–113
    logical ANDing, 113–115, **140–141**
    network addresses for, **286**
    number of subnets, deriving, 270
    subnet masks. *See* Subnet masks.
SVCs, 244, **258**
Switch ports, 52
switch(config)#vlan command, **220**
Switched networks, scalability of, **219**
Switched virtual circuits. *See* SVCs.
Switches, 54, **60–61**, 190
    booting up with TFTP, 67
    Cisco switches, 195–201
    collision domains, separating, **282**
    configuration, 197–200
    configuration, default, 198
    configuration, showing, **204–205**
    Fast Ethernet, **274**
    filtering and forwarding capabilities, 190–191
    IP address for, 198, 200, **204**
    LEDs, observing, 196–197
    loop prevention, 191–192
    MAC address discovery, 190
    management domains of, 211–212
    monitoring for errors, 197
    multiple LANs on, 208, **218**. *See also* VLANs.
    name-server address for, 200
    passwords for, 199
    port density of, 54, 203
    status of, 196–197
    switch startup, 196–197
    TCP/IP option configuration, 200–201
    for VLANs, 57
    Web interface, 201
Switching
    cut-through switching, 194–195, **203**
    error checking, 194–195
    fragment-free switching, 195
    frame throughput, 194–195
    LAN switching, 194–195
    store-and-forward switching, 194
SYN messages, 39
Synchronous Data Link Control. *See* SDLC.

T

Tab key, for command completion, **276**
TACACS, 89
TCP, 39–40
    acknowledgment windowing by, **267**
    checksums by, **268**
    destination and source port numbers, **268**
    error and duplication checking by, **267**
    functions of, **267–268**
    three-way handshake by, **267**
TCP header
    acknowledgment number field, 40
    checksum field, 40, **47**
    code bits field, 40
    data field, 41
    destination port field, 40, **47**
    filtering traffic by, 172, **184**, **186**
    format of, 40–41
    header length field, 40
    options field, 41
    reserved field, 40
    sequence number field, 40
    source port field, 40, **47**
    urgent pointer field, 41
    window field, 40
TCP/IP
    Application layer, 37–38
    background of, 36
    functions of, **47**
    Internet layer, 42–44, **48**
    layers of, 36–44, **45**
    mapping to OSI model, 36
    Network Access layer, 44, **48**
    protocols, 44
    Transport layer, 38–42
Telecommuting, bandwidth for, 236, **254**
Telnet, 37–38, 64, **73**, 120, **141**, **277**
    port number of, 42
    simultaneous sessions, 90
Terminal adapters (TAs), 237, **254**
Terminal emulation, Telnet for, 37–38
Terminal endpoints (TE1 and TE2), 237
Terminals, as DTE devices, **257**
TFTP, 37, 67–69
    at Application layer, **45**
    for copying configuration files, 87, **267**
TFTP server
    configuration files, copying from, 68–69, **100**
    configuration files, storing on, 68, **265**
    connectivity, testing, 67
    IOS files, backing up to, 67–68
    IOS files, copying to, 95–96, **104**
    IOS files, upgrading from, 68
    IOS files on, 96–97
    platform support for, 87
Thicknet, 13
Thinnet, 13
Throughput performance, of switches, 54
Ticks, 150–151, **159**
Time exceeded message, 44
Time-to-live. *See* TTL value.
Timers, acknowledgment, 39
Timestamps, for link state updates, 137
Token passing, 14
Token ring, 15, 44, **264**
Token ring encapsulation type, **160**
Tokens, 14

Topology changes, detecting and updating, 134–135
traceroute command, 65–66, 73, 120–121, **141, 277**
Traffic, permitting and denying, **271**. *See also*
  Access lists; IP access lists; IPX access lists.
Trailers, 26
Transmission Control Protocol. *See* TCP.
Transmission Control Protocol/Internet Protocol.
  See TCP/IP.
Transmission media, 12–13
Transport layer, TCP/IP model, services at, 38–42, **49**
Transport layer (layer 4), 19–21, 27
  end-to-end connection establishment, 19–20, **283**
  reliable data transport by, 21, **274**
  segment transmission at, 20–21
  services of, **274**
  SPX at, **158**
  upper-layer application segmentation at, 19
Trivial File Transfer Protocol. *See* TFTP.
Troubleshooting
  connectivity, 64–69, **70–73**
  IPX, 156–157
trunk command, 215
Trunk connections, 211–213
  creating, 214–215, **218**
  flooding prevention, 212–213, **220**
  verifying, 215
TTL value, 42
  setting, 65
  traceroute use of, 120–121
Tunneling, 27, **270**. *See also* Encapsulation.
Twisted pair copper cable, 12–13
  categories of, 13
  data rate capabilities, 13, **30–31**
  shielded and unshielded, 13
  types of, **31**
Type-of-service (TOS), 42

U
UDP, 41, **49**
  checksums by, **268**
  destination and source port numbers, **268**
  functions of, **47, 268**
UDP headers
  checksum field, 41, **47**
  destination port field, 41, **47**
  filtering traffic by, 172, **184**
  format of, 41
  header length field, 41
  source port field, 41, **47**
Unicast packets, 14
Upper-layer protocols
  flow control for, 24
  independence from LAN topology or protocols, 23
Urgent pointers, 41
User applications. *See* Applications.
User authentication, 89. *See also* Authentication.
User information, conversion into data, 27, **30**
User mode, 76–77, **279–280**
  restricting, 90
  show command keywords, 78–79
username *name* **password** *secret-password*
  command, 233
Users
  assigning to VLANs, 209–210, **218**
  grouping by security level or functional area,
    210, **218**

V
Vendor codes, **264**
Virtual circuit status messaging, 246
Virtual circuits, 244, **258**
  showing status information, 249
Virtual connections, between devices, **265**
Virtual local area networks. *See* VLANs.
virtual terminal password command, 90
Virtual terminals, 90
vlan command, 216
VLAN IDs, 210, **273**
vlan-membership command, 216, **221**
VLAN Trunking Protocol. *See* VTP.
vlan {*vlan*} **name** {*name*} command, **220**
VLANs, 57, 195, 208–210
  assigning to ports, 216–217
  benefits of, 210, **218**
  communication between, 208–209, **273, 275**
  configuration, 213–217, **284**
  configuration, dynamic, 213, **221, 284**
  configuration, port-centric, 213
  configuration, static, 213, **222, 284**
  configuration, verifying, 216
  creating, 216, **220**
  frame tagging and, 210
  ISL and, 211, **273**
  management of, 211–212, **219**
  spanning multiple switches, 209, 211, **218**
  trunk connections, 211–213
  user assignment to, 209–210
VTP, 211–212
  advantages of, **219**
  client mode, 212
  default configuration parameters, 212
  enabling, 214
  management domains, 211–212
  pruning, 212–213, **220**
  server mode, 212
  showing information, 214
  transparent mode, 212
vty password command, 90

W
WAN service connections
  peer device connection services, 228
  point-to-point and point-to-multipoint
    services, 228
  switched services, 227–228
WAN service providers, switches of, 226–228
WAN services
  Cisco-supported services, 227–228, **258**
  ISDN encapsulation of, 236, **254**
Wildcard masks, 167–168, 171, **183**
Window field, 40
Window size, changing, 40
Wireless networks, 12
write erase command, **102**
write terminal command, 81–82